UNDERSTANDING POLICY SU(

Also by Allan McConnell

Governing after Crisis: The Politics of Investigation, Accountability and Learning (*edited with A. Boin and P. 't Hart*)

Risk and Crisis Management in the Public Sector (*with L. Drennan*)

Scottish Local Government

The Politics and Policy of Local Taxation in Britain

State Policy Formation and the Origins of the Poll Tax

Understanding Policy Success

Rethinking Public Policy

Allan McConnell

First published 2010 by
PALGRAVE MACMILLAN

Palgrave Macmillan in the UK is an imprint of Macmillan Publishers Limited,
registered in England, company number 785998, of Houndmills, Basingstoke,
Hampshire RG21 6XS.

Palgrave Macmillan in the US is a division of St Martin's Press LLC,
175 Fifth Avenue, New York, NY 10010.

Palgrave Macmillan is the global academic imprint of the above companies
and has companies and representatives throughout the world.

Palgrave® and Macmillan® are registered trademarks in the United States,
the United Kingdom, Europe and other countries

ISBN 978-0-230-23974-6   hardback
ISBN 978-0-230-23975-3   paperback

This book is printed on paper suitable for recycling and made from fully
managed and sustained forest sources. Logging, pulping and manufacturing
processes are expected to conform to the environmental regulations of the
country of origin.

A catalogue record for this book is available from the British Library.

A catalog record for this book is available from the Library of Congress.

10 9 8 7 6 5 4 3 2 1
19 18 17 16 15 14 13 12 11 10

Printed in China

Dedicated to
(*in order of appearance*)
Rafael, Aibidh, Calum and Sofia

Contents

List of Tables, Boxes, Figures and Appendices

Tables

Boxes

Figures

Appendices

Acknowledgements

At the time of writing, Oprah Winfrey has reached a deal with an insurance company in a dispute over the right to use the phrase 'that aha moment'. Well, I distinctly remember using the term when learning to play the guitar back in 1974 (my moment was realizing that you could play two, three and even four notes with one stroke of the plectrum) and so I'm not convinced that she has a monopoly on the term. Indeed, I continue to have aha moments – one of them being the driving force behind this book. The person responsible was Dave Marsh, then of the University of Birmingham and now of the Australian National University in Canberra. During a lengthy sabbatical at the University of Sydney, he suggested that there was real gap in the policy literature, because there was virtually nothing written on the topic of policy success. He was absolutely correct and I realized to my astonishment, that on the fringes of numerous lectures I had given and papers I had written on various matters of public policy, I had unwittingly been building up a stock of ideas on 'policy success' that were so obvious that I had failed to realise their significance.

Dave suggested that we might write on the topic, and the product was an article published in *Public Administration*, together with a reply to Mark Bovens who published a commentary on our paper (see Marsh and McConnell, 2010a and 2010b; Bovens 2010). I then decided to develop the topic in much more extensive form – hence this book. I have many people to thank but first and foremost is Dave, whose suggestion produced my 'aha moment', but who was also most generous in discussing ideas and offering advice.

Several chapters were read and commented on by Paul 't Hart, Mike Howlett and Dave Marsh. Their suggestions were more useful than they probably realise and I thank them for taking the time to offer sage advice. The book is much better for their input. Ideas were also presented and formulated over several conferences: the Australian Political Studies Association (Brisbane), European Consortium of Political Research Workshops (Lisbon) and Asia-Pacific Science, Technology and Society (Brisbane). I thank all the participants for their helpful comments and suggestions. The dialogue with Mark Bovens in *Public Administration* was also influential in shaping my thinking.

At the University of Sydney, I had the good fortune to teach hundreds of public servants in the Department of Government and International Relations and the Graduate School of Government. The students kept me on my toes and I think I kept them on their toes by suggesting that they should not think of policy processes as (simply) 'rational' solutions to policy problems. Much public policy accords with what I would call 'good politics but bad policy'. This has become something of a mantra for the book and I thank all the students for passing on all their experiences and insights to me.

Erin Kelly performed a sterling job in undertaking initial research. Doing so helped kick-start my thoughts on case examples. The book was written partly at the University of Sydney and partly at the University of Strathclyde. I thank all my colleagues there for a supportive working environment, under the headships of Michael Jackson and David Judge respectively.

Steven Kennedy at Palgrave Macmillan has been incredibly supportive but also encouraged me to go beyond the scope I had initially envisaged for the book. There is no escaping Steven's persistence, but also no escaping the fact that he has a point. The book is immensely better for his suggestions. I also thank two anonymous reviewers for their suggestions and comments. I tried as best I could to address their concerns and there has been the occasional point where I have stood my ground. Overall, however, the comments have allowed me to clarify my arguments, as well as avoiding digging myself into analytical holes. I thank them for their efforts. Any errors or omissions remain my own.

My wife Iris has been the rock of my life – not a particularly easy task when she herself has been studying for PhD. I thank her for everything: space to write, moral support, encouragement and advice on research methods! In the process of writing the book, four little additions have come into the family – helped into the world by Lalla and Ivan, Steven and Violet, and Debbie and Patrick. I dedicate the book to the 'newbies' and their successes to come.

ALLAN MCCONNELL

Note: Material from a UK House of Commons debate in Appendix 5.1 is reproduced under Click-Use Parliamentary licence P2009000114.

Introduction: The Thorny Topic of Policy Success

The thorny topic of policy success permeates public policies. In recent years, countries ranging from Australia and Singapore to France, Sweden, Germany, Canada, the US and the UK have debated the successes and failures of public policies, such as Internet censorship, bailing out of banks, welfare cutbacks, privatization of utilities, deployment of troops overseas, removal of 'at risk' children from families, public–private infrastructure projects, subsidies to the arts, pollution controls, capital punishment, health and safety in the workplace, classification of certain drugs as illegal, and measures to tackle homelessness. One of the highest profile examples is policies to tackle climate change – epitomizing often polarized debate on whether policy initiatives are succeeding or failing. For example, the US and UK governments portrayed the outcome of the December 2009 Copenhagen summit on climate change as a pragmatic success story, given the complexity of reaching any deal at all. The Chinese authorities likewise perceived the outcome as highly successful in relation to China's perceived national interests. But other participants viewed it as an abject failure, with Lumumba Di-Aping, chairman of the G77 group of 130 poor countries, going so far as to say it was 'asking Africa to sign a suicide pact, an incineration pact in order to maintain the economic dependence of a few countries. It's a solution based on values that funnelled six million people in Europe into furnaces' (*Guardian* 2009).

Such cases, and more, give rise to broadly similar sets of debates. Complex social circumstances – including policy shortfalls, ambiguities and failures – are framed as 'success' by policy supporters, and 'failure' by critics. Recent assumptions about success, or otherwise, include studies of housing market stimulation in Norway (Stamsø 2008), e-governance reforms in Austria (Rodousakis and dos Santos 2008), US policies on intellectual disabilities (Pollack 2007), Spain's attempt to control HIV spread through blood transmission (Jordana 2001), public administration reforms in Northern Ireland (Knox 2008), youth justice policy at the federal level in Canada (Campbell *et al.* 2001), environmental policy in the Netherlands (Smith and Kern 2009), urban labour market reforms in France (Sintomer and de Maillard 2007), higher education reforms in Japan

1

(Goldfinch 2006), and Singapore's embracing of deliberative policy-making (Noh and Tumin 2008).

A substantial amount of political discourse is devoted to policy success and/or its absence. A Google search for the term 'policy success' (27 December 2009) revealed about 105,000 hits. Some recent news headlines are given in Box I.1. Claims of policy success emanate from government and politicians, the media, political parties, non-governmental organizations, interest groups, political consultants, academics, and ordinary citizens. Academic analysis often leans towards the explanatory rather than the normative, although many research papers and case studies have an underlying normative dimension in terms of whether a policy succeeded or not.

It is little wonder that the word 'success' is used so frequently amid societal complexity, policy problems and socio-economic inequalities. The word 'success' is pleasing to the eye and comforting to the ear. It is a 'feel good' word that neatly captures human beings' desires to achieve goals and attain happiness. The *Oxford English Dictionary* (2001: 93) defines success as: 'The prosperous achievement of something attempted; the attainment of an object according to one's desire; now often with particular reference to the attainment of wealth or position.' The word 'success' shares much in common with others, such as learning and improvement. Who does not want to learn and improve? Who does not want to attain success, even if it is only the modest achievement of personal goals?

Box I.1   Recent news headlines on the topic of policy success

'Housing Results Prove Policy Success'

'Efficient Delivery System Ensures Policy Success'

'Medics' Return A Foreign Policy Success For Bulgaria'

'In Improving Ties with India, Bush Can Claim a Foreign Policy Success'

'Why Has Microfinance Been a Policy Success? Bangladesh and Beyond'

'Deregulation Could Become Outstanding Policy Success'

'President Obama's First Foreign Policy Success'

'Funds Absorption Key for EU Rural Policy Success'

'Iraq Trip to be Major Foreign Policy Success for Iran Leader'

'Border Policy's Success Strains Resources'

'German Poll Shows Majority Sceptical About Climate Policy Success at G8 Meeting'

Success: much talked about but rarely studied

Despite an abundance of claims to success, there is surprisingly little written on the topic. The single and most thorough treatment of the topic can be found in *Success and Failure in Public Governance: A Comparative Analysis* edited by Mark Bovens, Paul 't Hart and Guy Peters (2001a). It covers four policy areas in six countries. Prior to that, an edited collection by Helen Ingram and Dean Mann (1980), entitled *Why Policies Succeed or Fail*, did not do justice to its title by concentrating almost exclusively on failure. Coupled with an earlier article by Donna Kerr (1976) in *Policy Sciences* and a more recent book chapter by Scott Prasser (2006a), this more or less constitutes the grand sum of what has been written directly on the topic. These works will be returned to in detail (Chapter 1) but, for the moment, they illustrate a point: the paucity of literature on policy success. Far more has been written on failure: a topic that will be crucial in the quest of this book to help understand policy success. A Google search for the term 'policy failure' (27 December 2009) revealed about 405,000 hits. More importantly, it is a burgeoning area of academic analysis. It cuts across disciplines such as political science, sociology, management science, geography and economics. It also straddles topics such as the politics of crises and disasters (Boin *et al.* 2005; Drennan and McConnell 2007), human error (Reason 1990; Dekker 2006), leadership and group pathologies (Janis 1982; 't Hart 1994, 't Hart *et al.* 1997; Post 2004), policy fiascos, pathologies and scandals (Hogwood and Peters 1985; Dunleavy 1995; Bovens and 't Hart 1996; Tiffen 1999).

It is understandable that failure is of greater interest than success. Dramatic and high profile failures such as 9/11, Bhopal, Chernobyl, Columbine, Lockerbie, the Asian tsunami, Space Shuttles Challenger and Columbia, Canberra bushfires and Hurricane Katrina help provide 'focusing events' (Birkland 1997, 2007), often bound up with human tragedy and political careers being terminated or revived. On media agendas, 'bad news' is more attractive than 'good news'. Failures also provide opportunities for reformers to advocate policy change, and for academics to study deeper systemic reasons for failure (Toft and Reynolds 2005; Boin *et al.* 2008).

The shortage of literature on policy success is a significant gap in our understanding of the world. Scholars and practitioners of public policy lack a framework with which to approach and make sense of the complex nature of policy success amid all its ambiguities, contradictions and accompanying political rhetoric by governments that their policies 'are working'. There is also the lack of a framework with which to understand many related and complex policy issues. For example, how can we explain the phenomenon that is known colloquially as 'good politics but bad policy'? The implication in this phrase is that policy can succeed on a political level but fail on a programme level. And how can we understand policy-making strategies that attempt short-term success fixes (such as putting together a loose coalition of interests, or marshalling evidence that suits a desired policy direction) but store up longer-term risks of failure? And what roles do claims to success actually perform? Are they simply political rhetoric or do they have deeper functions, such as legitimizing established policy trajectories and minimizing agenda-setting opportunities for those seeking to criticize the policy status quo?

The primary aim of this book to help demystify the complex phenomena of policy success. It does not claim to be the last word on the topic, but it does aim to provide a framework that allows us to explore this puzzling phenomenon in a way that has hitherto been almost absent in the public policy literature. The book also has a secondary aim. In essence, I am convinced that a 'success heuristic' has analytical depth that supplements and fills in many of the analytical gaps in existing policy analysis models, such as new institutionalism and rational choice. Hence, the secondary aim is to use the framework of policy success in order to rethink many of the established models of how we understand public policy. These are bold statements, and so some of the thinking and argument needs to be put forward. In order to do so, it is necessary to be clear on what constitutes 'policy'. Doing so is pivotal to the analysis throughout the book.

The importance of conceptualizing policy

It will come as no surprise to those steeped in the tradition of public policy that definitions of what constitutes 'policy' are highly generalized. For example, Easton (1953: 13) suggests that policy is a 'web of decisions and actions that allocate ... values'. Dror (1983: 14) defines it as 'general directives ... on the main lines of actions to be followed'. Dye (2005: 1) defines public policy as 'whatever governments chose to do or not to do'. To take this latter definition, governments do everything from building roads and regulating food safety, to consulting stakeholders, blaming opponents and calling elections. How can such policy complexity be captured in order to deal with the issue of success? A way forward lies in digging deeper in terms of the nature of public policy studies. While there is no strict agreement on the nature of public policy, different traditions and different analysts approach what 'governments do' from different vantage points. Three broad perspectives help us here.

The first tradition is that policy is about *process*. This is the classic policy cycle or systems approach, examined by Lasswell, Easton and others in the 1950s and 1960s, and continued today, for example, through Althaus *et al.* (2007) in the *Australian Policy Handbook*. In essence, what governments do is define issues, examine options, consult (or not, as the case may be), take decisions, decide how they will be put into practice and decide what procedures will be used to evaluate. For example, Chari and Heywood (2009) argue that the development of education policy in Spain has been driven by a strong core executive, effectively sidelining other actors who could be involved, such as parents' associations and teachers' associations. Clearly, the 'agency' of policy-makers to make process choices is contextual (in the Spanish case, this refers particularly to constitutional rules that allow national government a privileged position in educational policy-making) but, nevertheless, *process* is one of the things that governments do. They might have considerable powers to decide who, when and how to consult; the range of policy alternatives that will be given serious consideration; and the policy-making route, whether it be new legislation or refinements to existing legislation. Therefore, any credible examination of policy success needs to engage with the fact that processes can succeed, or fail.

The second tradition focuses on the decisions themselves, or the specific 'tools' that governments use (inaction, persuasion, resources, regulation, provision) to tackle policy problems (Eliadis *et al.* 2005; Hood and Margetts 2007). Such issues relate to the *programmatic* aspects of policy. Governments throughout the world have many programmes (even although they might not formally be called programmes, especially if they involve a decision not to intervene). Examples include US President Bill Clinton's long-time refusal to intervene in Rwanda (Burkhalter 1994), public information campaigns to prevent the spread of sexually-transmitted diseases in South Africa (Jeeves and Jolly 2009), reforming food inspection in Canada (Ugland and Veggeland 2004), banning smoking in public places in the UK (Cairney 2009), regenerating urban economies in France (Ambrose 2005), and the provision of public health care in Singapore (Ramesh 2004). Once again, an examination of policy success needs to explore the nature of programmes in succeeding, or failing.

The third tradition focuses on the *political* dimensions of policy – for example, in enhancing the reputation and electoral prospects of government, or reinforcing its broad governance agenda and the vision it promotes. Processes and programmes, coupled with the activities and choices made by government, can have a profound impact in enhancing/destroying government's electoral capacity and its ability, or otherwise, to steer the course it charted. The Thatcher government's intervention in the Falkland Islands was an important factor in turning around the Conservative Party's political fortunes and securing a victory in the 1983 UK general election. George W. Bush's response to the 9/11 attacks helped him attain heights of popularity unprecedented in US polling. Of course, the reverse can happen. The Icelandic government's prevarication over the global financial crisis led to protests and a resignation of the entire cabinet in early 2009. The political dimension of policy also leads into issues such as the possibility that policies might perform little more than the function of easing the business of governing and keeping a difficult or wicked issue off the government's agenda (Head and Alford 2008).

Conceiving policy in terms of process, programmatic and political dimensions is certainly not the only way of dividing up 'policy', but it does help capture the diversity of what government's do – such as making choices in terms of who to consult, whether to regulate, and what to spend in the run-up to an election. A definition of success will be dealt with later (Chapters 2 and 3) but, hopefully, there is already a sense that success can be achieved and/or constructed in each of the process, programmatic and political dimensions. A government, therefore, can be 'successful' in rushing through emergency legislation without getting bogged down in consultation, or regulating food standards to improve public health, or promising pre-election tax cuts and gaining electoral benefit. Policy is multi-dimensional and, hence, success needs to be seen in the same vein.

Plan and approach of the book

Outlining the structure of the book helps identify some of the arguments and analysis to follow. The aim is to provide a heuristic that will help others approach the topic of policy success. To use a colloquialism, I have tried to be as even-handed as possible. Inevitably, however, policy success is largely uncharted territory for public policy scholars and, hence, my own understandings and arguments are unavoidable. This is particularly the case in the final two chapters, where I reflect on long-term 'success' issues, as well as the broader implications of a policy success heuristic for the study of public policy. The book will contain a wealth of short, contemporary examples from countries (mostly, but not exclusively) throughout the western world, as well as several slightly longer case studies to provide examples of the complexities of success, and failure.

Chapter 1 reviews a diverse range of literature that will aid the understanding of policy success. As indicated earlier, there is a paucity of studies dealing explicitly with policy success, but this chapter will deal directly with them, notably the works of Kerr, Prasser, Ingram and Mann, Bovens, 't Hart, and Peters. Despite the near absence of works on the topic, there are substantial bodies of policy-related literature that deal explicitly, and often implicitly, with conditions considered to promote the greater good. The chapter explores literature on policy evaluation and improvement, public value, promoting good practice, and (of particular interest to the political dimension of policy) political strategy and survival. Importantly, the chapter also deals with the fairly extensive literature on failure, including crises, disasters, fiascos and catastrophes. Common themes emerge across these diverse sets of writings, such as differing perceptions on how we should conceive of and attain 'good' policy, as well as the fact that there are many grey areas between the polar extremes of success and failure.

Chapter 2 directly tackles the nature of what constitutes policy success. It begins by examining foundationalist and anti-foundationalist perspectives on success. The former would consider success to be a 'fact' while the latter would consider success to be a matter of 'interpretation'. An argument is then put forward for a realistic definition of success that recognizes objective dimensions of success (such as achieving intended goals), as well as interpretative ones (because not everyone will value or support the goals or the means of achieving them). The chapter provides a detailed outline of key criteria in the process, programmatic and political aspects of policy that can be used as measures of success. These include criteria such as government preserving its policy goals and instruments throughout the policy formation process (process success), achieving desired outcomes (programme success) and enhancing electoral prospects or reputation of government and leaders (political success).

Chapter 3 is crucial in further dissecting the nature of success and failure, focusing particularly on the complex relationship between them. In the real world of public policy, aspects of success and failure permeate all policies. Some are effectively insignificant in the broader scheme of things, while others are huge. Existing literature refers occasionally and loosely to phenomena such as 'mixed successes', 'partial success' and 'non-failures'. This chapter tackles explicitly the issue of how we can understand complex bundles of success and failure, in order to say meaningfully whether a policy has been a success; and, if the answer is yes, whether it is unproblematic/uncontroversial, or one that is struggling to hold onto the last vestiges of success. The chapter provides a framework based on moving across a spectrum containing: success, durable success, conflicted success, precarious success and failure. It examines this framework across the process, programme and political dimensions of policy.

Chapter 4 deals with the methodological problems of identifying and measuring success. It amalgamates many issues, flagged in earlier chapters, surrounding just how complex success actually is. It focuses on several issues, in particular:

- that success for one actor/group might be failure for another
- that identifying success is bedevilled by assessing phenomena, such as partial achievement of objectives, contradictory objectives and unintended consequences
- the difficulty in isolating policy outcomes from other societal factors that might have influenced those outcomes
- the problem of hidden agendas and lack of evidence
- the problems of time and spatial context. In the latter case, for example, a policy might be a short-term success but a long-term failure (and vice versa).

The chapter concludes by suggesting how, for practical purposes of policy analysis, analysts can confront such issues and navigate through them.

Chapter 5 focuses on the way in which political actors frame success, and the impact this framing has on agendas. It focuses particularly on how a range of actors, from government politicians to media opponents, will adopt different baselines to claim and also contest success. Sometimes the word 'success' will be used but, at other times, surrogates will be used, such as 'we did what we set out to do' and 'things are better than before'. These (and more) indicate a range of bases for claims, such as whether objectives have been met, whether outcomes have improved from a previous time period, whether the benefits outweigh costs, and whether the policy is morally right. The chapter then dissects actor narratives surrounding success into the scale of that success and the time-frame that applies. Finally, it examines the agenda impact of claims to success. This includes policy legitimation, deflection of criticism and justification for policy continuity.

Chapter 6 turns its attention to strategies for producing successful policy. The purpose is not normative. Rather, the purpose is to provide a framework that helps provide an understanding of different strategies for producing successful policy, coupled with the potential benefits and costs of each strategy. Strategies for success include striking a deal, engaging in stakeholder deliberation, bringing in ideas and practices from other jurisdictions, and using executive muscle to push through desired programmes. It then deals with the importance of context, and argues that strategies succeeding in one context are at high risk of failure in another. Accordingly, it identifies a number of variables, such as degree of issue politicization and degree of urgency, that point towards some strategies being more feasible than others. It concludes by examining low-, medium- and high-risk strategies for achieving policy success.

Chapter 7 continues with similar themes, but its aim is to provide a framework that can help provide an understanding of different elite strategies for shaping policy evaluations. Broadly, it identifies 'tight-grip', 'relaxed-grip' and 'loose-grip' strategies. The former involves (among other things) keeping a tight control over the format and parameters of evaluations, as well as intervening during the course of the evaluation to mould and/or discredit it; the latter involves granting more independence to evaluators through format and parameters, as well as resisting the temptation to discredit an evaluation that seems not to be going according to government's wishes. The analysis then uses similar contextual variables to the previous chapter to show that for policy-makers seeking process, programme and political success, a tight grip is generally the most feasible approach and a loose grip is highest risk. Ultimately, it points towards most policy evaluations as being designed to steer reports towards either the stamp of success (when maintenance of policy trajectories is sought) or the stamp of failure (when legitimation is needed for a new direction to be pursued).

Chapter 8 reflects on 'bigger picture' issues. It revolves around several key questions. First, are the conditions for cultivating success the same in different contexts, or are 'success' factors in one jurisdiction unlikely to work in another? This question has important implications for those who seek to promote universal principles and practices (such as privatization and public deliberation) that will work in virtually any context. Second, how sustainable are policy successes? In other words, do they tend to continue with only marginal refinement or are there factors that can lead to the termination of successful programmes? Third, are we more liable to learn from successes or failures, such as crises and disasters? This question is particularly pertinent because of the common argument than nothing gets fixed unless something goes horribly wrong. Fourth, and finally, is it possible to predict policy success? And if we can (or cannot), what does this tell us about our capacity to produce successful policies?

Finally, the Conclusion steps back further and suggests that we need to rethink our approach to public policy. It suggests that the policy success heuristic allows us to shine a light into the dark corners of public policy. If we can grasp the dynamics of policy success, then we can grasp many aspects of public policy that are certainly evident in the views of many practitioners and commentators, but are rarely written about in the field of public policy studies. These include good politics but bad policy, placebo policies, hidden agendas, policy 'on the hoof' and quick fixes. It also argues that the policy success heuristic can add value to most existing models of the policy process, such as rational choice and new institutionalist approaches. It concludes by going even further and suggesting that the policy success heuristic should be considered as a new model of the policy process, with (at worst) better explanatory power than the policy cycle and (at best) the capacity to explain policy outcomes with just as much credibility as mainstream models.

Chapter 1

Perspectives on Success: The State of the Discipline

There have been very few studies of what constitutes policy success, yet understanding the nature of policy success matters more than ever before. The slow decline of partisan politics and class voting patterns in many countries, coupled with the growth of the world-wide-web and the rapid availability of facts, arguments and policy stories, means that citizens (and the media) are scrutinizing and judging policies to an unprecedented degree. Claims of policy success and counterclaims of policy failure have become a key currency of political competition. Later chapters will help fill the gap in our understanding of policy success, but we should not assume that the paucity of literature on the topic renders existing writings of no interest. The opposite is the case. There is much that can be learned from several diverse sets of public policy-related literature focusing on what constitutes good and valuable policy, as well as literature that focuses on failure. Many of the assumptions about what constitutes success are implicit rather than explicit. The goal of this chapter is to draw out a set of issues that can be taken forward in subsequent chapters in terms of identifying, measuring and sustaining policy success. As will be seen, many similar themes run through disparate groups of literature.

The chapter is not exhaustive in its survey of writings dealing even implicitly with policy success. As Pollitt (2008: 31) notes in his book on time and public policy/management: 'It is a general law that large literature searches on almost any topic yield unmanageably huge quantities of potentially relevant material.' Research for this book is no exception, and sheer practicalities have necessitated choosing what to exclude and include. So, for example, I have chosen to exclude literature on good governance with its emphasis on systems of democracy and accountability, and game theory with its focus on 'good' strategy. The reason for exclusion lies in the logic I have adopted for inclusion. I have chosen to deal with mostly policy-related literature that contains quite strong assumptions about policy success (albeit implicit and couched in different terminology) and broader writings dealing with the political benefit to policy-makers of adopting particular courses of action. Therefore, the chapter deals directly with literature on policy evaluation and improvement, public value, studies of success and failure, promoting good practice, and political strategy and survival. The chapter concludes by highlighting issues to be developed in subsequent chapters. As will be shown, explorations of what constitutes good and valuable public policy have not been easy journeys for academic analysts.

Policy evaluation and improvement

In the traditional policy cycle framework, which sometimes doubles as both an explanatory and normative model of policy-making, 'evaluation' is found after the policy implementation phase. Evaluation, according to Dye (2005: 332) is 'learning about the consequences of policy'. Consistent with liberal democratic values of power dispersal and public accountability, policy-makers and others can find out what is 'working' and what is not, and follow through with policy refinements, policy improvements and policy learning. Wildavsky (1987: 7) encapsulates the spirit of this tradition in his statement that 'what we want from evaluation in political arenas ... [is] recognition and correction of errors, encouraged by social processes rich with varied reactions.'

Literature on evaluation has burgeoned in recent years, especially since the early 1980s. The world-wide financial crisis of the mid-1970s, high inflation, high unemployment, and the turn against Keynesian principles of public sector growth and the beginnings of public sector cutbacks, led to greater pressures to achieve value for money. Much of the new thinking drew on the free market ideas of Friedman, Hayek and others. The new agenda involved greater scrutiny of public services, attacks on big government, accusations of government overload, and manifestos for a limited steering role for government (see Hughes 2003; Pollitt and Bouckaert 2004; Prasad 2006). It became increasingly difficult, therefore, for public services to escape the scrutiny of (arguably) more pragmatic labour/left-leaning governments (Callaghan in the UK, Schmidt in West Germany, Hawke and Keating in Australia, Lange in New Zealand), as well as the more zealous conservatives and liberals (the Thatcher government in the UK, the Reagan and Bush Senior years in the US, and Howard in Australia). Therefore, the spotlight of policy evaluation shone increasingly brightly on public services. The mantra of the 1980s and 1990s was very much on value for money (Campbell-Smith 2008), while the more recent focus has been on performance improvement (Boyne 2003, 2004; Barber 2007; Hodgson *et al.* 2007).

Many policy evaluations are conducted within or commissioned by government from academics, consultants, non-governmental organizations, and through *ad hoc* committees/commissions of inquiry, particularly following crisis or disaster (Prasser 2006b; Drennan and McConnell 2007; Boin *et al.* 2008). Generally, however, there is less academic literature on evaluation than we might expect. For example, Hodgson *et al.* (2007: 362) found only 51 empirical studies in the UK focusing on public sector/service improvement.

Nevertheless, when evaluation research and writing from other countries is factored-in, particularly from the US, there is a rich and diverse body of literature with which to engage. This diversity in evaluation research helps provide some indication of the types of issues and debates that we need to contend with in terms of policy success.

First, the policy evaluation literature rarely uses the term 'policy success' but, nevertheless, it contains strong and implicit assumptions about what constitutes successful policy. For example, there is a strong normative strand in the evaluation literature (deLeon 1988; Radin 2000). This is especially so in the US (see, for example, Gupta 2001; Davidson 2005; Weimer and Vining 2005). The assumption is that evaluation is a tool used to help produce better policy and client-oriented advice to government. The implication is that 'good' policy is whatever serves the interests, vision and agenda of government. However, policy analysis can serve many purposes other than the wishes of government, and therefore policy evaluation itself can serve different purposes. It can solve puzzles (Winship 2006), facilitate democratic debate (Ingram and Schneider 2006) and critique existing institutions and policies (Dryzek 2006a). Balloch and Taylor (2005: 250) put the matter forcefully when they argue that evaluation should concern itself with challenging prescribed indicators and improving power-sharing. The deeper assumption here is that successful policy is infused with a healthy dose of equality, justice and fairness. Within the literature, many other explicit and implicit benchmarks of success can be found. For example:

- policy improvement – that is, success resides in services being better that they were before
- what matters is what works – that is, success resides in what the evidence base tells us about the policy and its impact
- economy efficiency and effectiveness – that is, success resides in the meeting of highly desirable criteria for the provision of public services.

Overall, therefore, some initial issues present themselves when thinking about the nature of policy success. In essence: a framework is needed for comprehending the existence of different measures of successful policy, ranging from (roughly) policy according with the wishes of government, to policy that adheres to and promotes certain key principles.

Second, and related, there is a diversity of opinion on evaluation techniques. Again, the implicit issue is: what is the best way to identify and measure success? A strong divide exists between science-based and value-based approaches. The former, described by Bovens *et al.* (2006) as 'rationalistic evaluation' and by Dunn (2004: 359–60) as 'pseudo evaluation', assumes that success or otherwise is an objective phenomenon, and it is the task of evaluators to gather information and data, compiling and presenting it in a neutral and impartial way. Such approaches are found particularly, but not exclusively, in the US. Typical evaluation techniques with the veneer of science include:

- benefit-cost analysis (see Weimer and Vining 2005; Miller and Robbins 2007)
- the balanced scorecard approach, involving weighing up different indicators in their context, rather than seeking the attainment of a clear target as a measure of success (Kaplan and Norton 1992, 1997)
- results-based monitoring and evaluation (Kusek and Rist 2004).

Even adherents to such approaches recognize the limits of scientific rationalism. As Bovens *et al.* (2006: 323–4) suggest: 'political realities have simply been too harsh to scientific rationalists'. Nevertheless, in the rationalist approach, grey areas and ambiguities tend to be presented as marginal issues to be addressed in an impartial manner. However, for other analysts, these 'marginal issues' are fundamental because within them resides issues of conflict resolution and power. For example, Taylor and Balloch (2005b: 1) argue that:

> Evaluation … is socially constructed and politically articulated … evaluation operates within discursive systems and … its social meaning is pre-constituted within wider relations of power independently of any particular use.

Essentially, therefore, evaluation from this latter perspective is much more about maintaining path dependencies and policy pathways than it is about redirecting them. As Dye (2005: 343) argues: 'Government agencies have a heavy investment – organizational, financial, physical, psychological – in current programs and policies. They are predisposed against findings that these policies do not work.' The general lesson for present purposes in terms of thinking about policy success is that there is no 'magic bullet' for evaluating policies (Fischer 2003: 8). Somehow, any examination of policy success needs to contend with different approaches to assessing success.

Third, a particularly useful aspect of the evaluation literature is that it alerts us to the complexities of assessing policies. Such complexities are given more, or less, emphasis depending on the particular perspective adopted, but they include:

- weighing up overall costs and benefits
- weighing up the impacts on differing target groups
- considering unintended consequences
- dealing with short and long-term effects
- indirect symbolic costs and benefits – that is, beyond the programme level
- how to deal with lack of evidence

- identifying standards to be used for evaluation – for example, before-and-after comparison, pre-identified targets.

Such issues will prove vital in the attempt in this book to deal with policy success (Chapters 4 and 7, in particular).

Fourth, the evaluation literature brings a diversity of assumptions in terms of how success can actually be achieved. One strand assumes, by and large, that success is a matter of refinement and learning. The literature on policy improvement typifies. It assumes that success is the incremental adjustment of existing policies, based on evaluations and learning lessons from them. Strategies for improvement, therefore, include increased competition, effective leadership, organizational reform, stakeholder participation and better quality management techniques (Boyne 2003; Hodgson *et al.* 2007). The more radical end of evaluation studies is critical of the narrowness of evaluations (Fischer 1995; Taylor and Balloch 2005; Pawson 2006) because they can be:

- conducted within strict value limits set by government
- commissioned from evaluators sympathetic to government goals
- conceived as one-off evaluations that do not take a longer-term and more systematic perspective.

Therefore, such evaluations carry the stamp of political authority but are often focused on 'proving' that a policy has worked, or only assessing whether it has been executed properly. A variety of critical issues can be excluded from such evaluations, including:

- whether or not the original policy goals were legitimate
- inputs into the evaluation that would be likely to lead to different results
- the impact of the policy on societal power relations.

Once again, therefore, the intensely political matter of what can be done to attain and identify success is an issue that the evaluation literature deals with, and that needs to be factored into the subsequent examination of policy success in this book.

Public value

The emergence of debates and thinking around public value since the mid-1990s gives further indication of the difficulties in dealing with the topic of policy success, as well as some of the issues that need to be addressed and explored further. In many respects, one of the most interesting aspects is less the nature of public value *per se*, than about the debates and issues that have emerged as practitioners and academics grapple with what public value actually is and how it can be achieved.

Discussion of public value typically begins with the seminal work from Mark Moore (1995) of Harvard's Kennedy School of Government; *Creating Public Value: Strategic Management in Government*. The context of his work is relevant. The general US antipathy to state intervention, and a mood captured by Osborne and Gaebler (1992) in their clarion calls for a leaner, more efficient and 'hands off' approach to government, provided the catalyst for Moore to promote an alternative vision. He envisaged public sector managers (defined widely to include elected representatives such as presidents, mayors and governors) as being successful when they: 'increase the public value produced by public sector organizations in both the short and the long run. Indeed, the idea that public mangers should produce value creating organizations matches the criteria of success used in the private sector' (Moore 1995: 10). For Moore, public value is a surrogate for success. It is an attempt to define what a successful public sector looks like. He suggests, in his strategic triangle framework, that three broad public value tests need to be met:

1.   production of things of value to overseers, clients, and beneficiaries at low cost in terms of both money and authority;
2.   legitimacy in terms of authority and political sustainability in terms of attracting money and authority from the political authorising environment;
3.   operational and administrative feasibility i.e. activities needs to be accomplished in order to meet organisational goals.

(Moore 1995: 71)

In a book with three main parts, Moore devotes the second part to 'Building Support and Legitimacy', and the third to operational aspects of delivering value. The implications for policy success, therefore, are that success resides not only in good services and good outcomes (Kelly *et al.* 2002), but also in issues of process. This important point will later form part of the argument in Chapters 2 and 3.

From such small seeds, the public value phenomenon has grown. It is now being conceptualized as a new paradigm supplanting new public management (O'Flynn 2007; Stoker 2006b) and has become the standard of appraisal for public sector policies as diverse as the arts (Gray 2008), bushfire control (Marton and Phillips 2005) and public infrastructure procurement (Charles *et al.* 2008). According to Rhodes and Wanna (2007), the public value phenomenon has meant that government intervention is now 'back in fashion'.

This simple outline of Moore's approach and its growth belies deeper complexities and debates surrounding public value. These issues also provide pointers on our journey to deal with policy success because they mirror many of the complexities surrounding it. Several are related but are worth treating separately.

First, public value is a slippery concept. Moore does not provide a direct definition, and subsequent debates confirm this (for example, Rhodes and Wanna 2007, 2008, 2009; Alford 2008). There is a similarity to other concepts such as the 'public interest' that are difficult to pin down. Rhodes and Wanna (2007) cite Schubert on how the public interest might be conceived as the electoral expressions of the popular will as implemented unwaveringly by public officials; or in higher, natural laws interpreted by officials; or in pluralist bargaining in order to mediate between and resolve conflicts. If a dose of free market critique is added, public value would equate with little or no public intervention, except for the protection of private property rights. It seems, therefore, that neither public value, nor its close relation policy success, is easy to define.

Second, and related, the point is made by van Gestel *et al.* (2008: 144) that 'the study of public values is as ambiguous as it is fundamental'. Indeed, Rhodes and Wanna (2007: 408) suggest that its attraction lies in its ambiguity: 'it is all things to all people'. Who doesn't want public value? Who doesn't want policy success? Both are simple wordings with positive connotations, but meaning different things to different people.

Third, and following on, public value is neither a homogeneous state of affairs, nor devoid of internal conflicts. To be precise, many studies of public value have revealed that, in practice, different public values compete with each other. For example, Steenhuisen and van Eeten (2008) in their study of Dutch Railways, a regulated organization providing the bulk of train services in the Netherlands, illustrate that the rail body had to cope with imperatives to satisfy competing values such as punctuality versus allowing passengers time to transfer between trains, and maximizing the number of trains versus reducing the number of trains to create spare capacity in times of irregularity.

Fourth, some analysis emphasizes the contextual aspects of public value. In other words, a policy delivering public value in one jurisdiction might not necessarily deliver value in another. A report commissioned by the Municipal Association Victoria into Bushfires in Australia, stressed the need for policy to be based on a strong local evidence base, rather than policy models being imported from overseas (Marton and Phillips 2005). Indeed, Rhodes and Wanna (2007, 2008, 2009) go as far as arguing that the concept of public value is less relevant and useful in Westminster systems because it pre-supposes a degree of managerial autonomy that is not provided in strongly hierarchical systems with disciplined political parties. Such arguments, therefore, steer analysis towards consideration of a policy's success (or even failure) varying according to context. These arguments dovetail well with the literature on the potential pitfalls of policy transfer (Dolowitz and Marsh 2000).

Fifth, many of the debates surrounding public value focus on strategies to achieve it. Options are many and, according to Moore (1995) involve aiming for the right level of abstraction in terms of goals, a balanced approach to the risks involved, and ensuring that strategies are aligned with public purposes. Rhodes and Wanna (2007) develop the risk dimension by proposing a 'ladder of public value', with strategies varying from low-risk marginal operational refinements in order to achieve public value, through to high-risk strategies driven by managerial ideas and priorities.

Sixth, different perspectives exist on the measurement of public value. For example, Kelly *et al.* (2002) envisage the public as the ultimate arbiters of value and recognize the difficulties in objective measurement and establishing causal connections between policy intentions and outcomes. Their framework focuses on the benchmarks of services, outcomes and trust, using polls and surveys to gauge opinion but recognizing the limits of knowledge. By contrast, Cole and Parston (2006) propose the Accenture Public Service Value Model, tilting much more towards value as 'fact'. They describe the model as 'a disciplined approach to public sector performance management focused on defining outcomes, quantifying results and identifying ways to achieve increased outcomes cost-effectively' (Cole and Parston 2006: 143). Overall, differing perspectives on how easily (or otherwise) public value can be measured indicate that any analysis of policy success needs to deal with broadly similar issues.

Finally, there is the issue of what Rhodes and Wanna (2007, 2008) describe as the 'dark side' of public policy. In other words, behind the upbeat language of public policy there is the reality that some policies involve spying, torture and arrest without evidence. Subsequent chapters of this book, therefore, need to deal with policies that might, in fact, be successful in achieving their aims, but are unpalatable and even sickening to many.

Studies of success and failure

Very little has been written explicitly on the topic of policy success. Far more has been written on failure. In this section, both sets of (occasionally overlapping) literature will be considered. The latter will be particularly important because it will lead towards thinking about how the most resounding of successes contain within them small aspects of failure.

Success

In 1976, Donna Kerr published an article in *Policy Sciences* entitled 'The Logic of "Success" and Successful Policies'. The preoccupations of the economic and political volatilities of the time seem to have been influential in her thinking. The analysis comes to assumptions about success by first of all visiting failure.

She argues that polices can fail because they cannot be implemented, or do not fulfil their intended purpose(s) or cannot be justified in terms of the norms they promote. It is only in the final summary to the article that success is dealt with explicitly. She argues that 'a policy that does not fail is successful' (Kerr 1976: 362). She proceeds to couch success in terms of the opposite of the conditions for failure; that is, implementation success, instrumental success and justificatory success. Nothing further is discussed on these matters but the article does at least indicate early policy analysis thinking about the nature of success. Success might be bureaucratic, in the sense that a policy is implemented according to the rules laid down. Success might also be the achievement of goals, akin to the *Oxford English Dictionary* definition given previously. And success might also be the meeting of valued moral criteria, such as fairness and equity. Yet, one aspect of her argument might seem quite bizarre: that policies succeed if they do not fail. This assumes that anything short of outright failure is a success; for example, 60 per cent of trains running on time is just as much a success as 90 per cent. Many people would surely disagree, but perhaps Kerr has a valid point buried here. Perhaps policies that are not outright failures contain some elements of success, even if they are hotly contested and beset by implementation failures.

Subsequently, in 1980, Ingram and Mann edited a book entitled *Why Policies Succeed or Fail*. Sir Isaac Newton's famous statement that he had 'stood on the shoulders of giants' does not apply in the case of Ingram and Mann. The fact that their bibliography contains not a single reference to any article or book on policy success indicates the paucity of literature in this field. The book, unfortunately, adds little to our understanding of success. Ingram and Mann (1980), in their editors' Introduction, do not define success and concentrate instead on failure, perhaps understandably in the context of the political and economic turmoil of the 1970s. Their only key observation is that: 'success and failure are slippery concepts, often highly subjective and reflective of an individual's perception of need, and perhaps even psychological disposition toward life ... policy success or failure is in the eye of the beholder' (Ingram and Mann 1980: 12). Stuart Nagel, in the Introduction, produces the only explicit definitions of success. He states that:

- 'In terms of *intent*, a policy is a success if it achieves its goals.' (Nagel 1980: 8).
- 'In terms of *reality*, a policy is a success if its benefits minus its costs are maximized.' (Nagel 1980: 8).

Ingram and Mann are more sympathetic to the latter, because a major focus of their argument is that unrealistic expectations are placed on modern government, and that government should not be judged by formal programme goals. Hence, the 'difficulty with policy is that it often begins with the selection of unrealizable aims' (Ingram and Mann 1980: 19). In developing their argument, therefore, they suggest that successful policy requires reasonable demands on government and realistic policy goals.

The disappointing level of engagement with success in Ingram and Mann's book, is compensated by Bovens *et al.* (2001a) in their mammoth volume *Success and Failure in Public Governance: A Comparative Analysis.* It is a product of 33 contributors, studying six countries and four policy sectors: decline of the steel industry, health care reform, innovation in banking, and managing blood supplies against HIV. Bovens *et al.* are more concerned with examining the state of public governance and its capacity to cope with new challenges, than focusing on a few disastrous issues and generalizing from them. Therefore, they make a conscious effort to think about 'success' rather than adding to existing bodies of work on policy failures and planning disasters. A key framework proposed is the distinction between programme and political dimensions of success. Therefore:

- 'In a *programmatic* mode of assessment, the focus is on the effectiveness, efficiency and resilience of the specific policies being evaluated.' (Bovens *et al.* 2001b: 20)
- 'the *political* dimension of assessment refers to the way policies and policy-makers become evaluated in the political arena.' (Bovens *et al.* 2001b: 20)

This distinction, and the book in general, provide the richest pickings to date for any scholar interested in policy success. The details of their argument bear closer examination, because these points will be picked up and developed in subsequent chapters.

It recognizes that 'success ... means different things to different people at different times' (Bovens *et al.* 2001b: 20). It also recognizes that assessments need to take temporal, spatial, cultural and political factors into account. Furthermore, it acknowledges the existence of conflict between the programmatic and political aspects of policy, while also tackling the conditions necessary (or at least conducive to) producing success. It focuses particularly on consensual styles of policy-making, and the building of collaborative networks within both the public sector and with the private sector.

There are, however, several issues either absent from the analysis or underdeveloped. They recognize briefly that success is not 'all or nothing' in their comment that 'It may be ... appropriate to label steel restructuring as a matter of non-failure than to speak of straightforward success' (Bovens *et al.* 2001c: 596). They also provide detailed criteria for assessing the programmatic and political dimensions, but only develop their framework up to a point. Programme indicators of success vary across each of their sectoral cases. For example, governance of the steel sector is assessed in terms of the financial costs of restructuring, the economic viability post-restructuring and the size of employment losses that are sustained (Bovens *et al.* 2001b: 21). By contrast, health sector reform is assessed in terms of how long the reform episode lasted, the ability to achieve short- and long-term reform ambitions, and the reduction of professional dominance. In many respects, such bespoke criteria are perfectly valid for diverse cases (indeed, broader *ad hoc* literature dealing with the success of individual cases also uses bespoke criteria). However, more generic criteria are needed for a success heuristic to have lasting impact beyond a select group of case studies. Finally, while they focus on the programmatic and political dimensions of policy success, they do not deal with the possibility that policy processes might themselves be successful. For example, a policy produced after extensive consultation with stakeholders is likely to be a process success (regardless of the specific programme developed) because it brings constitutional or quasi-constitutional legitimacy to the policy. Bovens (2010) recognized subsequently, in response to an article by David Marsh and myself (Marsh and McConnell 2010a) that the 'process' dimension is, indeed, a valuable addition to the study of policy. In subsequent chapters of this book, the issue of process success will be developed in detail.

The most recent writing on the topic of policy success (with the exception of Marsh, McConnell and Bovens) is a short book chapter by Scott Prasser (2006a) entitled 'Aligning "Good Policy" With "Good Politics" ' in a book edited by Hal Colebatch (2006) on how the 'policy cycle' is problematic in our understanding of policy processes. His concern is to separate policy and politics, based on the recognition that a policy might at times be successful in one of these spheres, but not in the other. Hence, a policy might be 'bad policy' put provide political rewards. He produces a long list of 15 criteria for good politics. It includes gaining favourable publicity, being seen as a winner, winning votes, showing leadership, appearing open and giving the impression of being politics-free. Indicators are fewer in number for good policy. They are: being seen as a credible policy, tackling the policy problem, having real substance (as opposed simply to rhetoric) and being fiscally responsible.

Prasser's chapter is certainly useful in pointing towards a number of issues with which a detailed examination of policy success will need to deal. However, it covers a great deal of ground very quickly, and lacks the kind of overarching framework that can be picked up and used easily by others. Also, it assumes that a feature of good policy is that it needs to have substance and that it directly tackles the problem. However, as I will argue later in the book, many policy programmes (especially involving 'wicked issues') are successful in terms of their goals precisely because they *do not* tackle root causes and complex symptoms. Prasser's chapter is a useful hint to the direction we need to take, but the ideas need to be developed in an extended and detailed manner.

Failure

Bovens *et al.* (2001b) deal with failure as the flip side of success and, hence, all the criteria above, and the various issues such as temporality and subjectivity, also apply. This work aside, literature on failure significantly outnumbers that on success. Failure is often an attractive topic to research, and policy failure is certainly a more media-friendly topic than success. In a competition for attention-grabbing headlines, 'New Health Care Plan is Working According to Plan' would barely get off the starting blocks against 'New Health Care Plan is Policy Fiasco'.

The sheer scope of literature on failure is impressive. It cuts across academic disciplines such as political science, economics, geography, sociology, planning, public health and more. Leaving aside literature on specific cases such as the UK poll tax, Hurricane Katrina, 9/11, space shuttle explosions, Bhopal, Chernobyl and others, literature on failures includes:

- human error (Reason 1990; Dekker 2006)
- organizational pathologies (Mitroff and Pauchant 1990; Anheier 1999)
- leadership and group pathologies (Janis 1982; 't Hart 1994, 't Hart *et al.* 1997; Post 2004)
- crises and disasters (Rosenthal *et al.* 2001; Boin *et al.* 2005; McEntire 2007)
- policy fiascos, scandals, disasters and pathologies (Hogwood and Peters 1985; Dunleavy 1995; Bovens and 't Hart 1996; Tiffen 1999; Thompson 2000)
- risk (Slovic 2000; Drennan and McConnell 2007; Althaus 2008)
- political system overload and failure (King 1976; Offe 1984)
- plagues, pandemics and viruses (Abraham 2004; Barry 2005; Withington 2005; Booker and North 2007)
- corporate failures (Hamilton and Micklethwait 2006; Ricks 2006)
- economic crises (Kindleberger and Aliber 2005; Oliver and Aldcroft 2007)
- state failure (Milliken 2003; Rotberg 2003)
- global calamity and catastrophe (Perrow 2007; Bostrom and Ćirković 2008).

It is difficult to do justice to the diversity of ideas and analytical frameworks therein but, nevertheless, the literature does give us a good sense of many issues relating not only to the nature of failure and how we understand it, but also its relationship to success.

First, there have been many attempts to define failure, but there is no universal agreement on what it is. Continual debates take place around the objective versus subjective nature of failure. Failure as 'fact' can be found most often in the literature on organizational failure and human error. Reason (1990: 17) defines error as 'planned actions that fail to achieve their desired consequences without the intervention of some chance or unforeseeable agency'. However, most other literature pays high regard to the subjective nature of failure, yet does not fully embrace a constructivist approach (that failure is purely in the eye of the beholder). For example, in their work on policy fiascos, Bovens and 't Hart (1996) lean heavily towards a social constructionist perspective on disasters, giving prominence to the contestability of phenomena, but stop short of a completely subjectivist view. They argue, for instance, that the Space Shuttle Challenger explosion and poverty in America's cities are 'real' failures (Bovens and 't Hart 1996: 147). There is nothing wrong with 'constructed' and 'real' dimensions co-existing. But it does indicate that any credible exploration of policy success must contend with both.

Second, there is the related issue of power and interests. A failure for one group or actor is not necessarily a failure for another. Corporate failures provide opportunities for competitors to flourish, policy failures benefit reformists who opposed the policies in the first place, and leadership damage in the wake of crisis provides opportunities for leadership contenders and opponents to rise to power. In terms of policy success, therefore, the issue of 'failure for whom' is very important indeed.

Third, there is some recognition of degrees of failure. Such recognition can be found, in a fairly limited way, in literature dealing with the differences between emergencies, disasters and catastrophes (Perry and Quarantelli 2005; McEntire 2007), ranging generally from emergencies as failures that can be coped with routinely by individuals and institutions trained for particular threats, through to catastrophes that are generally conceived of as beyond the coping capacities of institutions and processes. However, risk management literature, by its very nature of being a regularized assessment of the likelihood and likely impact of a graded series of risks, generally provides the most comprehensive treatment. For example, in their book on global catastrophic risks, Bostrom and Ćirković (2008) identify a range of risks from the personal to the trans-generational, each varying in intensity. The outcome is that the smallest failure is a personal one where someone loses a single hair on their head, through to larger failures such as country recession and a global flu pandemic, and then to the ultimate cataclysm, human extinction. For present purposes, the specific categories are not as important as the fact that failures can vary in magnitude. A framework for examining policy successes and their relationship to policy failures needs to do something similar. Chapter 3 will take up this challenge.

Fourth, there is recognition of different types of failure. Process failure is found most clearly in Hall's (1982) book *Great Planning Disasters*. He defines a disaster as: 'any planning process that is perceived by any people to have gone wrong' (Hall 1982: 2), before examining cases such as the Sydney Opera House and the Anglo-French Concorde. Indeed, process failures leading to crisis or disaster can be found throughout many works, such as that of Lee Clarke (1999) in his study of the tendencies of contingency planning for crisis to be little more than of symbolic value; Irving Janis (1982) on the role of groupthink in processing threats and producing 'bad decisions', and Patrick Dunleavy (1995) on the centralization of power within the British political system making it prone to producing 'bad' policies. Writings on programmatic failure can be found particularly in literature on implementation and reform failures (Pressman and Wildavsky 1984; Patashnik 2008), policy pathologies such as underfunding and delusions of grandeur (Hogwood and Peters 1985), and policy fiascos. Political failures are most often found in the literature on the politics of crisis management (Boin *et al.* 2005; Boin *et al.* 2008) on leadership damage in the wake of perceived mishandling, and governments being effectively forced to change from their desired course as a consequence of crisis.

Fifth, particularly in the crisis and disaster literature, there is recognition that change is ever present and, indeed, can occur exponentially. Therefore, undesirable states of affairs might not stay that way for very long. They could be catalysts for change. Boin *et al.* (2008) and also Birkland (1997, 2007) recognize that crises can open windows of opportunity for policy reform. To be explicit, government policy in a particular policy sector can be disastrous at point T1, but lead to reform and 'success' at point T2. For example, the UK government's policy in regulating safety in sports grounds was arguably a disaster at Hillsborough when 96 people died as a result of a crush, but arguably a longer-term success when all-seater stadiums became mandatory after the recommendations of the 1990 Taylor report.

More generally, it is evident from all these groups of literature, that there is limited exploration of the relationship between success and failure, treated more or less equally in terms of analysis. By far the most extensive is Bovens *et al.* (2001a) in the aforementioned work on public governance. In examining policy success, this book will need to tackle explicitly the issues of success, failure, and the grey areas in between. Chapter 4 takes up this challenge.

Promoting good practice in policy-making and programme management

Most public policy literature is explanatory rather than prescriptive, although there are often prescriptive elements to some degree, varying from small normative assumptions tagged onto primarily explanatory works, through to explicitly 'how to' books and articles. Most writings on good practice deal with issues of policy processes and (to a lesser extent) programme management and implementation. Literature that in some way promotes good process (policy-making, broadly defined) includes deliberation and engagement (Carson and Martin 1999; Gutmann and Thompson 2004; Creighton 2005), negotiation and bargaining (Lindblom 1965; Susskind and Cruikshank 1987) rigorous problem definition and options analysis (Dunn 2004; Bardach 2009), good people skills in policy analysis (Mintrom 2003), good policy design (Schneider and Ingram 1997), and the use of science to guide policy-making (Morgan and Peha 2003; Wagner and Steinzor 2006). A small number of authors also deal with how to implement and effectively manage programmes (Wanna 2007; Cohen *et al.* 2008).

Rarely will this broad field of literature use the word 'success', but it certainly contains strong assumptions of what constitutes 'good' policy. One of the most interesting issues for our purposes is the way in which it focuses on particular dimensions of policy. Broadly, they can be separated into issues of policy-making process and issues of programme management and implementation. Each can be dealt with briefly.

What constitutes good policy-making is almost self-evident to certain academics and practitioners. As a rough guide, there are three broad categories of literature here, each containing assumptions about what constitutes successful policy. Some writings arguably straddle more than one category but, nevertheless, the categories are sufficiently distinctive to highlight different assumptions about where successful policy resides.

First, one strand of work, with its roots in post-World War II social and political sciences, focuses on good policy as residing in rational, apolitical analysis. It can be termed as optimizing comprehensive rationality. It focuses on the ways in which goals can be achieved and is based on the thinking that policy should be informed by 'science' and epistemic communities of experts. The undercurrent here is that successful policy is policy devoid of 'politics'. Stokey and Zechauser (1978: 1) argue, for example, that societal well-being depends on government intervention to correct market failure, and that such interventions require the approach of a: 'rational decision maker who lays out goals and uses the best way to achieve these goals.' David Mitrany (1966), and his influential functionalist work on international peace and cooperation, argued that cooperation in economic and technical areas devoid of political contestation is the key to a gradualist approach to world peace.

A second strand proactively promotes a set of cherished values that are independent of government. Lindblom (1959, 1965), for example, was pre-eminent in promoting the virtues of incremental policy change, negotiation and bargaining, as was Crick (1962) in his classic *In Defence of Politics*. Lindblom (1959: 83) argued that the test of good policy is 'agreement on policy itself, which remains possible even when agreement on values is not'. Literature on the virtues of citizen engagement and public deliberation also contains strong assumptions about what constitutes good policy. Gastil (2008), drawing on Dahl, typifies with his suggestion that democratic policy-making requires inclusion, deliberation and enlightenment. Indeed, he argues that democracies cannot survive without meeting such tests. Also, Schneider and Ingram (1997:

203) advocate seven principles of good policy design that: 'will achieve a better balance among the multiple values that need to be served including solving problems, being responsive and accountable to the people, serving justice, and encouraging active empathetic citizenship'. Positions such as these point to success as residing in practices that accord with high level, moral and democratic values.

A third strand of literature is executive-centric, focusing on supporting government to 'do its job'. It is, in effect, a public/civil service type ethos, although writings come from academia as well as various think tanks and institutes. Some focus on establishing policy priorities in the initial phase of government (Daly *et al.* 2006), while others focus on issues such as effective management and implementation (Wanna 2007). In their book *The Effective Public Manager*, Cohen *et al.* (2008) suggest that the effective manger is one who overcomes obstacles and constraints in order to meet long-term objectives. The bottom line in terms of all such writings is that success equates with providing efficient and effective advice to government and its goals, whatever they might be.

Overall, one of the lessons for present purposes is that when policy analysts and commentators go in search of 'what works', they come up with widely different answers. Benchmarks vary from rationality through ethics to the wishes of government. Once again, later chapters of this book need to accommodate a diversity of views on what constitutes success, but to stop short of success and failure being nothing more than in the eye of the beholder.

Political strategy and survival

Most of the literature examined so far focuses on differing assumptions of what constitutes 'good' policy. It focuses particularly on what might constitute good policy processes and good policy programmes. An additional set of literature now needs to be introduced that deals explicitly with 'politics'. The simple reason is that, if public policy is broadly what governments choose to do (or not do), then government does not just 'do' processes or programmes, it also 'does' politics. It would be naïve to think that the processes of policy-making, or the types of policies chosen, are devoid of the political interests of parties or government. Success and failure of programmes can have a bearing on elections (campaigns, support, outcomes), strategic direction of government (helping keep policy trajectories on course or knocking them off course), and leadership career pathways (helping turn leaders into 'heroes' or 'villains'). As May (2005) and Althaus (2008) argue, the political viability of policy proposals is a reality of life. Policy options and alternatives have their own intrinsic merits and drawbacks, but their feasibility in terms of being adopted can depend on broader issues such as election timing and the challenges that policy options pose to key interest groups. To be blunt, therefore, consideration needs to be given to what constitutes successful politics because it has a bearing on the operational realities of policy-making and the programmes adopted. I would suggest that there are three broad groupings of literature on various forms of political strategy and survival that have a bearing on policy success.

First, there are works of political prescription. The founding father is Niccolò Machiavelli (1961) and his work *The Prince* (published originally in 1532), written arguably as an exercise to cultivate the favour of the Medici government in strife-torn Florence. Although much analyzed and disputed, his tract acknowledges and actively encourages, in a pragmatic manner, strategies for the acquisition and maintenance of political power. One implication is that success equates with doing what is necessary to obtain power and hold onto it. The spirit of Machiavelli lives on in the backrooms of politics. However, few academics and practitioners are prepared to advocate such apparent ruthless-ness and self-interest, but there are certainly some who write of such matters when others might only speak of them. For example, Dick Morris (1999, 2002), former adviser to Bill Clinton, offers pragmatic advice for politicians in terms of issues such as how to control your own party, how to court your own party, how to defeat bureaucratic inertia and how to win elections – even if you have no charisma! A plethora of books also exist on political campaigning and how to win elections (for example, Shaw 2004; Zetter 2007), although they are typically couched in mundane language. Who really wants to stick their neck out and advocate 'how to use your position in government to increase the likelihood that you will win the next election' or 'how to produce a quick fix policy that will not solve the problem but will get the media off your back'? Nevertheless, literature on political prescription reminds us that policies can have important political consequences. Hence, the achieving of political goals needs somehow to be factored into any assumptions of what constitutes policy success.

Second, the counter to Machiavellian instincts is the literature that recog-nizes, but critiques, the exercise of political power. For example, Bachrach and Baratz (1970), drawing on Schattschneider (1960) developed the concept of the 'mobilization of bias' to help explain the way in which the 'rules of the game' create biases in political agendas that favour elites and work against non-elites (in their case, an impoverished black community in Baltimore). Cobb and Ross (1997), in their work on agenda-setting, draw inspiration from some of this thinking and examine the way in which the strategic use of culture and symbolism denies some individuals access to the political agenda. Edelman writes from broadly the same tradition, although his works deals directly with some of the issues with which the present book is concerned. The title of his 1977 book captures the essence of his argument: *Political Language: Words that Succeed and Policies that Fail.* He writes of reassuring words and tokenistic policies often being sufficient to ensure the political viability of unsuccessful policies. Political viability accords with *not* disturbing existing hierarchies of power, income or status. The common denominator in all these works is the underlying implication that political success resides in policies that empower non-elites. To take Edelman's argument further, policy success actually *would* involve disturbing established hierarchies.

Third, and finally, perhaps the theoretical perspective that sits most easily with explaining political self-interest is rational choice theory (or public choice theory) and its assumption that rational self-interest among political actors is the driving force of political life and public policy. There are many variations within this approach (see Hindmoor 2006), with a particular emphasis on party positioning in relation to the electorate (Downs 1957), coalition building (Riker 1962) and bureaucratic growth (Niskanen 1971). Writing within this broad tradition, de Mesquita *et al.* (2003: 8), in *The Logic of Political Survival*, suggest that their: 'starting point is that every political leader faces the challenge of how to hold onto his or her job. The politics behind survival in office is, we believe, the essence of politics.' One does not need to be a rational choice adherent to accept that there is a grain of truth in this statement. Once again, it points us in the direction of needing to take seriously that, in terms of policy success, policies have political consequences and that political success is a fundamental component of broader policy success. In accordance with one of the continual themes of this chapter, not everyone agrees what success looks like (in this case, political success), but that is something we need to factor into our discussions in defining success.

Conclusion: taking stock of existing literature

This chapter has demonstrated that academics and policy practitioners often disagree and struggle with the nature of success, even if their concerns are not success *per se* but, rather, surrogates such as improvement and value. Yet, they provide a base on which to build. Five broad sets of issues have emerged in this review of the literature.

First, it is clear that success, whether explicit or implicit, means different things to different people. For some it is policy improvement, while for others it is achieving public value, or meeting benchmarks, or simply the faithful execution of government policy. A coherent framework is needed to accommodate and draw together these widely differing perspectives. Second, there are differing views of what aspects of a policy can succeed. Some, such as the rational choice and political survival literature, focus particularly on political success, while much conventional policy analysis literature concentrates on success related to programmes. Others, ranging from incrementalists to the new breed of deliberative democrats, emphasize 'good process'. Again, a policy success framework is needed that can accommodate such diversity. Third, success is not 'all or nothing'. While some literature, especially that dealing with success and failure, alludes to grey areas between the extremes of success and failure, a robust analytical framework needs to capture a range of possible outcomes, many of which will contradict one another.

Fourth, there are many different views, usually implicit, on how success can be achieved. For some, such as adherents to rational evaluation and traditional policy analysis, success is a product of a careful, comprehensive and non-politicized examination of policy problems and solutions. For others, success is a product of careful political strategy or, in the case of rational choice, the product of the pursuit of self-interest. A comprehensive examination of success strategies needs to be able to link together all these differing perspectives, whether we find them agreeable or not. Fifth, and finally, a series of issues has emerged that provide food for thought. How can a policy be successful if many abhor it? Are the conditions for success the same in every policy context? How stable is success once it has been achieved? These issues and more will be tackled in subsequent chapters.

Chapter 2

Policy Success: Definitions and Dimensions

Claims of policy success are in abundance. They permeate political life and emerge in forums ranging from local councils to parliamentary assemblies and global forums. Yet, as was shown in Chapter 1, the academic world has barely begun to dig beneath the surface of this key policy phenomenon and the rhetoric that surrounds it. When it does – either directly through the 'success' literature, or indirectly through examination of public value, policy improvement and so on – it tends to be based on loose assumptions of what are desirable characteristics of public policy. With the exception the work of Bovens *et al.* (2001a), the phenomenon of policy success is rarely tackled directly and systematically. As Law (2004) argues, it seems that the world is messy and our attempts to understand it only serve to compound the mess.

In order to help understand this seemingly intractable and messy phenomenon of policy success, this chapter provides a heuristic to aid our understanding. It begins by dealing explicitly with the issue of whether success is an objective state of affairs or simply a matter of interpretation, before fine-graining the analysis and identifying three main forms of success: process, programmatic and political. The analysis ventures at times into the more philosophical realms of the nature of success, but remains grounded in real-life cases to help illustrate that there are perfectly valid reasons for rejecting common managerialist and political assumptions of 'success' as an indisputable 'fact', as well as rejecting the often commonsense view that success is 'all a matter of interpretation'. An argument is developed that straddles both, emphasizing the political nature of policy success.

The scope of the chapter is limited simply to providing an initial analytical framework for examining success. It should be read in conjunction with Chapters 3 and 4, which illustrate that, while the tripartite classification provides a useful framework for examining different types of policy successes, there is a host of methodological and complexity issues that render 'success' far from straightforward. These include the complex relationship between success and failure, multiple policy goals (some of which can be met, while others are not) and the capacity of some policies to succeed in the short term, while incubating conditions for long-term failure.

What is policy success?

Students and analysts of political life know that understanding the world is far from simple. Even if we take basic political concepts such as democracy, human rights, power and politics, we are liable to find little agreement. For example, what is democracy? Supporters of liberal democracy would see democracy as rooted in political freedoms of constitutional and personal self-expression, while marxists would equate democracy not with political rights as such, but with material rights and freedom from capitalist exploitation. We could go further through third world dictatorships and fascist regimes, and find that democracy has multiple meanings, most of which stand in direct opposition to the others, but are linked by the powerful and positive language of 'democracy' (Macpherson 1966). What hope, therefore, is there of defining policy success? We certainly cannot escape the nature of political science as a pluralistic discipline that is divided in terms of theoretical reflections and research strategies (Hay 2002; Marsh and Stoker 2002). However, many of the unexplored issues surrounding policy success can at least be unpacked in order to produce a definition for others to reflect on, and that can guide subsequent analysis in this book.

As a starting point, we need to be aware that debates surrounding 'what is' (in our case, what is policy success) constitute ontological issues. As Marsh and Furlong (2002: 18) argue:

> Ontological questions are prior because they deal with the very nature of 'being' ... The key question is whether there is a 'real' world 'out there' that is independent of our knowledge of it. For example, are there essential differences between genders, classes or races that exist in all contexts and at all times?

Consequently, the question that emerges for present purposes is: does there exist a phenomenon of policy success that is independent of our knowledge of it, and that transcends space, time and culture? I begin by examining two different sets of arguments on this issue, before drawing them together with a third. Table 2.1 provides an overview.

A foundationalist position: policy success as 'fact'

Put simply, the crux of a foundationalist position is that there is an objective state of affairs that constitutes policy success, regardless of our interpretation, our cultural beliefs and so on. This perspective on the undisputable nature of success is close to 'official' assumptions and official language surrounding success. When French President Nicholas Sarkozy hailed the November

Table 2.1 *Foundationalist, anti-foundationalist and realist perspectives on the nature of policy success*

	Core assumption	Rationale	Example of government programme to build a nuclear power plant
Foundationalism	Success is a fact. It can be assessed against identifiable standards.	Objectives can be met.	Government builds plant on target.
		Desired outcomes can be achieved.	Plant achieves government outcome of generating enough energy for 10 per cent of nation's power supply.
		Some policies can promote universal human values; e.g., right to life and freedom from harm.	Safety is paramount. Plant operates safely to promote healthy working environment for employees and healthy living for residents in local areas.
			(Outcome = Success)
Anti-foundationalism	Success is purely a matter of interpretation. No identifiable standards exist for success.	Objectives and outcomes will be supported and opposed by different actors. We cannot call a policy a success. All we can do is recognize interpretations of success or otherwise.	Local residents and campaigners did not want the plant in the first place. They perceive it as a failure for the local community. The government perceives the plant as a success, but this is simply their view.
		Debates on universal human values are typically controversial. A policy that seems to promote such values will always be perceived differently by different interests: some perceiving success and some perceiving failure.	Local residents and campaigners feel at risk and disempowered, despite government assurances. They argue that the plant is jeopardizing their health and well-being. The government holds the opposite view.
			(Outcome = Simply different interpretations of success and failure)
Realism	Success is both fact and interpretation. A policy can be successful in some senses (e.g., meeting objectives), but not everyone will perceive it be a success.	Objectives and outcomes can be achieved. In this sense, a policy is successful. Different interests will support and oppose the objectives and the means of achieving them. Only supporters are likely to perceive a policy success.	The government's programme to build and operate the nuclear plant has been successful, insofar as the plant has been built as intended, generating energy as intended. However, it is perceived as a failure by local residents and campaigners, despite the government perceiving it as a success.

(Outcome = Success in some respects, but interpretations differ in terms of whether it is a success or failure) |

2008 G-20 summit to tackle the global financial crisis as a 'success'; when US President George W. Bush stated that the toppling of Saddam Hussein's regime was one of the greatest successes of our times, and when UK Prime Minister Gordon Brown stated that measures to control a new outbreak of foot and mouth disease in 2007 were highly successful, the underlying assumptions were that success was a matter of fact, not judgement. Such arguments are explored here in a more systematic and philosophical manner. Nevertheless, it is vital to remember that they are grounded in the realpolitik of political actors (often governments and officials) espousing statements – backed by facts and figures – that seem to indicate that a policy's 'success' is indisputable.

It is possible to identify several variations of the argument that success is a 'fact'. The first is a simple *instrumental* or *bureaucratic* one, suggesting that a policy is successful if it is implemented in accordance with original objectives. So, for example, if a government aims to put 2,000 more police into local communities, build 100 new schools or spend $2 billion on new submarines, then 'perfect implementation' (Hood 1976; Hogwood and Gunn 1984) of these goals constitutes policy success. The second variation is *outcomes-based*, which would suggest that a policy is successful if it achieves the desired outcome. For example, a government that intended to and then achieved a 15 per cent increase in the early detection of breast cancer among women under 40, or a 20 per cent increase in commuters using public transport could be construed as having achieved a policy success. A third and more philosophical variant on the foundationalist position is one based on *universal human values*. It would suggest that there are universal values – such as the right to life and free speech – that transcend nations and cultures. Therefore, any policy that protects such values constitutes a success. According to this position, for example, the criminalization of murder would be a success, because it protects the right to life and ensures harsh penalties for those who take the lives of others. Or, the building of levees and dykes to protect communities ranging from New Orleans to the Netherlands (see Box 2.1) would constitute a success, because they protect life and liberty. Therefore, according to this position, policies that protect universal human values are indicators of 'real' success.

It is easy to critique many aspects of the foundationalist argument. *The instrumental* or *bureaucratic* measure of success in terms of the achievement of implementation goals is based on the assumption that successful execution equates with successful policy. However, a policy might be successfully executed, but be undesirable to many. Suspected terrorists can be subject to torture in order to provide information, ordinary citizens can be subject to surveillance on the grounds of protecting national security, and wars can be fought that bring loss of life in the thousands and even millions. Such policies might achieve their goals, but are they 'successful' when they are opposed, and even abhorred, by some? Foundationalists would say 'yes, because policy-makers did what they set out to do. However, a crucial matter is confronted

Box 2.1 An example of programme success: flood control in the Netherlands

Background

Approximately 60 per cent of the population of the Netherlands lives below sea level. The country is protected by an elaborate series of dams (or dykes), storm surge barriers, drainage works and other measures. The two largest and most recent public projects are the Zuiderzee Works built in 1932–03 and the Delta Works completed between 1950 and 1997. Both projects involved land reclamation.

Programme success

Flood control defences in the Netherlands are not without debate. In 2007–08, the Delta Commission was established in order to examine how the Netherlands could best upgrade its defences in light of the challenge of climate change. Nevertheless, it is reasonable to suggest that, at the present time, the Dutch system of flood control defences meets all the criteria for programme success.

Meeting objectives: The clear objective has been met of holding back the waters of the North Sea, Wadden Sea and Western Scheldt (as well as discharges from the rivers Rhine and the Meuse), and preventing incursions onto dry land.

Producing desired outcomes: If not for the dams and other defences, about a quarter of the land mass of the Netherlands would be underwater and more than half the 16 million population would probably die. Flood controls defences help avoid such outcomes and create feasible and safe living/working conditions. Also, the Dutch economy would be decimated if the dams failed. Roughly 65 per cent of GDP is generated in low-lying areas, including Amsterdam, the Hague and the Port of Rotterdam. Other positive outcomes include avoidance of damage to nature, landscape, culture and reputation.

Creating benefit for target group: The main target group is the roughly 11 million people living below sea level, who can live and work safely as consequence of successful flood defences. Effective flood control is also a collective good and, hence, it also benefits the entire population.

Meeting policy domain criteria: The key criterion in this policy sphere is safety. The dams help meet this criterion. There have been no floods since the great flood of 1953 in Zeeland in the south-east of the country, killing at least 1800 people.

Source: Based on Delta Commission (2008).

here. As argued in Chapter 1, success is a 'feel good' word, perfectly captured in the definition in the *Oxford English Dictionary* (2001: 93), which defines it as 'The prosperous achievement of something attempted; the attainment of an object according to one's desire; now often with particular reference to the attainment of wealth or position.' Whether we like it or not, the word 'success' is part of the fabric of language; it has emerged to denote affirmation, prosperity, support and desirability. The word leaves no room for coldness and dispassion. Hence, foundationalist assumptions that see the bureaucratic attainment of objectives as indisputable evidence of success will always struggle against competing perceptions, from citizens, stakeholders and opposition parties, and media, but even at times within governing parties and bureaucracies themselves.

The *outcomes-based* version confronts similar difficulties. Groups, interests or individuals might feel that a particular policy has actually been unsuccessful because they oppose the policy aims, or at least believe them to be badly put into practice. It would certainly be easier to find widespread agreement on some outcomes, such as increased breast cancer detection, than on others, such as increased reliance on nuclear power or easing health and safety regulations to reduce 'red tape' for businesses. Once again, the language of success cannot be divorced from normative issues on the part of different policy actors.

The *universal human values* perspective on success is more difficult (although not impossible) to criticize. Who wants the freedom to see people murdered without sanction? Who wants to see entire communities destroyed? We would not expect very many people, if any at all, to desire death and destruction. Therefore, policies that protect universal human values seem to bring us closer to objective 'success', regardless of time, space and culture. However, we are not quite as close to grasping the universality of success as it might seem. Several objections can be made.

First, even a brief delving into the history of philosophical inquiry reveals disagreement on what many of us might be expect to be a given. In their book *Practical Ethics in Public Administration*, Geuras and Garofalo (2005) draw on a variety of rich traditions from Aristotle to Bentham in order to produce four different approaches to ethical issues in the public sector: teleology, deontology, intuitionism, and virtue theory. Each has implications for success. If we felt that it were proper and ethical for government to protect the life of citizens within its jurisdiction, then we would confront several alternative positions; if we assumed that such actions pointed towards objective, undisputable success:

- *Teleology*: Does protecting life produce the greatest happiness of the greatest number? Some would argue that there are many instances where it does not, and so alternative measures are acceptable – for example, capital punishment, abortion, sending troops to inevitable death in battle, legalized euthanasia, not prescribing expensive cancer medications on cost grounds. In other words, success can reside in *not* protecting life.

- *Deontology*: What principle is relevant here and can it be applied consistently? If the principle is to protect life regardless, then a policy of protecting citizens' right to life could only be a success, for example, if there were no wars and no financial barriers to treating all cancer patients.
- *Intuitionism*: What does my conscience tell me about the principle of government protecting life? As debates between those advocating a 'women's right to choose' and anti-abortionists reveal, not every individual has the same conscience. Success according to the conscience of one individual will be a failure according to that of another.
- *Virtue theory*: Is it virtuous to protect human life? Some people would consider legalized euthanasia to be entirely virtuous, while others would consider it to be dishonourable. Again, success judged by the morality of one individual will be a failure judged by the morality of another.

A foundationalist response might be that such debates are precisely that, and do not detract from the real existence of inalienable human values and the 'success' of policies that uphold them. Nevertheless, it is impossible to escape issues of interpretation and judgement on core human values. Even at the most abstract of levels, political philosophers ranging from Kant and Dewey to Hegel and Habermas dispute the nature of moral absoluteness. Indeed, if we factor in economic debates that rest on matters such as the universal desirability of individual preferences or efficient resource allocation, it seems that equating success with the promotion of universal human values is fraught with difficulty. Judgements are unavoidable.

Second, where would we draw a dividing line between policies that protect universal human values and those that do not? Again, it is a matter of interpretation. Law and order and national security policies, for example, would seem to be prime contenders for such a category, because they aim to protect life and property, but they are among the most contentious areas of public policy. Furthermore, many people might assume that 'typical' public policies (such as the building of roads, regulation of restaurants, licensing of taxis, the building of water processing facilities, and granting planning approvals) are not concerned with high-level values, but others might disagree. There is a plausible argument, for example, that the regulation of restaurants is rooted in deeper societal values about health and safety, as well as market values such as fair exchange. As such, it is difficult to say which policy areas might be candidates for 'objective' success and which might not. Interpretation is again needed, rendering success, at least to some degree, in the eye of the beholder.

Third, there are typically multiple public policy solutions to public policy problems (notwithstanding the issue of problem definition and its limiting of the range of policy solutions, see Schön and Rein 1994; Peters and Hornbeek

2005). Some individuals, groups or interests would support certain solutions over others. The death penalty is an example. Supporters and opponents would share values in seeking to reduce murder rates, but would be in vehement opposition to each other about whether imposing the death penalty would be the best policy solution. Therefore, vastly differing views on the 'success' of the death penalty are likely.

Fourth public policies are not stand-alone solutions to policy problems. Rather:

- there is overlap between policy sectors – for example, industry, environment, transport, commerce, trade
- there is overlap between constitutional areas of policy responsibility – for example, national, state/province, regional, local
- there is overlap between quasi-constitutional areas of governance – for example, quasi-autonomous non-governmental bodies, public–private partnerships
- there are decision-making trade-offs to be made – for example, allocating resources to one policy area and not to another.

Even if a policy achieves its intended outcomes, it might be to the detriment of other policy areas. In other words, success for some jurisdictions or policy areas might be at the expense of failure for others. For example, a successful policy of reducing income tax rates might leave less funding for health and education. Or, a policy of successfully redistributing a national tax to a rural region with a low tax base and a widely-dispersed population spread might be to the detriment of an urban region with a high tax base and a concentration of population. Such issues will be dealt with in greater depth in Chapter 4 but, for the moment, they indicate, once again, that a foundationalist position on policy success (as indisputable fact) is difficult to sustain wholeheartedly. Context and interpretation matter.

An anti-foundationalist position: policy success as 'interpretation'

Many different theoretical perspectives emphasize, to varying degrees, the socially constructed nature of political life. These include a focus on discursive politics (Fischer 2003), interpretation (Bevir and Rhodes 2003) and meaning (Edelman 1988; Hodgson and Irving 2007). While all would depart from a foundationalist position of success as 'fact', they do not provide a diametrically opposite view and so we need to go a little further to make a point. The basis of an 'idealized' anti-foundationalist position is that policy success is a matter of interpretation, rather than a reality. Put simply, whether or not a policy is successful is a matter of judgement, rather than a matter of fact. Neither success nor failure exists objectively, only judgements on whether a policy has succeeded or failed. So, even if a government executes a policy to perfection, this does not constitute success (according to an anti-foundationalist position), because the policy will have its supporters and detractors, depending on the degree to which they are affected by the outcomes, the values they hold and so on. Opposition might come from outside government (media, citizens and non-governmental organizations) but also inside it (governing parties, public bureaucracies).

An example of the former is a tax on carbon emissions with 100 per cent collection rates, but which is unlikely to be viewed as a successful policy by those who are opposed to increased taxation or who are sceptical of the argument that global warming is 'man-made'. Similarly, the achievement of policy outcomes does not constitute success because of differing perceptions of the merits or otherwise of the policy. For example, the policy in Sweden of requiring the minority partner (usually the father) to take two months of paternity leave is not a success for those who argue that fathers should not get paternity leave (as is the norm in countries such as Australia and the US). Likewise, when we enter the realm of core human values (such as policy debates surrounding abortion, capital punishment, euthanasia and stem cell research) we enter a world of often hostile debate, rather than universal agreement.

At first glance, much is attractive about the argument that success is simply a matter of interpretation and can always be contested. It is politically realistic in recognizing that, in plural societies with free speech and competing values, debate and differing viewpoints are the order of the day. As Stoker (2006a: 5) argues: 'To understand politics, one must, above all, understand the inevitable *partiality* of judgement.' We would, for example, expect environmentalists and ecologists to disagree over the need for controlled burning in order to prevent bushfires, and for supporters of ethnic diversity to disagree with those who want heavy restrictions on immigration. However, it is difficult wholeheartedly to embrace the idea that success is nothing but interpretation in disguise. There are two key reasons.

The first refers to attainment of objectives. It is easy to get caught up in issues of interpretation and forget that government can set out to do something and then do it. If it wants to build a nuclear power plant in a remote coastal location and does it, we can surely say that, at least from government's perspective, the attainment of its objective constitutes a success. Similarly, if a government wants to raise income tax by 1 per cent and does it, then the move also constitutes a success in relation to goal attainment. This is not to deny that some might disagree with government's aims and means of achieving them, but I would argue that it is virtually impossible, except at the most abstract of levels, to question where a government really did build its nuclear power plant, or really did raise the rate of income tax. The argument that success is simply a matter of interpretation cannot realistically be sustained.

The second reason to question an entirely interpretative approach to success is more complex: the issue of power. Debates in this area of political science are many (see, for example, Scott 2001; Lukes 2005), but a common (although not exclusive) theme is that power equates with the advancing of interests, such as A over B, one class over another, and one state or another. Public policies, by their very nature as authoritative choices in terms of the distribution of rights and rewards in society, are facilitators of power. Pawson and Tilley (1997: 20), for example, write of 'asymmetries of power which are assumed in and left untouched by the vast majority of policy initiatives'. The implication is that, regardless of the interpretation of success (or otherwise), policies have real impacts on interests and so can produce real successes for those interests. This is the very essence of a range of interest group perspectives such as policy communities (Richardson and Jordan 1979), advocacy coalitions (Sabatier and Jenkins-Smith 1993) and policy monopolies (Baumgartner and Jones 2009), which focus on policy domains effectively being 'captured' by key groups(ings). Differing perspectives on the dominance of socio-economic power, class, race and gender tend to focus on the capacity of political (and economic) systems to reproduce dominant inequalities. Regardless of whether we are sympathetic to any of these perspectives, or none, it is difficult to deny the fact that policies, by virtue of allocating and redistributing, benefit some interests over others; often continually so. Therefore, the issue of 'success for whom' is vital.

Anti-foundationalists might respond that even issues of power inequalities are primarily a matter of how they are socially constructed and given meaning, rather than being objective truths. Lukes (2005), in his defence of using the term 'real interests' to support his argument that power includes domination by one individual/group that affects an individual's real interests, makes us realize how difficult it is to escape constructivism when he argues that there is no magical canon that states what the 'real interests' of any particular individual or group actually are. A Marxist, for example, would argue that 'real interests' are material ones, whereas a liberal democrat would argue that real interests are based on political freedoms within a liberal democratic framework. Indeed, Flathman (1966) argues that the public interest is so fluid and dependent on context that it is virtually impossible to define. Such differences seem to lead us down the path of saying that we cannot say that a policy is a success for A (remembering that A might be inside or outside government), because we do not have a definitive understanding of what is in A's interests. However, there is a danger that, in accepting the anti-foundationalist defence of its position, we completely reject what A articulates as their interests. For example, if A is a pressure group and argues in favour of policy X, to provide it with outcome Y, and this happens, or it supports the benefit it obtains from policy X, then it seems reasonable to argue that policy X can be considered a success for group A.

For example, if a group representing local businesses wants to pay less taxes and lobbies for a below inflation rise in property tax rates and the government does so, then it seems reasonable to suggest that the reduced tax rate policy is a success for local business. If success is purely and simply in the eye of the beholder, then we are rejecting the reality that policies provide rights and rewards to some interests (and not to others), as well as the reality that policy-makers might identify objectives and actually meet them.

Policy success: a realistic definition

I would argue that we need a definition of policy success that accommodates issues of interpretation, but does not become infatuated by them; and accommodates issues of goal attainment but leaves room for interpretation. I advance what I consider to be a pragmatic and realistic definition of policy success, straddling both foundationalist (success as fact) and anti-foundationalist (success as interpretation) approaches. Hence:

> A policy is successful insofar as it achieves the goals that proponents set out to achieve. However, only those supportive of the original goals are liable to perceive, with satisfaction, an outcome of policy success. Opponents are likely to perceive failure, regardless of outcomes, because they did not support the original goals.

There are several advantages to this definition. First, it recognizes that some actors will see a policy as a success, while others will see it as a failure. As an example, the levying of a road toll across a new bridge might be perceived as a success by those who support a stream of income to fund the project, but a failure by those who feel that free public access to public infrastructure is a right of citizens. Second, and following on from the above, the definition can accommodate the 'success for whom?' issue, because policies might benefit some interests and/or accord with their values, and not do so for others. For example, if government makes available a large national competitive infrastructure grant for refurbishing an airport and makes the award to city E as opposed to city F, the former is likely perceive the programme as a success and the latter a failure. Third, the definition can encapsulate 'commonsense' usages of the term success, in terms of setting goals and achieving them. If government wants to build a new town hall and does so, there is something to be said for the attaining of this goal to attract the label 'success', regardless of issues such as whether we might think the new building is necessary or an efficient use of resources. Fourth, the definition can accommodate aspects of policy that are successful (government meeting its goals, actors/interests/groups benefiting) without any assumption that such outcomes are desirable. In other words, the definition is not normative.

Finally, as will be evident shortly, the definition can cope with the reality of public policy-making: multiple goals, as opposed to just one. Goals might range from wanting to present a political party as fit to govern in the context of the next election to wanting to ensure that a policy has 'legitimacy'.

Much more is needed over the next few chapters to expand on these points. The first stage is to examine, in detail, three forms of success: process, programmatic and political. In reality, they can overlap (Chapters 3 and the Conclusion in particular will deal with this issue) but, for initial ease of understanding, they can be treated separately.

The three dimensions of policy success

Different actors might be involved in different aspects of policy. Some are much more involved in processes of policy-making, others are more involved in programme implementation, while yet others are involved more in the political sphere of electioneering and managing party reputation. Criteria for success in each sphere are not definitive, but I would argue that they capture the vast majority of ways in which policies might be considered successful.

Importantly, it should be noted that analysts might disagree on whether any particular criterion has been met. For example, one of the conditions for programme success is achievement of desired outcomes. Some might argue that a before-and-after comparison is the most suitable indicator, while others might argue simply that the benefits need to outweigh the costs. Such issues will be dealt with in detail in Chapter 4 (offering practical advice to analysts) and Chapter 5 (dealing with the ways in which success can be framed by policy proponents).

Process success

The process of policy formation is a vital, but often neglected element in consideration of a policy's success or otherwise (see Marsh and McConnell 2010a, 2010b; Bovens 2010). In broad terms, 'process' refers to policy-making and implementation. We will concentrate on the former when dealing with issues of process, because implementation will be covered in the programme aspects of policy. Hence, the concern here is with the emergence of issues, the way in which problems are defined, options examined, stakeholders consulted and decisions made (see Hogwood and Gunn 1984; Althaus *et al.* 2008; Howlett *et al.* 2009). Particularly from the 1950s onwards, with the emphasis on policy systems and decision-making processes (Lasswell 1956; Lindblom 1959; May and Wildavsky 1978; Dror 1983), it has been clear that public policy is about more than just policy decisions or their impact on society, it is also about the process that produces policy. A caveat is necessary. The development of political science and public policy studies (deLeon 1988; Radin 2000), particularly since the early 1970s, indicates that not all policy-making follows the sequenced and rational assumptions of the policy cycle. Rather, it might be driven, for example, by the self-interest of political actors, locked-in by path dependencies or agenda-managed in advance by 'garbage can' solutions. Such perspectives do not deny the importance of process. Rather, they affirm its importance by examining issues that traditional policy cycle theorists are not good at dealing with, such as the issue of agenda manipulation and political self-preservation. Therefore, processes *are* important, in both practical and symbolic terms. This point can be taken further by identifying key ways in which process can be considered successful. Box 2.2 refers to process success surrounding electoral reform in British Columbia, and covers all the detailed criteria that follow.

Preserving government policy goals and instruments

From a policy-maker's perspective, a legislative process during which a bill is scrutinized, but the outcome is the preservation of the broad values and detailed policy instruments, is likely to be considered a success. Of course, policy-making interests might at times be served by opposition amendments that help make proposals more workable, or by making small concessions in order to gain sufficient numbers for support in voting chambers. Such issues will be dealt with later (Chapter 6) and do not detract from the basic point that political executives typically want to see their policy proposals become law, and that achieving these goals can be perceived as a success as far as they are concerned. For example, in November 2005 the Australian Prime Minister John Howard introduced a bill proposing controversial reform of industrial relations law. It was designed as a 'union busting' end to collective bargaining, to be replaced by a new national system of individual workplace agreements, negotiated between employers and employees. Amid high profile media publicity generated by government, its supporters and critics, the bill was passed swiftly through the House of Representatives and the Senate within six weeks. From the coalition government's perspective, the outcome can be considered a process success because, despite some minor amendments, the government achieved its goal. Its core policy proposals remained intact, as did the flagship of its neo-liberal, economic rationalist agenda. This example is also useful in flagging up a complexity issue that will be dealt with in Chapter 4. Howard's policy (a short-term process success) might have helped lose them the 2007 election and so have been a long-term political failure (Brett 2007).

Ensuring policy legitimacy

A policy that is produced through constitutional and quasi-constitutional procedures will confer a large degree of legitimacy on policy outcomes, even

Box 2.1   An example of process success: a decision not to reform the electoral system in British Columbia

Background

Particularly since the mid-1990s, the electoral system in British Columbia (BC), Canada had proved very controversial. In 1996, the New Democrats won a majority of seats in the legislature, despite obtaining only 39 per cent of the vote and their opponents the Liberal Party obtaining 42 per cent. The Liberals committed themselves to establishing a Citizens' Assembly on Electoral Reform when they next took office. When they gained power in 2001, they incorporated that promise into a wider package of constitutional measures.

Membership of the Citizens' Assembly was 160 citizens, selected at random from stratified populations. Membership comprised a 50:50 gender split, including two representatives from First Nations. Its first meeting was held in January 2004, and a final report was produced in December of the same year. Work was undertaken in four stages, over a one-year period. After 50 public hearings across the province in town hall meetings and extensive e-consultation, it recommended that the existing system (simple plurality) be replaced with a more proportional one, based on the Single Transferable Vote. The core impact of the proposal would likely be, depending on voting patterns, a move from a more adversarial to a consensus-based system.

The proposals went to a referendum in 2004, were accepted by 58 per cent of voters and had majority support in 77 of 79 electoral districts, but this was short of the required 60 per cent majority in electoral districts. The Liberal government, led by Gordon Campbell, felt that the result was sufficiently close to warrant further consideration.

In May 2009, a second referendum was held in conjunction with provincial elections. Only 38 per cent of voters supported the electoral reform proposals, and the Liberals were returned to power. The existing system would not be reformed after all.   ◊

when those policies are contested. Even an emphasis on 'evidence-based policy' or 'good negotiations' and debate, the very heart of 'politics' (Crick 1962), brings a measure of legitimacy and authority to whatever final decision is reached. Indeed, as Issalys (2005: 154) argues: 'insofar as legitimacy resides in the acceptance both of an authority and of the rules laid by this authority, it has obvious repercussions for the effectiveness ... of any mechanism of public

⚡ Process success

The referendum result was decisive and, in public policy terms, it conforms with 'policy as inaction'; that is, the decision not to proceed. It can reasonably be argued that the process that produced this decision constitutes a process success, because it conforms to all the main criteria for the same.

Preserving policy goals and policy instruments: This case is a subtle example of meeting this criterion. Normally, government might have a preferred policy option from the start, and 'success' comes for government because, after a period of scrutiny, its preferred option remains intact and becomes law/policy. In this case, the government's goal was not so closed. It was to introduce electoral reform, only if a system recommended by the Citizens' Assembly was endorsed in a referendum. Therefore, the process preserved government's goals and did not become distorted to the point where it found itself with no choice but to implement a system it did not support. Even if we assume that government had a hidden goal simply to defuse the issue, it managed to achieve this end.

Conferring legitimacy: Despite some concerns surrounding the first referendum that many people were unaware of the work of the Assembly, its work plus two referendums gave popular legitimacy to proceeding no further on the issue of electoral reform.

Building a sustainable coalition: A decisive province-wide referendum, plus support of government, is liable to ensure that advocates of 'no electoral reform' remain dominant and sustainable for the foreseeable future.

Symbolizing innovation and influence: The BC Citizens' Assembly experiment was a radical and innovative way of tackling a politically difficult issue. It attracted attention from deliberative theorists, practitioners and journalists from throughout the world. It symbolized forward-thinking and contributed to process legitimacy.

Sources: Based on Lundberg (2007); Carty *et al.* (2008); Flinders and Curry (2008); Ward (2008).

intervention'. In effect, process legitimacy can help ensure successful programme implementation. Edelman (1977) goes further and argues that policy processes that co-opt participants into discussions are effectively rituals that legitimate existing power arrangements. Process legitimacy can therefore lay the conditions for political success.

Every policy will have some claim to legitimacy attached to it (even if it is based only on the moral authority of the leader), although legitimacy depends on subjective interpretation among a variety of political actors and is not an 'all or nothing' phenomenon (Knoepfel *et al.* 2007; Wallner 2008). Nevertheless, recognition from stakeholders and citizens that a policy produced through constitutional and quasi-constitutional processes is a success for government because it can do what it set out to do, without any significant questions over its right to do so. In France in 1977, for example, the Jospin Government was successful in using the legitimating factor of needing to meet Maastricht Treaty rules for budget deficits in order rapidly to push through a series of tax reforms (Adolino and Blake 2001: 197). In Australia, the liberal government under John Howard held a referendum in 1999 on whether Australia should become a republic. In essence, the conservative government got what it wanted (a majority 'No' vote), with the authority of a nationwide referendum to legitimate the decision.

Building a sustainable coalition

A successful process from the perspective of policy-makers and policy-supporters can be (and be presented as) the building of sustainable alliances. Sometimes, of course, sustainability is a luxury than can be ill-afforded under circumstances such as minority government or party-divisive issues. Here, obtaining formal approval (perhaps in cabinet or the floor of the legislature) is a key goal. Such circumstances aside, it seems reasonable to suggest that programme success (or even avoiding low-level failures) is more feasible if the policy process is successful in engaging and reflecting the interests of powerful coalition of interests. A sustainable coalition of support is more liable to have the authority to ensure successful implementation, and/or to carry sufficient power and authority to ensure that small failures are less liable to be constructed as damaging to the overall success of the policy. In the Canadian province of Alberta, for example, a package of successful educational reforms introduced by the Klein government was aided by process success in building support among the educational professions and among the public at large (Wallner 2008).

It should be noted that determining what constitutes a sustainable coalition is far from an exact science. Academics have approached the issue from many different angles, such as minimum winning coalitions (Riker 1962), advocacy coalitions (Sabatier and Jenkins-Smith 1993), policy monopolies (Baumgartner and Jones 2009) and veto players (Tsebelis 2002). However, such debates do not negate a fundamental point; that is, from the vantage point of policy-makers, a strong alliance that supports a particular policy initiative can be portrayed as the basis of successful policy. George W. Bush, for example, launched Operation Iraqi Freedom with the backing of a 49-member 'coalition of the willing'. He continually utilized the level of multi-lateral support as an indicator of how successful the incursion actually was. In other words, an assumed legitimacy of process success was considered a vindication of the programme overall.

Symbolizing innovation and influence

Innovation and influence can also be indicators of successful process, regardless of eventual outputs or outcomes. Old problems tackled in new ways fit the bill here. In the Canadian Province of British Columbia, the 1990s produced a number of high-profile corruption scandals, generating widespread disenchantment with politicians, parties and policy-making processes. In order to tackle this anti-establishment mood, the ruling Liberal government sought to reform the electoral system, not through a top-down initiative but through a Citizens' Assembly on Electoral Reform, comprised of 160 citizens selected at random. The details of this case are intricate (see Box 2.2 for a detailed examination) but the key point for present purposes is that the Liberal government could take credit for an innovative initiative that cast aside the machinations and political partisanship that typically surround electoral reform.

Innovation can also stem from a policy being transferred from another political jurisdiction (Dolowitz *et al.* 1999; Dolowitz and Marsh 2000; Evans 2009). A range of measures can be transferred from detailed policy instruments to broad visions – all on the assumption that there is some value to the 'receiving' country or jurisdiction in doing so. Naturally, the value of the policy being transferred is often disputed. Just because a policy seemingly works elsewhere does not always guarantee further success when 'exported' (Chapter 8 will discuss this in detail). Nevertheless, from the perspective of policy-makers, transfer can be used to legitimate their own policy proposals. For example, Japan's reform of its higher education system took inspiration from and was legitimated by the UK's higher education reforms and broader approach to disaggregating the civil service, and the public sector more generally, into a multitude of agencies and quasi-independent bodies run on new public management principles and practices (Goldfinch 2006).

Programme success

As indicated in Chapter 1, success in programme terms has become synonymous with successful policy among most western-style democracies with their focus on evidence-based policy-making and policy improvement (Davies *et al.* 2000; Parsons 2002; Head 2008). As former British Prime Minster Tony Blair famously stated: 'what matters is what works'. This statement exemplifies the

Table 2.2   *The three main dimensions of policy success*

Process	○ Preserving policy goals and instruments
	○ Conferring legitimacy
	○ Building a sustainable coalition
	○ Symbolizing innovation and influence
Programmes	○ Meeting objectives
	○ Producing desired outcomes
	○ Creating benefit for target group
	○ Meeting policy domain criteria
Politics	○ Enhancing electoral prospects/reputation of governments and leaders
	○ Controlling the policy agenda and easing the business of governing
	○ Sustaining the broad values and direction of government

argument that our assessment of success should be based on outcomes and evidence rather than political ideology (Parsons 2002; Sanderson 2002). For governments keen to show that they are governing in the public or national interest, equating success with evidence can create (or at least be intended to create) the appearance of neutrality and the avoidance of partisanship. Chapter 4 will deal explicitly with the issue of how amenable success actually is to empirical verification. For present purposes, we can concentrate simply on various ways in which programmes can be considered a success. In practice, they are not mutually exclusive but, for analytical purposes, they can be treated independently of each other.

Meeting objectives

This is a classic 'we did what we set out to do' measure of success. In programme terms, it encapsulates the bureaucratic objectives of implementation, as well specific programme objectives. It sits easily with many of the dictionary and commonsense assumptions about success. There is little difference between a transport agency wanting to build a new road and doing so, and a government space agency wanting to send a rocket into space and doing do. Both constitute objectives that have been met. It is therefore unsurprising that, for both explanatory and normative reasons, goal attainment has a central place in much academic analysis (see Chapter 1). For example, rational choice theory focuses on how decision-makers strive for utility maximization (Mueller 2003; Hindmoor 2006), while theories of bounded rationality explain why there are limits to rational goal attainment (Simon 1957; Jones 2001). Many different policy traditions also confer a central role on goal attainment, with implicit and occasionally explicit assumptions that achieving goals equates with success. Much of the US-based policy analysis literature focuses heavily on goal attainment as bureaucratic achievement of objectives, while relegating to the margins issues surrounding the political desirability or otherwise of policies (Gupta 2001; Weimer and Vining 2005). Classic continental European bureaucratic and legalistic assumptions of public administration also focus on the necessity for policies to be implemented according to the objectives laid down when they were approved. Therefore, meeting objectives can also include implementation in accordance with intentions.

By focusing on meeting objectives, many policy protagonists can claim policy success. We might debate the issue of 'how much of a success' a programme has been (Chapter 3 will tackle this issue directly) but examples of broad policy objectives that were fulfilled include the 1990 constitutional integration of East and West Germany; the 1995–99 creation and opening of a bridge between Denmark and Sweden; and the switchover to digital television in countries such as Luxembourg, Finland and Switzerland. In essence, governments did what they set out to do.

Producing desired outcomes

The nature of programmatic success can also encapsulate the subsequent impact on society; that is, outcomes. Objectives and outcomes might overlap, but not necessarily so. Sometimes the outcome is focused narrowly on a target group. In Norway, for example, a government grant aimed at first-time entrants to the private housing market was successful in ensuring vertical equity; that is, redistribution towards lower-income families (Stamsø 2008). At other times, the target group is broader and even societal-wide. In Switzerland, for example, legislation to increase home ownership achieved its target of doubling home ownership within a 15-year period (Knoepfel *et al.* 2007: 232). Also, in Singapore, from the early 1960s to the early 1990s, a variety of housing provision and supply policies led to roughly 90 per cent of citizens owning their own homes, with a general improvement in living conditions and amenities (Ramesh 2004). The goals here were to ease severe housing shortages; yet, in other cases, goals are part of government's political rhetoric accompanying policy proposals. The 2001 US 'No Child Left Behind' law introducing a standards-based approach to school education is an example, as is the pledge in 1987 by Australian Prime Minister Bob Hawke that no Australian child would be living in poverty by 1990. Such aspirations might be difficult, if not impossible, to achieve (indeed, some 20 years later, Bob Hawke expressed regret at making his rash promise in a speech that was a departure from what had been distributed to the media). Nevertheless, they indicate that, beyond specific targets or the bureaucracy of implementation, the broader impact or outcome that policy actually has can be used as an identifier of policy success.

Creating benefit for a target group

A further aspect of programme success is the benefit it brings to a particular target group, interest or actor, based on issues such as class, territory, gender, religion and race. In South Korea, for example, young children benefited from the huge expansion in the number of kindergartens over a 30-year period until the mid-1990s, with enrolments increasing from 1 per cent of the population to 88 per cent (Ramesh 2004: 180). In the UK, civil partnerships legislation in 2004, which entitled gay and lesbian couples to legal recognition of their relationships, can be seen as a success for gays and lesbians in terms of securing rights in relation to practical matters such as property and finance, as well as helping erode societal discrimination.

Importantly, as will be discussed extensively in Chapters 3 and 5, a programme that is successful for some interests does not mean that everyone agrees. Contestation is an inescapable feature of programme successes. An interesting example is indigenous land rights in Australia. In 1976, legislation enabled over 40 per cent of land to be handed back to its traditional owners (Aboriginal and Torres Strait Islander peoples) and the installation of a 'permit' system for entry. The move was promoted widely as a success for indigenous peoples whose land had been defined by colonists as *'terra nullius'* (land belonging to no one). In 2007, however, the commonwealth coalition government, led by John Howard, instigated a highly controversial move to remove many aspects of the permit system in the Northern Territory as part of broader measures aimed at tackling child abuse in indigenous communities. Critics perceived it as 'land grab' and the escalation of crisis-type conditions for political advantage (see 't Hart 2008). The importance for our purposes of these moves, 20 years apart, is that granting *and* removal of indigenous land rights in Australia have each been proclaimed as a success by the governments who instigated the reform. Competing discourses are a natural aspect of public policy in plural societies (Schön and Rein 1994; Stone 2002).

Meeting policy domain criteria

Public policies encompass a vast range of different policy domains, including energy, industry, agriculture, environment, intelligence, defence and foreign affairs, policing, health, social services and many more. Most, if not all, policy sectors have values that are widely held by its community of actors; for example, secrecy (intelligence), efficiency (budgeting), patient care (health). Often, these values are enshrined in industry standards or benchmarks, such as risk management standards, accounting standards for public bodies, best value or public value tests, emissions standards for motor vehicles, and Geneva Conventions and protocols relating to armed conflict. In effect, such standards are indicators of success in that policy domain. Austria, for example, ranked first place for two years running in the EU's annual benchmark survey of online availability of public services, and was the first country to reach 100 per cent in the category 'full on line availability' (Rodousakis and dos Santos 2008). Meeting standards can also include passing tests such as balanced scorecards (Kaplan and Norton 1992, 1997) and benefit-cost analysis (Miller and Robbins 2007).

Other criteria for success might cut across policy domains. Efficiency is a particularly important one. The issue of resource success and cost containment is one that has risen high on public agendas in developed countries since the mid-1970s' world economic crisis. The growth of public audit agencies, efficiency reviews, value-for-money studies, productivity commissions, competitiveness councils and suchlike are indicative of resource efficiency as a measure of successful public policy. In Germany, for example, most health care reforms since the mid-1970s have focused on controlling costs, beginning with the Health Care Cost Containment Act 1977 (Adolino and Blake 2001: 226–7). In the real world of public policy, the word efficiency has become something of an umbrella term to encapsulate a broad range of imperatives and initiatives to reduce waste, cut costs, do more with less and so on. Several studies, for example, have suggested that waste collection in Switzerland of roughly one collection site per 2,000–3,000 inhabitants is an efficient use of public resources (Knoepfel *et al.* 2007: 234). More generally, targets are common, and achievement of targets is assumed to equate with success. In the UK, a report by the Home Office on efficiency and productivity in the police service stated clearly in response to the issue of 'what success looks like', that it included:

> Authorities/forces achiev[ing]... cashable efficiency & productivity gains worth at least 9.3% over three years, net of costs – sustainably deployed to where they are most needed. This is the basis on which taxpayers have provided the Service with funding.
>
> (*Home Office 2004: 4*)

Efficient use of resources has become common currency for programme success.

Political success

If policy broadly equates with what governments do, then they do not simply oversee policy processes or take programme decisions, they also *do* politics. There are, of course, many different definitions of politics, ranging from those focusing on generic issues of conflict and cooperation (which can reside anywhere from the micro-level of the family to the super-macro level of global actors and institutions) to those focusing more on policy-making arenas and their satellite of actors and interests (for example, parties, lobby groups, elected representatives and bureaucrats). The use here of the word 'political' is rooted more in the latter camp, purely for explanatory purposes rather than any assumption that politics is simply the preserve of the formal institutions and actors of politics. In this light, political success is defined in relation to government, its capacity to govern, the values it seeks to promote and so on. In other words, process and/or programmatic success can, depending on the circumstances, bring political success to government. Let us break down this contention further into three categories. They are treated separately here but can overlap. Box 2.3 gives an example of all three, in Australian Prime Minister Kevin Rudd's history 'sorry' speech to Aboriginal peoples.

Enhancing electoral prospects or reputation of governments and leaders

One hardly needs to be a rational choice theorist to recognize that parties holding political office want to stay elected. Governments want to continue to govern. The implication is that a policy that helps sustain, or even boost their prospects at the ballot box can be considered successful. The Thatcher government seemed doomed to electoral failure in 1982 until its intervention in the Falkland Isles paved the way for a 'heroic' victory. Venezuelan President Hugo Chávez has spent much of his time since 1999 gathering extraordinarily high levels of populist support, on the back of pursuing policies aimed at bridging the gap between rich and poor.

A small field of political science has also devoted itself to studying issues such as 'populist policy-making' and 'poll-driven government', as well as 'political business cycles', 'election giveaways', 'electoral bribes' 'election budgets', 'vote buying' and more (for example, Alesina *et al.* 1997; Schaffer 2007). Sometimes, as some of these categories indicate, policies stray into illegality, such as the Building Stable Communities programme of Westminster Council under its Conservative leader Dame Shirley Porter selling council homes in marginal wards, which an inquiry (in a judgement later upheld by the House of Lords) found to be unlawfully aimed at improving the party's electoral prospects (Hosken 2006). Beyond specific instances of verifiable corruption, however, it is very difficult to prove empirical connections between programmatic aims and hidden political agendas. Despite, such links remaining in the grey areas of political study, it is not unreasonable to suggest that the prospect of forthcoming elections can cultivate environments where policy programmes are capable of being used to facilitate political success.

A further dimension is added to the mix when considering circumstances of crisis, traditionally where severe threats are imminent, uncertainty is high but there is a need for rapid decision-making (Rosenthal *et al.* 2001; Drennan and McConnell 2007). While crises do have the capacity to destroy government and leaders (Spanish Prime Minister José María Aznar after the 2004 Madrid bombings; the Icelandic cabinet in 2009 after a popular backlash against its handling of the global financial crisis), they also have the capacity to galvanize and renew (Boin *et al.* 2008). Crises can create opportunities for government and leaders to prove their fitness for office and emerge as heroes (Peruvian President Alberto Fujimori and the 1996–7 hostage crisis, George W. Bush and 9/11, German Chancellor Gerhard Schröder and the 2002 river floods). In fact, crisis circumstances can be cultivated and/or exploited for precisely this purpose (Boin *et al.* 2009; McConnell 2009). Once again, therefore, political success can stem from programme implementation.

Controlling the policy agenda and easing the business of governing

Governments face a difficult task. They face a never-ending stream of problems (some chronic and long-standing, others short-term episodes), are lobbied by countless groups who are often in complete disagreement, have limited resources at their disposal and are scrutinized by a host of often hostile players from political opponents to the media. Therefore, an aspect of the business of government involves producing programmes that might arguably leave much to be desired in terms of dealing with policy problems, but help sustain its capacity to govern. Therefore, a programme can be considered politically successful if it:

- involves a narrow definition of the problem in order to make it manageable (Rochefort and Cobb 1994) – for example, defining riots as a problem of individual bad behaviour rather than defining them as a product of deeper socio-economic factors
- gives the appearance of dealing with the problem – this might involve a 'token' or 'placebo' policy, such as the creation of a new programme without any additional funding, which does little more than keep a 'wicked issue' off the political agenda (Head and Alford 2008)
- helps buy-off/counter critics or gain support from key interests/actors through concessions or promises of future reform.

Such examples help explain why modest or minimal policy programmes can manage an issue down or even off the agenda, bringing political success in helping ease the business of governing.

Sustaining the broad values and direction of government

Governments all have vision because a government with no vision will not be elected. Greek Prime Minister Andreas Papandreou came to power in 1981 with a vision of change away from the behind-the-scenes influence of powerful,

> ## Box 2.3   An example of political success: Australian Prime Minister Kevin Rudd's 'sorry' speech
>
> ### Background
>
> One of the most controversial periods in Australia's history is the forced removal of many Aboriginal and Torres Strait Islander children from their families. Precise numbers have been impossible to determine, but a national inquiry in 1997 estimated that between one-in-three and one-in-ten children had been forcibly removed over the period 1910–70.
>
> Reasons for the removal are disputed by historians, politicians and others, with some arguing that the removal was to protect the children themselves, and others arguing that it was a racist policy designed to assimilate children of mixed-descent into white families. In 1997, after a two-year national investigation, the 1997 *Bringing Them Home* report was produced. The report suggested that one of the first steps towards healing was a national apology. Despite widespread support, Prime Minister John Howard (1996–2007), head of a Liberal-led coalition, refused to say 'sorry'. His argument was that he could not say sorry for something for which his government was not responsible. When the Liberals were defeated at the 2007 general election, one of the first acts by the new Labor Prime Minster Kevin Rudd was his historic 'sorry' speech at Parliament house on 13 February 2008. He apologized on behalf of the government and the Australian people, for all the pain and suffering that had been caused to Aboriginal and Torres Strait Islander people as result of the forced removal of children from their families.   ◊

traditional and affluent right-wing influence in Greek society. Japanese Prime Minster Junichiro Koizumi reformed and brought his Liberal Democratic Party to power in 2001 on an agenda of economic restructuring and revitalization. Swedish Prime Minister Fredrik Reinfeldt took office in 2006, ending a long reign of social democratic dominance with an agenda of labour market and welfare reforms. Governments tend to want policies that align with such vision, although often the rhetoric of adversarial politics, while in opposition, often gives way to strong continuity between governments when in political office (Rose 1984). Regardless, policies can be politically successful if they promote the values desired by government, and help maintain the broad trajectory of government and its programmes. For example, Japan's acceptance of very small numbers of asylum seekers in a country where ethnic and cultural homogeneity

Political success

Use of language to persuade and convince is a policy instrument (Hood and Margetts 2007). Official statements by leaders constitute policy, in the sense that they are something that government does, with an attempt to exercise influence. Rudd's speech can reasonably be seen as a political success by all the stated criteria for political success.

Enhancing electoral prospects/reputation of governments and leaders: The speech symbolized Rudd's image of a new, young and energetic leader. His government had already won the election but, after the speech, his opinion poll ratings increased.

Controlling the policy agenda and easing the business of governing: Although the issue is far from over (notably on the issue of compensation), the speech was nevertheless effective in diffusing an exceptionally difficult and sensitive issue. Doing so allowed the government to pursue its other high-priority items in the fields of education, telecommunications and industrial relations.

Sustaining the broad values and direction of government: The speech symbolized a new direction in the governing of Australia. It symbolized a government that was more tolerant, inclusive, socially conscious and respectful of social diversity.

Sources: Based on *Bringing Them Home* (1997) and numerous newspaper sources.

is paramount is, arguably, as Adolino and Blake (2001: 116) suggest: 'in the interest of maintaining an image of international cooperation and humanitarianism rather than a wholehearted commitment to fulfil Japan's international obligations'.

A variation on this category of sustaining government trajectory relates to the situation where a government explicitly wants to change direction. A policy might be successful, therefore, in helping forge *new* values and new pathways. In response to the global financial crisis that emerged in 2008, many governments throughout the western world began undertaking what was previously unthinkable – nationalizing banks and/or providing major rescue packages for banks, as well as generating public expenditure deficits in order to stimulate growth. Therefore, such programmes helped open policy windows, making it easier to legitimate further reform. In essence, therefore, programmes might be successful from government's point of view precisely because they cultivate momentum along particular political pathways, whether it is one broadly of continuity or change.

Conclusion

This chapter has provided an important starting point in our understanding of policy success. For heuristic purposes, it has straddled the divide between success as 'fact' and success as 'interpretation'. To do otherwise would be to ignore the realities that governments can meet objectives; programmes can benefit a range of interests (from governments to target groups); and that what one person views a success, another might view as a failure, depending on values, vision and interests. The 'realistic' vision of success allowed us to break down success into three key components. Put simply, if public policy is broadly what government chooses to do (or not to do), then governments *do* process (defining issues as problems, examining options, consulting and so on), programmes (using a wide variety and combinations of policy instruments) and politics (engaging in activities that can influence electoral prospects, maintaining capacity to govern and steering policy direction). Success can reside in each of these spheres when government achieves what it sets out to achieve, although the contestability of success means that not everyone will agree, depending on whether they support government goals and the means used to achieve them

Clearly, there is much work to be done on building and refining this model, as well as recognizing its limitations. The next two chapters will do just this. Chapter 3 will explore the complex relationship between success and failure, indicating that success is not all 'all or nothing' phenomena. Chapter 4 will also introduce further complexity issues surrounding temporal, spatial and cultural aspects of policy success, as well as examining the types of evidence that can be used to demonstrate or disprove success.

Chapter 3

Dissecting Success: The Spectrum from Success to Failure

The previous chapter divided success into process, programme and political dimensions. These are analytically convenient categories, as well as helping capture the dynamics of different dimensions of public policy. However, one vital part of the equation has still to be considered; namely, the fact that success (whether in the realms of processes, programmes or politics) is not an 'all or nothing' phenomenon. Policies have multiple process, programme and political goals, all of which can be met (or not) to a greater or lesser degree. Total policy success is uncommon, as is total policy failure. How, therefore, is it possible to comprehend bundles of complex outcomes between the polar extremes of success and failure, as well as factoring in the role of varying perceptions? This current chapter tackles these issues head-on. First, it maps out a spectrum of outcomes, ranging from policy success, through to policy failure, including 'grey areas' in between. Second, it uses this framework to examine in greater detail, different types of successes and failures across the process, programme and political dimensions of policy. Finally, it examines contradictions between different forms of success, including what is known colloquially as 'good politics but bad policy'.

The general relationship between success and failure

While there is a scarcity of literature on policy success (see Chapter 1), there is much more literature on policy failure. In particular, there is a rapidly expanding body of literature on crises (Rosenthal *et al.* 1989; Rosenthal *et al.* 2001; Boin *et al.* 2005), disasters (Perry and Quarantelli 2005; Rodriguez *et al.* 2006), catastrophes (Posner 2004; Perrow 2007; Bostrom and Ćirković 2008), fiascos and scandals (Bovens and 't Hart 1996; Tiffen 1999; Thompson 2000). This literature covers everything from human error through to organizational failure and, ultimately, societal collapse. Common concerns cross the boundaries of political science, sociology, geography, psychology, business management and organizational studies. Despite the preponderance of literature, especially in the periods since 9/11 and Hurricane Katrina, there is considerable disagreement on what constitutes failure. In many respects, the issues mirror those of success. Some literature focuses on failure as an objective phenomenon (for example, Reason 1990; Gerstein 2008), particularly when the focus is on technological failures, infrastructure damage and loss of life. Other work focuses on the constructed and subjective nature of failure (for example, Bovens and 't Hart 1996; Brändström and Kuipers 2003; Boin *et al.* 2009), and emphasizes the ways in which different policy actors can play up or play down its significance, even to the point of denying that failure exists.

In order to help understand the relationship between the rarely-written-about phenomenon of success and the more-often-written-about phenomenon of failure, as well as dealing with the objective versus subjective dimensions of policy, it is useful to begin by restating the definition of success developed in Chapter 2. Therefore:

> A policy is successful insofar as it achieves the goals that proponents set out to achieve. However, only those supportive of the original goals are liable to perceive, with satisfaction, an outcome of policy success. Opponents are likely to perceive failure, regardless of outcomes, because they did not support the original goals.

If this same logic of dealing with the attaining of goals and the level of support for those goals is applied to 'failure', it can be said that:

> A policy fails insofar as it does not achieve the goals that proponents set out to achieve. Those supportive of the original goals are liable to perceive, with regret, an outcome of policy failure. Opponents are also likely to perceive failures, with satisfaction, because they did not support the original goals.

One example will suffice, indicating that polar opinions can exist on the success of the same programme. The US rendition programme, whereby suspected terrorists are sent to other countries for interrogation, has generated considerable controversy. When senior CIA official Michael Scheuer, one of the architects of the programme, was questioned as part of a congressional inquiry, he stated that:

> the Rendition Program's goal was to protect America, and the rendered fighters delivered to Middle Eastern governments are now either dead or in places from which they cannot harm America. Mission accomplished, as the saying goes.

> (*Committee on Foreign Affairs 2007: 14*)

In stark contrast, a report from Amnesty International (2008: 8) stated that:

> Renditions violate international law because they bypass judicial and administrative due process ... [they] have typically involved multiple human rights violations, including unlawful and arbitrary detention; torture or other ill-treatment; and enforced disappearance. Torture and enforced disappearance are not only grave violations of the international legal obligations of states, they are also international crimes for which individuals may be held criminally responsible.

In essence, a governing administration met its goal, but attainment of that goal was viewed as a success by supporters of rendition, and a failure (indeed, a crime) by its critics. This example illustrates the gulf that often exists between policy supporters and critics over the success, or otherwise, of the same policy phenomenon. As such, it allows us to think about the extremes of success and failure. However, the analysis now needs to go much further in order to explore the issue of what lies between such policy extremities. Some analysts have dabbled with these grey areas. For example, Bovens *et al.* (2001c: 596) write of the 'non-failure' rather than straightforward success of the restructuring of the steel industry in various European countries, while O'Neill and Primus (2005) examine the 'mixed success' of mid-1990s federal welfare reform in the US, and Pollack (2007) examines the 'partial success' of US policy on intellectual disabilities. However, none of these provide detailed criteria to flesh out what such terms might mean. Therefore, it is important to develop a systematic framework to help grasp a range of possible policy outcomes (see Tables 3.1, 3.2 and 3.3). The framework is based around a spectrum of outcomes starting with policy success and moving through durable success, conflicted success, precarious success and then policy failure.

These five categories require detailed explanation. Each is a combination of the extent to which the policy meets goals and the level of support for those goals. It is crucial to deal with both, if we are to provide a framework to aid our understanding, rather than merely asserting that particular outcomes are intrinsically desirable or undesirable. In addition, each category has three sub-dimensions (process, programmes and politics), as discussed in detail in Chapter 2. Initially, I discuss the five main categories on a broad policy level, before drilling down into processes, programmes and politics.

Policy success

At one end of the spectrum is the category of 'policy success' that has been examined in the previous chapters and that was defined earlier in this chapter. Strictly speaking, this is an ideal-type category because it assumes the full and unambiguous achievement of all process, programme and political goals. Pragmatically, this category would also include cases where there are very minor failures in meeting goals, such as insignificant time delays (for example, a three-year road building programme that is one week late), isolated and quickly remedied decision failures (for instance, giving incorrect and then corrected advice to an implementing agency), marginal shortfalls in meeting targets (such as 97.5 per cent of trains running on time as opposed to a target of 98 per cent). In addition, levels of controversy are either non-existent or very low and eminently containable. The reason might be a lack of political space for criticism because there are no significant gaps between government intentions and outcomes and/or the issue itself is not particularly controversial.

Many policy areas contain numerous policies that do essentially what they set out to do, with virtually no controversy. For example, UK transport policy is successful in ensuring that people drive on the left-hand side of the road and that drivers have passed their driving test (a few rogue drivers aside). Numerous regulations on water quality ensure that drinking water is fit for human consumption. Laws and regulations in developed countries successfully manage to ensure that the bodies of those who have died are buried or cremated, rather than disposed of in unorthodox ways. Almost by definition, once issues generate greater degrees of political controversy, then 'policy success' is not possible, other than at the very broadest of policy levels. For example, it is reasonable to suggest that there are numerous areas in which policy does more or less what it sets out to do and has cross-party support. Firefighters fight fires, police fight crime, doctors treat patients, planners assess development applications and so on. However, digging deeper and focusing upon detailed policy instruments and the resources devoted to them reveals that 'total' policy success is elusive, as a consequence of high levels of contestation and/or significant performance shortfalls on specific programmes. Nevertheless, an outright 'policy success' category is needed as a point of comparison against which to assess the vast majority of public policies that fall short of government aspirations to varying degrees and attract substantial disagreement, and even controversy. In essence, policy success means that the government does precisely what it sets out to, backed by constitutional legitimacy and gathering no opposition of any significance.

Durable success

Many policies fall short of their aims to small or modest degrees. However, they tend to be quite resilient, relative to the other categories towards the failure end of the spectrum, because of a lack of significant space for contestation over performance and decision-making, and fairly low or manageable levels of controversy. By and large, they do what they set out to do and, hence, they can be termed durable successes. There are a number of types of shortfalls that are certainly not unproblematic, but that do not inhibit substantial progress towards goals:

- small or modest shortfalls in meeting targets – for example, the introduction in over 90 countries of the MMR (measles, mumps and rubella) vaccine has substantially reduced the incidence of the three diseases, despite alleged links to autism and the exposure of children to other forms of health risk
- small or modest time delays – for example, launch delays on space shuttle flights
- small or modest resource shortages or budget over-runs – for example, a new rail project that is 5 per cent over budget
- small or modest decision failures – for example, a new departmental IT structure is put in place under contract with supplier B, despite some initial errors in assuming that the contract should be awarded to supplier C
- small or modest communication failures – for example, the UK's intelligence system fulfils its role of alerting and warning the public, but is weaker in explaining why occasional, and sometimes inconclusive, disruption is necessary (Gregory 2007)
- small or modest criticism that does not disturb the government's broad agenda and direction – for example, as part of a broader drive for efficiency, national government provides a below-inflation grant to local authorities, with the move attracting criticisms from the main opposition party, local authority association and some sections of the media.

It is important to note that there is no magical state of affairs where success becomes durable, rather than 'total', or where modest shortfalls or decision failures become big. Such matters are contested. Nevertheless, this category is useful in identifying many so-called 'policy successes'. They might not quite be policy exemplars, but they are survivors. Small departures from intentions have not prevented the attainment of broad policy goals or the normative values underpinning them. For example, bans on smoking in bars and restaurants have been introduced in countries such as Ireland, Scotland, Austria, Italy and Australia. Research has shown that the bans do, in essence, what they set out to do (see, for example, Mulcahy *et al.* 2005; Juster *et al.* 2007). They reduce exposure to passive smoke inhalation on the part of customers and employees, and so reduce the risk of health-related diseases. The policy formation process in all these countries was also relatively straightforward for government, and bans are generally seen as 'good politics' because of high levels of public support. Criticisms and implementation problems are certainly not absent. Pro-smoking groups have resisted; there are often detailed arguments from hotel/club/restaurant/gaming groups about what constitutes indoor areas, and there has been some evidence of pubs flouting the bans. By and large, however, it seems reasonable to consider smoking bans as durable successes. Put simply, as with all durable successes, they do, more or less, what they set out to do, and are generally capable of weathering any criticisms levelled at them.

Conflicted success

In this category, success is heavily contested between supporters and opponents as a consequence of the political space opened up by quite substantial departures from original goals, and/or because the issue itself is intrinsically controversial. Following the previous categories, the types of departures from goals might involve:

- considerable shortfalls in meeting targets – for example, hospital waiting lists reduced by 30 per cent, rather than 60 per cent
- substantial time delays – for example, troops sent on a peace mission six months later than initially promised
- considerable resource shortfalls or budget overruns – for example, the cost of the 2004 Athens Olympic Games was almost double its initial estimate of €4.5 billion
- a series of decision failures or a few of greater significance – for example, a war being won, despite a number of strategic policy misjudgements leading to loss of life
- substantial communication failures – for example, poor risk communication by public authorities regarding public health scares (Leiss and Powell 2004)
- substantial criticism forcing government into a concerted effort to maintain its broad agenda and direction, perhaps with some modifications – for example, a new tax on local businesses, constantly being reformed in terms of exemptions and calculations in response to pressures from industrial and commercial lobbies.

There is no clear line dividing durable success and conflicted success (and between the latter and the next category, precarious success). Rather, they should be seen as broad positions on a continuum. Conflicted success is still a 'success', in the sense that policy norms and instruments survive intact (the policy is not terminated and there is no fundamental rethink of underpinning norms because proponents continue to support it), but there is a high level of conflict over whether the policy has succeeded or failed.

A good example of conflicted success is NAFTA, the North American Free Trade Agreement between the US, Canada and Mexico, which was established in 1993. There has been reasonable progress towards meeting the original goals of trade liberalization and the promotion of fair competition, but this has been accompanied by accusations that it has caused trade deficits and failed to stem the tide of immigration (in both cases for the US in relation to Mexico). NAFTA continues to survive, but attracts staunch supporters and vehement critics in almost equal number. The EU's Common Agricultural Policy is similar, portrayed by supporters and critics as either the 'flagship' or the 'Titanic' of European integration, depending on whether the focus is on the successes resulting from ensuring stable supplies and maintaining income for farmers, or the failures associated with its heavy calls on the EU budget and the production of wasteful surpluses.

Precarious success

Policies in this category operate on the edge of failure. There are major shortfalls or deviations from original goals (although there might be a few minor successes somewhere within), producing high-profile and bitter conflicts over the future of the policy. Even proponents might doubt whether the policy is viable for much longer. Precarious programme success can include:

- little or no progress towards meeting targets – for example, Wisconsin's Learnfare programme, which linked welfare payments to school attendance (for those aged 13–19 with a dependent child), had only marginal success in improving school participation and school completion rates (State of Wisconsin Legislative Audit Bureau 1997)
- time delays, to the point that implementation has more-or-less halted – for example, building of a new public–private tunnel project is still officially in progress but with barely any work being undertaken until extended legal disputes are resolved
- lack of resources meaning that core tasks and responsibilities can barely be carried out – for example, government requires that municipal authorities conduct annual inspections of safety procedures in sports grounds, but no extra resources have been allocated and local authority inspections are minimal and *ad hoc*
- decision failures are either so frequent or so significant that the reputation of the policy is severely damaged and meeting goals is very difficult – for example, in 2001 the heavily flawed response to foot and mouth disease by the UK's Ministry of Agriculture, Fisheries and Food (Taylor 2003)
- communication failures are either so frequent or so damaging to the policy's reputation and operation that it is exceptionally difficult for progress to be made towards achieving goals – for example, widespread public confusion about an alert to boil water in response to a water contamination incident

- very strong and pervasive criticism, with government struggling to maintain its broad agenda and direction, which results in major concessions or rethinks – for example, the Blair government in the UK eventually scrapped a controversial policy that gave local authorities strong financial incentives to remove children from their natural families and place them with adoptive parents.

Precarious success is often a stage on the road to outright failure, as with the Child Support Agency in the UK. Almost from its inception in 1993 until its termination in 2008, it continued to survive and make some progress towards targets and making absent parents pay child maintenance, but was overwhelmed by a series of reviews and investigations revealing lengthy time delays for assessment, high incidences of incorrect calculations and cost inefficiency in processing claims (see Harlow 2002).

Policy failure

As argued previously, a policy fails insofar as it does not achieve the goals that proponents set out to achieve and no longer receives support from them. Those supportive of the original goals are liable to perceive, with regret, an outcome of policy failure. Opponents are also likely to perceive failures, with satisfaction, because they did not support the original goals. In a similar vein to 'policy success' at the opposite end of the spectrum, there are probably very few policies with zero progress towards goals. Therefore, this category includes very minor successes in terms of meeting goals and benefiting target groups that are, nevertheless, overwhelmed by pathologies. Often, policies that fail have previously been precarious successes, struggling to survive before collapsing completely and being terminated. As the definition of policy failure indicates, supporters and opponents, albeit with different emotions, are liable to perceive failures. The poll tax was one of the classic failures of British government (Butler *et al.* 1994). It proved unworkable in terms of collection, produced an unprecedented level of civil disobedience in modern Britain and consumed resources the equivalent of 4p in the pound income tax, as well as being a significant factor in the downfall of Prime Minister Margaret Thatcher. The aspiration of the Thatcher government to have a 'flagship' policy that spread the tax burden and made local authorities more accountable was in tatters. The poll tax has now become symbolic of both programmatic and political failure *par excellence* (see Chapter 6, for a detailed examination of this case).

In other instances, policies might fail before they are even put into practice. In New South Wales (NSW) in Australia, an integrated Tcard transport ticketing system was abandoned in 2008 after the company contracted to implement the system failed to deliver on time. Consistent with one of the themes in this book about the importance of the constructed nature of success, the NSW govern-ment argued that it was essentially a good policy that failed because of a poor project management by the contractor, whereas the contractor argued that it was a badly designed and overly complex policy that was virtually impossible to deliver.

Put simply, policy failures do not do what they set out to do, and prove incapable of weathering the storms around them.

Processes, programmes and politics: from success to failure

The framework this chapter has presented now allows us to drill down deeper, following through the logic of the success–failure spectrum and applying it, in turn, to the process, programme and political dimensions of policy. An impor-tant point of clarification is needed before proceeding further. The process, programme and political dimensions of the same policy can often be located at different points on the success–failure spectrum, rather than all being identical. For example, many policies fail, or are 'precarious' in the programmatic sense, but the consequences are confined largely to bureaucratic arenas and have negligible political repercussions. As Bovens *et al.* (1998: 195) suggest: 'Perhaps the most important aspect of policy failure and policy disasters is how mundane they really are'. In addition, some policies might bring huge political success, but perform poorly in programmatic terms. These points will be dealt with in greater detail later in the chapter.

A further point of clarification is that policies that can be labelled overall as a particular type of success (for example, a precarious programme success) will not necessarily have all characteristics falling neatly into the precarious success category. For example, London's Millennium Dome is often written about as a policy fiasco or disaster (see Gray 2003; McGuigan 2003) and, in many respects, it is plausible to put it into the category of precarious programme success. Visitor numbers were less than half those anticipated in original estimates, immense controversy followed and it was finally sold for £1. How-ever, costs were within 0.5 per cent of its original budget target and it was the most popular UK visitor attraction in 2000. Differing outcomes such as these are not particularly surprising – especially in light of the discussion of public value in Chapter 1, where it was evident that organizations typically pursue many different values, some being more important and/or more realistic than others.

The key point, therefore, as we explore each of these dimensions of success in detail, is that placing policies in particular categories is an art, rather than a science. There is no shame in acknowledging this point. Interpretation and judgement is a legitimate part of political analysis (Hay 2002). As Wildavsky

(1987) argues, policy analysis requires imagination. Unless a framework is provided to help scholars approach the complex relationship between success and failure, then analysis will continue to flounder on little more than generalized assumptions such as 'mixed success' and 'partial success'.

Process: from success to failure

At one end of the spectrum there is outright policy process success (see Table 3.1). Process success basically 'gets the job done' for government in the sense that it puts in place the policy that government wants, bringing constitutional legitimacy to the outcome, with a strong coalition of interests behind it. Others might not agree with government's goals and, so, the contestability of success is inescapable, but strong success here is about *process* – not programmes. Strong political executives throughout the world often produce process success because there is typically little difference between the broad aims and content of bills and the broad aims and content of legislation (Lijphart 1999; Patapan *et al.* 2003). A combination of inbuilt government majorities on the 'floor' and committees, with cohesive parties in adversary systems, means that the governing party typically has an inbuilt majority for the scrutiny of its own proposals. For example, although the UK opposition parties disagreed with the government's proposal to raise the upper earnings threshold for national insurance contributions (the Conservatives viewed it as a 'backdoor' increase in tax) when it was introduced in November 2007, the National Insurance Contributions Bill received Royal Assent some eight months later and the Labour government received constitutional approval to do what it set out to do. More generally, if a policy is also innovative, it can, depending on the circumstances, cultivate an image of 'good process'. For example, a strategic policy making review by the UK Cabinet Office entitled *Professional Policy Making for the Twenty First Century* stated that one of the five criteria for modernized policy is that it should be: 'Flexible and innovative – tackles causes, not symptoms and is not afraid of innovation' (Cabinet Office 1999: 9).

Durable success in terms of policy processes is close to outright success, but with minor, rather than significant, problems along the way. For example, in February 2008 the UK government rushed a bill through Parliament to nationalize the troubled Northern Rock Building Society. The speed of the move was criticized by the Conservative and Liberal Democrat opposition, but, armed with the need to respond to a 'crisis', the government got what it wanted in terms of authoritative powers that had been approved by Parliament after all-party scrutiny. As such, the passage of the Bill preserved government goals and conferred legitimacy on the policy.

Conflicted success in terms of process is much more of a struggle for government. It broadly does what proponents set out do, but not without

Table 3.1 *Policy as process: the spectrum from success to failure*

Process success	Durable success	Conflicted success	Precarious success	Process failure
Preserving government policy goals and instruments	Policy goals and instruments preserved, despite minor refinements.	Preferred goals and instruments proving controversial and difficult to preserve. Some revisions needed.	Government's goals and preferred policy instruments hang in the balance.	Termination of government policy goals and instruments.
Conferring legitimacy on the policy	Some challenges to legitimacy, but of little or no lasting significance.	Difficult and contested issues surrounding policy legitimacy, with some potential to taint the policy in the long term.	Serious and potentially fatal damage to policy legitimacy.	Irrecoverable damage to policy legitimacy.
Building a sustainable coalition	Coalition intact, despite some signs of disagreement.	Coalition intact, although strong signs of disagreement and some potential for fragmentation.	Coalition on the brink of falling apart.	Inability to produce a sustainable coalition.
Symbolizing innovation and influence	Not ground-breaking in innovation or influence, but still symbolically progressive.	Neither innovative nor outmoded, leading (at times) to criticisms from both progressive and conservatives.	Appearance of being out of touch with viable alternative solutions.	Symbolizing outmoded, insular or bizarre ideas, seemingly oblivious to how other jurisdictions are dealing with similar issues.

serious controversy or having to backtrack or modify its goals and preferred policy instruments along the way. In 2008, the Swedish government sought parliamentary approval for legislation to sanction the cross-border interception of electronic communications (email, text, telephone and fax) in order to combat terrorist threats. However, the debate was one of the most heated in modern Swedish history, with a focus not only on programme goals, but also on the process. The centre-right government was strongly criticized by a wide variety of opposition parties and civil liberties groups who argued that the government was abusing its power by introducing vague legislation giving enormous powers to intelligence authorities. The government eventually got its way and the bill was approved with amendments, leaving lingering accusations that legislation had been pushed through that contravened citizens' rights to privacy. Box 3.1 provides a further example of conflicted process success: the legislative process in France to ban, in state schools, the wearing of Islamic headscarves and other conspicuous religious symbols.

Precarious process success is something of a pyrrhic victory and does not bode well for the future of a policy. Precarious process successes are most likely when new processes are created, or existing ones radically adapted, that challenge conventional norms and elicit accusations of the abuse of power. Bachrach and Baratz (1970) describe this as a strengthening of the 'mobilization of bias'. The US policy of interning suspected terrorists in Guantanamo Bay prison camp is a good example. The Bush administration managed to establish processes to preserve its goal of securing and dealing with suspected terrorists who had the potential to attack the US at some time in the future. However, it had to contend with widespread and persistent accusations of policy illegitimacy, rooted in human rights violations and the bypassing of international law. The fact that Barack Obama's first public decision within hours of becoming President was to close the camp within one year, and reform the processes in the interim, indicates the fragile and intensely contested nature of the camp and its procedures.

Finally, outright process failures are essentially a brake, often abrupt, on the ambitions of government. They might be extensions of the latter example, where government stretches processes beyond what is considered acceptable, even by its own supporters. However, outright process failure can be more mundane in the sense that a policy proposal or bill is channelled through normal processes and is defeated. For example, in September 2008 the US House of Representatives delivered one such example by defeating the Bush administration's $700 billion bank rescue package to tackle the impact of the global financial crisis. Of course, the capacity of political systems to retackle pressing problems is immense and a modified package was approved a few days later. An example of a more enduring process failure occurred in November 2008, when Australian Prime Minister Kevin Rudd's proposal for FuelWatch legislation to increase transparency in fuel pricing was defeated in the Senate, prompting the government to abandon the proposal altogether.

Programmes: from success to failure

Again, leaving issues of interpretation and method aside, it is possible to get a sense of a range of ways in which programmes can succeed or produce some combination of success and failure, through to outright programmatic failure (see Table 3.2).

Table 3.2 *Policy as programme: the spectrum from success to failure*

Programme success	Durable success	Conflicted success	Precarious success	Programme failure
Implementation in line with objectives.	Implementation objectives broadly achieved, despite minor refinements or deviations.	Mixed results, with some successes, but accompanied by unexpected and controversial problems.	Minor progress towards implementation as intended, but beset by chronic failures, proving highly controversial and very difficult to defend.	Implementation fails to be executed in line with objectives.
Achievement of desired outcomes	Outcomes broadly achieved, despite some shortfalls.	Some successes, but the partial achievement of intended outcomes is counterbalanced by unwanted results, generating substantial controversy.	Some small outcomes achieved as intended, but overwhelmed by controversial and high-profile instances of failure to produce results.	Failure to achieve desired outcomes.
Meets policy domain criteria	Not quite the desired outcome, but sufficiently close to lay strong claim to fulfilling the criteria.	Partial achievement of goals, but accompanied by failures to achieve, with possibility of high-profile examples; e.g., ongoing wastage when the criterion is efficiency.	A few minor successes, but plagued by unwanted media attention; e.g., examples of wastage and possible scandal when the criterion is efficiency.	Clear inability to meet the criteria.
Creating benefit for a target group	A few shortfalls and possibly some anomalous cases, but intended target group broadly benefits.	Partial benefits realized, but not as widespread or deep as intended.	Small benefits are accompanied and overshadowed by damage to the very group that was meant to benefit. Also likely to generate high profile stories of unfairness and suffering.	Damaging a particular target group.

Box 3.1   An example of conflicted process success: the production of legislation to ban the wearing of conspicuous religious symbols in France

Background

This controversial issue has been debated for many years in France. For some, headscarves symbolize a tradition antithetical to France's secular tradition, as well as being considered a symbol of women's oppression and a reminder (for some) of the extent of immigration in France. For others, the right to wear headscarves, amounts to religious freedom of expression, and should be tolerated in any society with respect for religious diversity and minority rights.

In December 2004, the French President, Jacques Chirac, said he would introduce legislation to ban the wearing of Islamic headscarves and other conspicuous religious symbols in state schools. The bill was quickly processed through Parliament in early February 2004: 494 deputies voted in favour, 36 against and 31 abstained. The ruling conservative party (Union for a Popular Movement) and the establishment socialists (Socialist Party) both supported it. The bill became law on 10 February 2004.

Assessing success against process criteria

Preserving policy goals and instruments: Chirac did meet his goal of introducing legislation. In order to obtain the support of the Socialists, two last-minute amendments were accepted: that schools must attempt, initially, to resolve the issue with the pupils concerned, rather than resorting immediately to disciplinary measures; and the ban would be reviewed after a year.

On these criteria alone, the issue is best described as a conflicted process success for Chirac. He got his way and managed to preserve his goal of introducing a ban, but generated substantial controversy and made a concession to review in one year's time.

Programme success is a more-or-less interrupted achievement of what government set out to achieve, free of any significant performance failures and with any criticism coming from those with different views on the problem or the solution, rather than coming as a consequence of scandals, bureaucratic errors, or media frenzies. Some public policies that protect life and property can be found in this category; for example, the vast Delta Project of dykes in the

Ḋ

Conferring legitimacy: The law-making process was constitutionally legitimate, although the controversial nature of the issue, and the way in which it was processed through Parliament within less than two weeks, gave rise to concerns from some Muslim and human rights groups that the government was acting illegally and in contravention of the European Convention of Human Rights. These concerns were not sufficiently widespread or long-lasting to taint the constitutionality of the law making process; hence, on these criteria, the issue is best described as a durable process success.

Building a sustainable coalition: Chirac managed to produce a coalition that supported the legislation, despite the fact that his party already held 364 seats in the 577 seats in the National Assembly. However, the coalition was an uneasy one, and strong disagreement was problematic for Chirac, until the Socialists put forward amendments that were accepted. On this criterion alone, the process is best described as conflicted success.

Symbolism innovation and influence: Chirac and his supporters pitched the legislation as progressive, while others perceived it as harking back to the dark ages. Opinion was strongly divided. Against this criterion, policy-making is best described as conflicted process success.

Overall summation

Placing outcomes in particular categories involves judgement, as does assessing the significance of each criterion. In this case, conflicted success seems the most appropriate term for capturing the introduction of legislation banning the wearing of conspicuous religious symbols in France. The President got his way, but not without concessions and the generating of controversy that will last for many years to come.

Source: Miscellaneous news sources.

Netherlands that prevents the province of Zeeland from being at significant risk of flooding. It does what proponents set out to do and has cross-party support (see Box 2.1).

Durable programme success is technically a 'second best', but is probably the most realistic scenario and one that is generally perfectly acceptable for policy-makers, given the potential for broadly pluralistic polities to upturn the desires

---

Box 3.2 An example of durable programme success: microfinance in Bangladesh

Background

In 1971, the Grameen Bank began as an academic initiative, led by Muhammad Yunus, to lend small amounts of money to (mostly) women in poor households. In the decades since its inception, microfinance institutions and practices have evolved over the years to involve principally non-governmental microfinance institutions. The broad goal of microfinance is to alleviate poverty in impoverished areas by giving credit to those who would otherwise not have access to it. Despite the fact that the development of microfinance in Bangladesh has involved a range of non-governmental organizations, they operate in an environment that has been enabled by government – partly through allowing the schemes to flourish, partly through regulation, and partly through government-sponsored and statutory banks. Hence, given that public policy is broadly what governments chooses to do or not to do, then governments' role in the development of micro-finance involves the policy instruments of *laissez faire*, regulation and direct provision.

Assessing success against programme criteria

Implementation in line with objectives: The schemes operate broadly as intended, although there have been some cases of donor misuse of funds and gender discrimination in the allocation of finance.   ⇩

---

of determined governments. Patashnik (2008), in his study of reinventing government-style public procurement reforms in the US, recognizes the basic success and durability of the reforms, despite some worries about new forms of 'red tape' returning. Durable programme success does not require the hitting of each and every programme target. Box 3.2 provides a detailed example of durable programme success: microfinance in Bangladesh.

Conflicted programme successes are unlikely to be what policy-makers hoped for, but there is enough achievement of goals to bring a modicum of satisfaction, and perhaps even a sigh of relief that the problems did not escalate to disastrous level. The BBC licence fee, which funds the state-owned British Broadcasting Corporation, is successful in providing about 75 per cent of the Corporation's income, but has persistently proved controversial in terms of level of the fee, value for money and its funding of allegedly sub-standard journalism (such as Andrew Gilligan's claim that the threat from Iraq's weapons

▷ *Achievement of desired outcomes:* There are approximately 25 million active clients, with about 70 per cent of these among the 'poorest'. Microfinance accounts for more than half the annual poverty reduction of those who participate. However credit is not available for the very poorest – those most in need, but with no means of repayment.

Meeting policy domain criteria: Efficiency is an important and widely held feature of resource distribution. Systems are in place to make sure that resources are allocated efficiently through targeting; unviable clients are screened out, and repayments are paid on time. Some inefficiencies exist; partly through instances of corruption, but particularly through default on loans.

Creating benefit for a target group: Households benefit by enhancing their productive capacity, allowing them to avoid alternative credit at high cost. However, some critics argue that is still essentially a fragile, market-based solution to poverty, rather than deeper socio-economic structural one.

Overall summation

Micro-finance in Bangladesh seems best captured within the framework of a durable programme success. It is not a policy exemplar because it is not without difficulties, but it does broadly what its proponents seek of it and has proved resilient in coping with problems and criticism.

Source: Adapted from Hulme and Moore (2007).

of mass destruction had been 'sexed up' by the Blair government). The BBC example is an enduring one, but, as with most conflicted success, there is strong potential for instability. At the very least, conflicted successes are subject to periodic controversy, regular review and often reform. The BBC licence fee is no exception.

Precarious programme successes are policies gone seriously 'wrong' for policy-makers. They are often snapshots of programmes that hang on before collapsing into outright failure. An example is Railtrack, the group of private companies that owned most of Britain's rail network before being placed into liquidation in October 2002. However, precarious programme success can be saved from outright failure by a major reform or replacement. The Belgian criminal justice system in the 1990s is a case in point (Van Outrive 1998; Staelraeve and 't Hart 2008). After a series of child sex scandals and allegations of corruption – and, indeed, allegations of offering of protection to criminal networks – it retained little policy legitimacy before being subject to major reform.

Programme failures might contain very small elements of success but, in essence, are failures. They simply do not do what they set out do. For example, early attempts in Spain during the period 1983–85 to control the spread of HIV through blood transmission were virtually useless and contributed to Spain having the highest incidence of AIDS cases some ten years later (Jordana 2001). Similarly, in the State of Queensland in Australia in the period 2002–04, the government's attempt to introduce a levy on property in order to fund free ambulance services for the elderly, could scarcely have been worse in terms of its implementation (Prasser 2006a).

Politics: from success to failure

Policy has political repercussions, not just programmatic ones (see Chapter 1). Once again, locating a particular policy in any of the categories in Table 3.3 comes down to judgement. As Gray (1998: 12) argues: 'it often proves impossible to label events in ways which will command universal acceptance'. Nevertheless, the categories help us comprehend the broad types of political outcomes that can be generated by programmes.

Political success stemming from policy is the nirvana of political elites. At its height, it is the classic 'vote winning' or reputation-building policy that sustains – and even defines – a regime, helping set the direction for the future. Mrs Thatcher's protection of the Falklands Islands from Argentinian invasion, George W. Bush's immediate response to 9/11, Australian Prime Minister Kevin Rudd's 'sorry' speech to indigenous communities (see Box 2.3, p. 000), are only a few examples where a policy intervention has brought huge political benefits and helped define the direction of government.

Durable political success is a pragmatic version of outright success. Political realities are such that most politicians would probably settle for Bismarck's depiction of politics as the 'art of the possible, the attainable – the art of the next best'. Durable political successes weather criticism, stumbling blocks and any attempt to knock government off course with relative ease. An interesting example is the Blair government's granting in 1997 of operational independence for the Bank of England. Despite periodic accusations of government neglecting responsibilities, the policy has allowed governments to pursue broader economic policies without disruptive accusations of using interest rates for political purposes. Furthermore, as King argues:

> New Labour's decision to give the BoE [Bank of England] operational
> independence was a political decision, not an economic one. It estab-

lished New Labour's anti-inflationary credentials and delivered on the party's campaign promise to de-politicise the setting of interest rates. This promise was crucial for attracting the support of homeowners – the median voter in the UK – who gave their majority support to the Labour Party over the over the Conservatives in the 1997 election for the first time in over 30 years.

(King 2005: 94)

Further along the spectrum are conflicted political successes. Here, policies tend to produce substantial controversy; garnering both strong support and strong

Table 3.3 *Policy as politics: the spectrum from success to failure*

Programme success	Durable success	Conflicted success	Precarious success	Programme failure
Enhancing electoral prospects or reputation of governments and leaders.	Favourable to electoral prospects and reputation enhancement, with only minor setbacks.	Policy obtains strong support and opposition, working both for and against electoral prospects and reputation in fairly equal measure.	Despite small signs of benefit, policy proves an overall electoral and reputational liability.	Damaging to the electoral prospects or reputation of governments and leaders, with no redeeming political benefit.
Controlling policy agenda and easing the business of governing.	Despite some difficulties in agenda management, capacity to govern is unperturbed.	Policy proving controversial and taking up more political time and resources in its defence than was expected.	Clear signs that the agenda and business of government is struggling to suppress a politically difficult issue.	Policy failings are so high and persistent on the agenda, that it is damaging government's capacity to govern.
Sustaining the broad values and direction of government.	Some refinements needed but broad trajectory unimpeded.	Direction of government very broadly in line with goals, but clear signs that the policy has prompted some rethinking, especially behind the scenes.	Entire trajectory of government is being compromised.	Irrevocably damaging to the broad values and direction of government.

opposition. Often, such splits are not unexpected. They might, in fact, be anticipated, and even cultivated. Leadership writings are full of statements from self-avowedly 'conviction' politicians (or 'narcissistic' leaders, as Post (2004: 108–10) more scathingly refers to them), prepared to do what they feel is 'right', rather than what is popular. Political controversy over the impact of policies can even be a means of dividing opponents or providing a distraction from what is going on elsewhere in government. In August 2001, in the run-up to national elections, Australian Liberal Party Prime Minister John Howard controversially turned back a boat of asylum seekers headed for Australian shores, using the tactic to split the Labor Party. The 'Tampa' incident helped galvanize supporters and pave the way for the Liberals' success at the polls, although for many opponents the episode was a shameful indictment of the government and a blow to Australia's reputation overseas (Marr and Wilkinson 2004).

Precarious political successes are too 'hot' to handle. They are not without some political merits from government's perspective, but they are on the verge of producing a fully-fledged political disaster. Martin (2007) uses the term 'backfire' to refer to policy issues that rebound on perpetrators. Precarious political successes, in policy terms, tend not to stay that way for very long. The earlier process example of the Bush Administration and Guantanamo Bay prison camp is pertinent here. Politically, the 'tough on terrorists' rhetoric helped buttress Bush's 'War on Terror' post-9/11, but was more than counter-balanced by the political damage (particularly among the international community) because the camp was seen as symbolizing a government that had mismanaged the war on terrorism and that had behaved illegally and immorally in doing so. Box 3.3 provides a more detailed examination of this case.

Finally, there are political failures. Some policies are so close to producing political casualties that a major review or reform is needed, but the most extensive are those policies that bring down governments or leaders. For example, the Icelandic government resigned en masse in January 2009 after its response to the global financial crisis prompted widespread civil unrest. Similarly, the Dutch Cabinet resigned en masse in 2002 after a critical report on its role in the Srebrenica massacre, while in 1990 the 'flagship' poll tax was a major factor in the downfall of British Prime Minister Margaret Thatcher. Baumgartner and Jones (2002) argue that 'negative feedback' counterbalances policies that are too radical or too conservative. One does not have to be a pluralist to recognize that policies that produce political failures are not an everyday occurrence, but they are a near inevitable feature of pluralistic societies where there is potential for aggrieved and 'losing' groups, as well as government rivals, to mobilize against government.

Contradictions between the three dimensions of success

Success in one aspect of policy does not always go hand-in-hand with success in another. Indeed, the process, programme and political dimensions of policy often sit at different points on the success–failure spectrum, because of inherent conflicts between the different types of success that are sought. For example, Howlett (2009) argues that policy design and instrument choices (issues of process) are constrained within a 'nested relationship' with broader governance arrangements and abstract policy aims (for example, market governance) plus policy regime logic (for example, correcting market failures and governance failures). Meeting the latter criteria can be construed as helping meet the criteria for political success. The implication is that success in policy design processes might often be sacrificed, consciously or unconsciously, in order not to fall foul of the criteria for political success. This is only one example of conflict and trade-offs between success criteria in the realms of process, programmes and politics. Three others are worth highlighting.

Good process versus bad programmes

If success relates partly to achievement of goals (even though some might disagree with the goals), then a successful policy process is essentially a policy formation process, with constitutional legitimacy and a strong alliance, that allows policy-makers to do, in essence, what they set out to do. However, successful process can lead to failed programmes. To explain: one criticism of strong executive power – as implicit in incrementalist theory (Lindblom 1959, 1965), the pluralistic and discursive nature of politics (Crick 1962; Stoker 2006a) and the constitutional design of consensus democracies, such as Austria, the Netherlands and Switzerland (Lijphart 1999) – is a lack of sufficient scrutiny, limited checks and balances and a poor capacity for adjustment to policy goals and proposed instruments (hence, some would see process 'success' as process 'failure').

Small and large failures are not inevitable in programmes as a consequence of 'strong' and 'efficient' policies process. Nevertheless, Dunleavy (1995), for example, argues that the British political system has a propensity to produce policy failures because centralization of power and limited checks and balances can allow 'bad' policy proposals to be given serious consideration. He cites examples such as the poll tax, the Child Support Agency and the entry and exit from the EU's Exchange Rate Mechanism. This argument also resonates with much modern thinking on policy design. Schneider and Ingram (1997: 5) argue that 'Some contexts encourage choices of design elements that reproduce and accentuate antidemocratic tendencies leading to degenerative designs that are detrimental to democracy.'

Box 3.3   An example of precarious political success: Guantanamo Bay detention camp and the Bush administration

Background

The camp opened in early 2002, and is a product of the 9/11 attacks on New York and the Pentagon. It was a major component of the Bush administration's War on Terror. It was located in Cuba, on land that, according to US authorities, was outside US legal jurisdiction. Broadly, the purpose of the camp was to detain suspected and potential terrorists, with a view to protecting the security of the US. The camp detained approximately 800 individuals. In some respects, the camp did achieve its programmatic aims because, among other things, it is reported to have detained a small number of highly dangerous individuals, including some closely connected to 9/11. However, there were substantial departures from goals, criticism, and controversy surrounding individuals being wrongly incarcerated, maltreatment of prisoners during interrogation, absence of due legal processes and infringement of human rights.

Assessing success against political success criteria

Despite small signs of benefit, policy proves an overall electoral and reputational liability: Politically, the existence of the camp did appease those within the Bush administration, its supporters and citizens generally, who felt that the existence of the camp was justified as part of the broader war against terrorism. In opinion polls, roughly 45–50 per cent of citizens continued to support the camp, but roughly the same felt it should be closed. Over time, the issue became a reputational liability for a president whose approval ratings were in the region 85–90 per cent in the months after 9/11, but had fallen to 28–35 per cent in the last year of his presidency.

The counter-argument is that pluralistic policy-making, with multiple inputs and constant refinements, is in danger of producing programme failure. It expands goals and creates such a degree of complexity and compromise in order to satisfy a plurality of interests, that it is prone to creating volatile interdependencies, bureaucratic conflicts, policy stasis and policy failure.

Regardless of which argument (if any) seems most reasonable, it is certainly important to highlight the potential for conflict between process success and programme success. The creation of the Department of Homeland Security in

Clear signs that the agenda and business of government is struggling to suppress a politically difficult issue: The controversy gradually overtook the administration's capacity to deal with it. No sooner would it deal with one high-profile issue, than another would emerge soon after. Much of the criticism was given credence by opposition from bodies such as the European Parliament and the United Nations' Human Rights Council, but came particularly from leaders across Europe such as Tony Blair and Angela Merkel, who had supported the coalition in Iraq and Afghanistan.

Entire trajectory of government is being compromised: The camp seemed to symbolize the difficulty of a no-holds-barred approach to dealing with terrorists and those suspected of terrorism. On the one hand, it attempted to wage a War on Terror. On the other, doing so involved operating on the fringes of (and, arguably, beyond) regard for international law, fair judicial process and respect for human rights. Hence, the Camp seemed to symbolize what many saw as fault lines running through the incursions in Iraq and Afghanistan. Colin Powell, former US Secretary of State, said that 'Essentially, we have shaken the belief the world had in America's justice system by keeping a place like Guantánamo open ... it is causing us far more damage than any good we get for it' (*The Times* 2009).

Overall summation

It seems reasonable to locate the 'politics' of Guantanamo Bay uniformly within the three 'precarious political success' criteria and within the broader spirit of precarious success. It was beyond 'conflicted success', because the political balance sheet eventually overtook the Bush administration, but it stopped short of outright political failure, by virtue of its sheer survivability and enduring appeal to Hawkish elements of public and political sentiment. It was a classic precarious political success, operating on the edge of failure.

Source: Miscellaneous news sources.

the US is a good example. In process terms, it was a success (most realistically, a durable success) because the Bush administration achieved its aim of legislation to conduct the largest reorganization in the history of US public service, but in programmatic terms it is widely regarded as being located more towards the failure end of the spectrum (most likely a conflicted success) beset as it was by numerous problems because of the disruption, complexity and lack of coherence that it creates (May *et al.* 2009).

Good programmes versus bad politics

At first glance, it might seem strange to argue that programme success can lead to political failure. After all, it might be expected that 'good' programmes, effectively putting government aims into practice, will produce 'good' political outcomes for government. The counter-argument put forward here, is that well-run programmes can be risky for policy-makers, precisely because critics can focus on framing the policy as 'ruthlessly efficient' and 'inflexible'. Weare and Wolensky (2000), in their study of reforms in Japan's banking sector, illustrate this point. The reform programme focused on efficiency to the neglect of 'politics'. They argue that:

> This policy failure was a dramatic example of a ubiquitous but bedeviling aspect of policymaking: the multiple and conflicting goals that confront policymakers. Improving the efficiency of Japan's capital markets was clearly perceived to be important. Nevertheless, single-minded pursuit of efficiency conflicted with central goals pursued by stakeholders, including the protection of constituents from adverse consequences of policy changes, the maintenance of bureaucratic authority, and the preservation of stable financial markets.
>
> (*Weare and Wolensky 2000: 10*)

The outcome was defeat at the 1998 elections for Prime Minister Hashimoto's Liberal Party and, in effect, a vote of no confidence in the government's ability to revive the ailing Japanese economy.

More generally, bad political outcomes are not the inevitable product of good programmes, but the seeds of conflict are there. Most policies carry political risks (Althaus 2008), and a smooth policy process does not automatically produce smooth programmes.

Good politics versus bad programmes

This is a crucial issue and is revisited in the Conclusion to this book. In colloquial terms, it is known as 'good politics but bad policy'. The inference is that some policies can succeed in political terms, but fail in programme terms. In order to understand this phenomenon, we need to consider the symbolic dimensions of what governments do. Political symbolism is vital to the understanding of political life (Edelman 1964, 1977; Stone 2002). We know, for example, that programmes involve government deploying policy instruments in order to tackle policy problems. Yet, policy programmes do not operate in a vacuum. The way in which programmes operate, from the specific instruments deployed to the timing of their use, can help cultivate impressions of government and its capacity to govern. Governments can appear strong, decisive, rational compassionate, and fair; or, they might appear weak, indecisive, irrational, uncaring and unfair. Such impressions can have huge repercussions for the capacity to meet the criteria for political success:

- enhancing electoral prospects and reputation
- controlling the policy agenda and easing the business of governing
- sustaining the broad values and direction of government.

If governments do well through the impressions they give, they can help foster political success. However, if they do badly, their political capital could decline, they lose control of agenda, and they find it difficult to steer government and its values in the desired direction.

Crucially, programme success and political success need not go hand-in-hand. Political success can thrive, despite – and, at times, because of – programmes that tilt towards the failure end of the spectrum. A crisis can be one such circumstance. Despite a poor and chaotic response at the programme level, leaders can actually emerge as 'heroes', perhaps because societies often need heroes as part of the coping and healing process after tragedy (Boin *et al.* 2005). For example, the programmatic response to 9/11 has been criticized for its lack of intra-agency coordination (National Commission on Terrorist Attacks Upon the United States 2004), yet Mayor Giuliani became a hero, despite many allegations that his personal response was weak and indecisive (Barrett and Collins 2007).

A more common version of good politics versus bad programmes refers to responses to wicked issues (Head and Alford 2008). Wicked issues, in essence, are complex policy problems without clear solutions. Usually, they refer to complex social issues (such as poverty, homelessness, drug abuse and others) where causal factors are highly contested and can range from individual failings and institutional weaknesses, to broader societal factors. Political actors often play the blame game. Some would perceive chronic social problems as caused by individual lack of responsibility or recklessness. For example, poverty can be seen as a product of individuals' inability to look for work, or lack of motivation to do better. Correspondingly, others would look more towards societal causes, such as economic cycles (helping cause unemployment) or poverty and lack of life chances (helping create an environment where drug taking is a form of escape). Arguably, therefore, there is a placebo or symbolic dimension to many of the programmes designed to tackle such problems. They help create the appearance that government is doing something to tackle the appropriate problem but, in reality, they might do little more than help alleviate symptoms. Therefore, programme outcomes might tend towards the failure end of the spectrum, but can aid political success because they:

- help cultivate the impression of responsible government
- help government retain control of the policy agenda by keeping complex issues further down the agenda than they might otherwise be
- help government pursue its broader governance society, without being impeded by having also to tackle the complex societal causes of the problematic issue.

A more concrete example can be found in a paper by Schultz (2007) on the dysfunctional nature of much policy diffusion. He points in the US to the Reagan administration's use of tax incentives to attract inward investment and regenerate local communities. The programme was certainly 'good' politics because it fitted easily into Reagan's assumption that high taxes were a barrier to wealth creation and prosperity, but it did little in programme terms. All the research showed that financial incentives did not have a significant impact on business location decisions, job creation was patchy, and schemes were financed to the detriment of job creation and business development in other jurisdictions.

As Edelmen (1977) argues, governments, reputations and political stability can all thrive, despite the realities that programmes can perform poorly. We should not judge policies simply by programmatic outcomes. We should be prepared to consider their political repercussions, which are often at odds with their programmatic ones.

Conclusion

This chapter has broken new ground in providing a framework that brings some order to the complex mixes of success and failure, while also factoring in degrees of political controversy. Yet, the analysis is far from complete. At the end of their seminal book on policy fiascoes, Bovens and 't Hart (1996: 157) argue that 'Success ... is a contextual phenomenon. It is a function of standards and philosophies of government that are variable across time and culture, malleable by political argument and institutional impression management.' The next chapter identifies and assesses the analytical limitations engendered by 'context', as well as the sheer methodological difficulties in saying that a particular policy has succeeded or failed.

In some respects, such issues seem to erect considerable barriers to our quest. However, the argument put forward is that there is room for analytical pragmatism, while retaining a healthy respect for its limitations. Understanding policy success is not 'hard science' and is exceptionally complex, but this should not stop us being more focused in terms of how this multifaceted topic is approached.

Chapter 4

Complexity: The Problems of Identifying and Measuring Success

Chapter 2 identified three main forms of success: process, programmatic and political. These form the bedrock for the analysis in this book. Chapter 3 developed this framework by introducing a number of typologies that allow us to conceive of a spectrum from success to failure along each of these three dimensions, with many policies residing somewhere in between. A key message was that the nature of policy success is far more complex than headline grabbing term 'success', or its polar opposite 'failure'. Yet, understanding policy success is complex for many *more* reasons than simply the success–failure spectrum. This chapter amalgamates and expands on additional complexity issues – some of which have been flagged in previous chapters. It explores the issues of 'success for whom?'; partial achievement of goals; weighing-up multiple objectives; reconciling conflicting objectives; dealing with unintended consequences; success being greater than planned; the difficulty of isolating the policy effect; dealing with hidden agendas and lack of evidence; assessing short-term impact versus assessing long-term impact; factoring-in spatial conflict; and weighing-up the importance of differing outcomes in the success of the process, programmatic and political aspects of policy. A central theme of the chapter is that assessments of success require judgements and choices to be made relating to the significance we give to factors such as target shortfalls, ambiguities and unintended consequences.

In some respects, there might seem to be pessimism running through the analysis. In other words, the nature of policy success could be considered so complex and value-driven that it is not possible to come to any legitimate conclusion that a policy has 'worked' (or not). However, I consider that any credible framework for policy success needs to recognize the realities and difficulties of studying complex phenomena. To do otherwise would be a disservice to political analysis, and would gloss over crucial issues of power and politics. On a more pragmatic note, however, the chapter concludes by providing advice to help analysts approach the many difficult issues involved in assessing whether or not a policy has been successful. Some of the thinking in this chapter builds on Hogwood and Gunn (1984), Bovens and 't Hart (1996), McConnell (2003) and Marsh and McConnell (2010a, 2010b).

Complicating factors

Success for whom?

The successful achievement of policy goals typically creates winners and losers. Therefore, any understanding of the phenomenon of policy success must deal with the question: success for whom? Each of the process, programme and political dimensions of policy can be considered. It should be noted that the issue of 'success for whom' is scarcely dealt with in existing literature, apart from the more radical end of evaluation studies (see, for example, Pawson and Tilley 1997; Pawson 2006; Taylor and Balloch 2005a). The issue of 'success for whom' can refer to any actor or interest affected by public policy, from target groups and interest groups to government itself, including public servants. Here, for the purposes of simplicity, examples will be drawn only from target groups and interest groups.

Policy processes are not neutral, value-free exercises in policy formation. They are authoritative agenda-setters that steer processes of 'winning' and 'losing'. They decide:

- the way in which a policy problem is constructed – for example, unemployment can be considered a demand-side problem because of low levels of economic activity (implying the need for government policies to boost demand for jobs), or unemployment can be considered a supply-side problem because of lack individual initiative in seeking employment (implying the need for government to link entitlement to welfare benefits with evidence of seeking employment)
- the strategic goals and priorities of the process – for example, rapid policy-making in response to terrorist attacks, prioritizing issues of security over those of freedom of movement and communication
- the range of policy alternatives to be explored – for example, in education policy, reforms designed to improve pupil–teacher ratios, ruling out any policy initiatives that will place demands on the budget
- which interests to include and exclude in the policy-making process – for example, consultation within a small policy community versus consultation with a broader issue network
- mechanisms, parameters and timing for consultation – for example, consulting with community groups on how best to implement the installation of wind farms versus consulting on whether wind farms are needed at all.

Agenda-steering processes towards winners and losers are not purely top-down exercises. They can be influenced, shaped and even knocked off course in their iterative relationship with a wide range of non-governmental, and even governmental, interests. Nevertheless, policy processes are powerful agenda-setters, whether forming part of a 'mobilization of bias' or rules of the game (Bachrach and Baratz 1970: Rochefort and Cobb 1994; Cobb and Ross 1997). In effect, they steer policy processes towards the interests of some, and often against the interests of others. In 2009 in Germany, for example, the agricultural minister used her constitutional autonomy to permit trials on genetically-modified potatoes. In essence, the policy process was a success for, among others, German chemicals company BASF, because the process steered political choices along a route that the company supported and in which it had invested financial resources. However, the process was a failure from the perspective of opposition environmentalists, because they could effectively do nothing to stop the decision being taken.

Winners and losers from the programmatic dimension of policies are also inherent in the detailed policy instruments that governments use (Hood and Margetts 2007; Eliadis *et al.* 2009). The examples below can be subject to debate, not least because of what constitutes either the public interest or the 'real interest' of any particular group. Nevertheless, they illustrate on a basic level how Lasswell's 'who gets what' dictum, is inherent in the nature of public policy. The issue of 'success for whom' is inescapable, whichever policy instrument is deployed.

- *laissez-faire*: doing little or nothing, leaving the resolution of problems to the free market, voluntary groups, individuals and families – for example, a policy that rejects the setting of a minimum wage level can be a success for employers (because they pay low market rates) but a failure for vulnerable, unskilled workers (who receive low returns for their labour)
- *advice, information and persuasion*: persuading others to change their behaviour in order to deal with the problem – for example, government health warnings on cigarette packets can be a success for tobacco companies and governments because it helps create and legitimize revenue streams (which, in theory, could be cut off), but a failure for smokers and their health (such failures being legitimized as the personal choice of smokers)
- *raising revenue and distributing resources*: dealing with a problem by using government financial powers to award grants and create financial incentives or disincentives – for example, the introduction of a 'polluter pays' tax on industrial pollution is liable to be successful for all those in the local environment, but a failure for the polluter who is either penalized financially, must cut back on production, or find new ways of reducing pollutants
- *legislation and regulation*: a stronger attempt to deal with a problem by regulating behaviour, even to the extent of imposing legal obligations and

rights – for example, regulation of company mergers in order to prevent excessive market concentration is a success for those who believe that consumer interests are best served by market diversity, but a failure for companies who would otherwise seek to merge

- *direct government provision*: the strongest and most interventionist way of dealing with a problem. Government uses its own resources, staff and institutions – for example, provision of public health care systems benefits the users of such services and hence can be considered a success for them, but at the expense of those who fund it and for whom it might be considered a failure. Users and funders are not always the same people and, even if they are, some will benefit more than others, depending on the tax system and levels of usage. Hence, there are often debates over issues of equity and choice, leading to debates about for whom the system is actually a success.

Most policy programmes, by their very nature, have differential impacts and benefit some interests over others. For example, Fol *et al.* (2007), in their study of public aid loans in France, the UK and the US to allow poor households access to cars for employment purposes, found that the programme is structured in such a way that, in the US, it only benefits the 'solvent' poor who are in the position to repay the loan. The programme is of no benefit to those families further down the ladder. A separate study by Ashworth and Heyndels (2005) of Flemish municipal budgetary reforms illustrates how the move to a new allocation system created significant winners and losers; a situation that needed managing through phasing in the reforms. More generally, public policy-making involves tough decisions, many of these around who wins and who loses. It is little wonder, therefore, that what constitutes success for one interest might not be success for another.

The political dimensions of policy also, needless to say, benefit some more than others. If we think about the main political dimensions of political success (enhancing the electoral prospects or reputation of governments and leaders, keeping control of the policy agenda to help the business of governing, and sustaining the broad values and direction of government), then opponents and critics are 'losers' if government is successful in its aims. For example, in 2007 when new Australian Prime Minister Kevin Rudd made his historic 'sorry' speech to generations of aboriginal children that had been forcibly removed from their families, the speech symbolized (among other things) a popular government that was charting a different course to that of its Liberal-led predecessor. The Liberals were clear losers as political opponents, struggling to come to terms with a political move that they had resisted throughout their decade in office (see Box 2.3). Another example can be found in Laufer's (2003) research on equal employment policy in France. In essence, she found that equal opportunity reforms did more for government by symbolizing that it had coherent policies to tackle gender discrimination in the workplace than it actually did for women, particularly among the ranks of the less-skilled and lower paid.

The sum of the parts is that, for those evaluating the success or otherwise of policies, a key difficulty (and, indeed, choice) is the issue of *whose success?* Such matters are not confined simply to matters of high politics. As Bovens *et al.* (2006: 322) argue:

> [Even in relatively] uncontroversial instances, policy evaluations are entwined with processes of accountability and lesson drawing that may have winners and losers. However technocratic and seemingly innocuous, every policy programme has multiple stakeholders who have an interest in the outcome of an evaluation: decision makers, executive agencies, clients, pressure groups.

With the exception of rare examples where there are winners all round and it is difficult to consider seriously the prospects of losers (such as the building of dykes in the Netherlands to prevent over half the country's population from being submerged), the vast majority of public policies allocate, redistribute, regulate and so on. Hence, focusing on whose interests are advanced by a particular policy implies, *de facto*, that other interests are not advanced by the policy and, indeed, might suffer. Government intervention or non-intervention to resolve conflicts is part of the very nature of public policy, whether it is between farmers and environmentalists, trade unions and industrialists, or tobacco companies and anti-smoking groups. Success for one group, typically, is not success for another. Therefore, in considering the nature of policy success, the issue of 'success for whom' is a key issue that any assessment needs to take into account.

Partial achievement of a goal

The word 'success' has an elegant completeness about it. There seems to be no room for ambiguity or failure. In the world of sport, for example, few would disagree that David Beckham is probably one of the most successful footballers of all time, in terms of goals scored, reputation, international appearances, earnings and more. However, if we cast our mind back we remember the time in 1998 when he was sent off in a World Cup qualifying match against Argentina and vilified by many English supporters and tabloid newspapers for a couple of years afterwards. Policy is little different. As detailed in Chapter 3, it is very rare to find success criteria achieved one hundred per cent. Nevertheless, as indicated in Chapter 3, policy can still be framed as 'successful' to a greater or lesser degree, depending on the significance we give to failures or shortfalls in meeting objectives.

How close to an objective does one need to be to be able to ascertain success? Imagine a government with the objective of eliminating a $100 billion budget deficit. Is a reduction to $40 billion a success? $20 billion? $10 billion? $2 billion? Or is $0 the only indicator of success? Evaluators need to make a judgement on where to draw the line. In the real world of politics, when governments throughout the world attempt to eliminate a budget deficit but only partially meet their targets, they typically attract plaudits from their supporters for their success in reducing the deficit, and criticism from opponents who focus on their failure to produce a balanced budget. Deciding what outcome constitutes success and what outcome constitutes failure is a matter of political judgement rather than scientific precision.

Weighing-up multiple objectives

A more complex variation is the issue of what significance is given to multiple objectives. This is similar to the public value debate explored in Chapter 1, which alerted us to the fact that public organizations typically have multiple mandates. For example, the Swedish Police Service has the roles of:

- reducing the opportunities for crimes to be committed
- prosecuting more crimes and increasing the quality of crime investigations
- executing other tasks based on public need, through prompt and correct handling, good service and a high level of availability.

(*Swedish Police 2009*)

Yet, as any analyst of police services knows, there are conflicts, trade-offs and prioritization involved in the carrying out of such roles. A study by Andersson and Tengblad (2009) of policing in Sweden found a conflict between new expectations to tackle the causes of crime as well as investigating crimes themselves. What value do we attach to each? Few people would want to give percentage figures against each objective. Regardless, this point illustrates the difficulty of ascertaining success when multiple objectives exist. Again, a judgement needs to be made in terms of which objectives are the more important indicators of success, and by how much.

Reconciling contradictory objectives

This issue is a starker variant of the previous one. What if there are two conflicting objectives, where one is met and the other is not? In 2001, for example, the British government resolved the oil blockade dispute and acts of civil disobedience by negotiating with protestors. Ending the dispute might be considered a success, because an objective was met. However, the government had previously refused to enter into dialogue, opting for a law-and-order solution in dealing with protestors who had been portrayed as 'enemies of the state' (Robinson 2003). In this case, determining political success depends on the weight we give to the competing goals of ending the dispute by means of a negotiated solution with those engaged in civil disobedience, and ending the dispute without negotiating with those resorting to civil disobedience. The case highlights the fact that policy objectives can be in direct opposition to one another. When decisions or judgements are needed, on success or otherwise, a choice has to be made as to which should take priority.

Factoring-in unintended consequences

Policies can have unintended consequences. Such outcomes might enhance and/or detract from policy goals, but any assessment of policy success or otherwise would need to identify the nature and scale of these consequences, as well as their significance in buttressing or detracting from original policy objectives. Cornelius (2001), for example, examines post-1993 US border control policy. In relation to unintended consequences, he suggests that:

> The available data suggest that the current strategy of border enforcement has resulted in rechannelling flows of unauthorized migrants to more hazardous areas (resulting in more death), raising fees by people smugglers, and discouraging migrants already in the USA from returning to their places of origin. However, there is no evidence that the strategy is deterring or preventing significant numbers of illegal entries.

> (*Cornelius 2001: 661*)

Unintended consequences can backfire on government and damage political reputations and careers, often because a localized event or series of events embodies deeper tensions surrounding societally-sensitive issues (Drennan and McConnell 2007; Martin 2007). For example, the atrocities at Abu Grahib prison encapsulated deeper concerns about the US role in Iraq.

Importantly, unintended consequences need not necessarily have negative repercussions. They can also produce success. Unexpected negative consequences, (often manifested through scandal, crisis or disaster) might prompt positive change. In Ontario, for example, a neo-liberal hands-off approach to water regulation was a contributory factor in the 2001 Walkerton contamination crisis, but the longer-tem outcome was a much more stringent regulatory regime (see Snider 2004; Schwartz and McConnell 2009). Success can also be a spin-off from an already successful programme. Government research funding for designated scientific and even non-scientific projects can generate many new and unexpected breakthroughs, ranging from new thinking on a related issue or new products such as medicines and vaccines. Indeed, spin-offs might be hoped for, and even anticipated to some degree. Many of the founders of the European Coal and Steel Community hoped (as per the neo-functionalist view of European integration) that successful cooperation would spill over into other sectors. It would lead to a harmonious and incremental ceding of powers to the European level, based continually on the idea that success breeds success.

The sum of all these points is that, when policy produces some consequences that were not anticipated, a choice has to be made on how significant they are, and the extent to which they damage or make no difference to the original policy goals.

What if success is greater than planned?

Following on from this, and continuing the theme of unintended consequences, there are instances where success is greater than planned. In 2004, George W. Bush described the sudden and unexpected collapse of Saddam Hussein's regime as a 'catastrophic success' (*Washington Post* 2004). The implication is that success that is speedier or greater than planned can bring huge problems. The EU's Common Agricultural Policy (CAP) is an example *par excellence*. By the mid-1960s, it commanded about 13 per cent of the Community budget but, less than 20 years later, such was its success in providing production incentives to farmers and prompting self-sufficiency that it was absorbing roughly 80 per cent of the budget, bringing the Community to near bankruptcy, and generating considerable adverse publicity through enormous surpluses. In essence, success greater than anticipated can lead to failure. In evaluation terms, the problem created with 'excess success' is whether to allow the 'excess' to enter the evaluation and, if so, what weight to give it. In reality, the answers lie in political judgement rather than science. In the CAP example, proponents of the EU continued through the 1980s and 1990s to reform to CAP as the 'flagship' of the EU, while opponents labelled it the 'Titanic'.

Difficulty in isolating the policy effect

In order to say that successful outcomes are the product of a particular policy initiative, we would need to ascertain that the policy actually produced those outcomes. In other words, we would need to be sure that the outcomes were not produced by other factors, such as changing societal attitudes, media awareness, private actors or changing economic circumstances. Doing so might be exceptionally difficult, regardless of the sophistication of policy modelling. In the 1980s, for example, when the world was coming to terms with the emergence of AIDS/HIV, governments ran public education campaigns such as the Grim Reaper advertisements in Australia. Most would accept that such campaigns helped change attitudes to sexual behaviour and reduce the infection rate. However, such outcomes are difficult to attribute directly and solely to the campaigns. Successful outcomes might have been the product of factors such as media awareness and peer learning. Complexity is exacerbated because it has hard to separate such factors from government campaigns. Hence, isolating the 'policy effect' creates huge, if not impossible methodological challenges. Somehow, any assessment of policy and its impact needs to be able to cope with complexity and ambiguity.

On this point, a further complication is the fact that many policies can be knocked off course by external shocks, crises and disasters. How do we assess success in such circumstances? We would need to judge whether extraneous factors such as financial crises or terrorist attacks were knowable and predictable; that is, accidents waiting to happen. A policy derailed by crisis could be considered successful, because policy-makers implemented according to plan and could not conceivably have known what would happen. Throughout the world in 2008 and 2009, many public infrastructure projects were abandoned because of the global financial crisis. Are they successes (because they were implemented successfully up to the point of being abandoned) or failures (because they were not built)? Conceivably, both frames could be deployed, depending on what criteria we employ and whether we feel that policy-makers should be held culpable for unexpected events. Some such as Schwartz (2003) and Clarke (2006) argue that we need to be more imaginative and creative in our thinking because the seeds of future calamities exist in the present. Put crudely, the disasters of the future are broadly 'knowable', if we put our minds to the task. By contrast, Shapiro and Bedi (2007a) suggest that there are many alternative futures and contingencies that are beyond the realm of human action and beyond any realistic capacity to conceive of in advance. In essence, emphasizing either 'misfortune' or 'mismanagement' (Bovens and 't Hart 1996: 76–84) is a judgement that needs to be made, prior to labelling a policy as a success or failure. These issues will be examined further in the Conclusion to this book.

What would have happened if the policy had not existed?

Compounding the intricacies of policy assessment further still, is the 'what if?' question: in other words, what if the policy had not existed? In theory, this is highly pertinent to assessing the success of a policy, because its value is compared with an alternative future existing without it. No doubt many of us have seen the classic Frank Capra film *It's a Wonderful Life*. James Stewart plays George Bailey, a small-town businessman who only realises his worth in life when he is shown what the world would be like if he had never been born.

Cinema can take such artistic licence but public policy analysis cannot. What if the National Health Service in the UK did not exist? What if Sweden had not adopted a corporatist model of policy-making after World War II? What if the German education system had been starved of funds by successive post-war governments? What if the Spanish government did not have a disaster response to the 2004 Madrid bombings? To answer such questions leads us into speculating about alternative futures, and making assumptions about the types of policies (if any) that would have taken their place and the forces behind them. The issue of predicting success will also be examined in the Conclusion to this book.

More broadly, this point indicates that the waters become murkier, the more we try to isolate 'policy' to ascertain its success or otherwise. Public policy does not emerge in a laboratory, to be controlled and examined under a microscope. Analyzing public policy involves art, craft, creativity and imagination (Wildavsky 1987).

Dealing with hidden agendas and lack of evidence

Assessing the success or otherwise of a policy depends, at least to some degree, on the availability of evidence surrounding both policy goals and policy outcomes. Both are entwined and can be problematic. Identifying policy goals is hampered by the existence of hidden agendas. Identifying policy outcomes can be hampered when there is lack of evidence. Each can be considered in turn.

Hidden agendas are rarely studied in public policy, yet the reality is that many policy goals are unstated. It seems reasonable to suggest that hidden programme goals tend to be political, simply because for policy-makers to speak of them is to run the risk of accusations of process and political failure (that is, illegitimate policy-making) because it defies an established consensus, puts private interests above public ones, constitutes an abuse of power and so on. Some instances of policies that have attracted accusations of hidden political and programme motives are:

- the highly competitive and bureaucratic system for applications and entrance to high schools and universities in Japan has a hidden socio-economic agenda of creating a bureaucratic personality that matches the needs of large Japanese companies (Takeuchi 1997)
- the creation of the euro having a hidden agenda to challenge the supremacy of the dollar on world markets (Wyplosz 1997)
- the US-led invasion of Iraq having the hidden agenda of controlling oil reserves and reducing dependence on Saudi Arabia (Israeli 2004).

Hidden agendas can also reside in the process aspect of policy. For example, much of the criticism of the trend towards deliberative democracy (for example,

Bishop and Davies 2002; Shapiro 2003) hinges on scepticism of the role of public consultation. The core critique is that, while consultation processes can have formal goals in seeking wide and varied input into policy formation in order to 'improve' the policy, the reality often is more akin to a form of 'cosmetic consultation' or what Arnstein (1969) famously calls 'therapy' or 'manipulation'. In other words, the primary purpose of consultation is to quell dissatisfaction and give legitimacy to the policy, rather than consulting in order to ascertain whether policy goals or instruments should be altered, or even pursued at all.

The key issue raised is: how can we judge a policy to be successful when one or more of its goals are hidden? If we assume that only 'the facts' should be part of the analysis, we will have ignored what might be the driving force behind a policy. If we rely simply on judgement and hunches, we are open to accusations of unprovable speculation. Later in this chapter we will return to this matter. The Conclusion to this book will also revisit the issue of hidden agendas, arguing that the policy success heuristic can help explain the role of hidden agendas in public policy-making. It will argue that policy success can actually reside in preventing an issue getting on the policy agenda – raising echoes of the 'mobilization of bias' as a feature of public decision making (Bachrach and Baratz 1970).

The second major issue to consider here is the reality that 'evidence' might not always be available to inform an assessment of the success of a policy. There are many reasons why information might not be available, regardless of issues surrounding how we interpret such evidence. Reasons include:

- formal refusal – for example, many police services throughout the world have refused to provide information on the numbers of times tasers have been used
- lack of mechanisms or incompetence – for example, a national urban policy initiative in France was aimed at the 44 most deprived zones in the country, but a requirement that 20 per cent of new jobs in such areas be given to local residents could not be evaluated because the programme did not build in any administrative requirement that this information be gathered (Green *et al.* 2001)
- impossibility of obtaining information – for example, level of compassion shown to people dying after disasters.

In a similar vein to the discussion on hidden agendas, the difficulty for evaluators of policy success is that they need to contend with the 'unknowable' and decide to what extent (if at all) it really matters in an overall evaluation of policy success.

Assessing short-term versus long-term

Time is a growing subject of study in the political sphere (for example, see Pierson 2004; Pollitt 2008) and there is undoubtedly a temporal dimension involved in assessing policies. The process, programmatic and political dimensions of success can be examined over the short, medium and long term. The outcomes might be different, depending on the time period we examine. Short-term success can be long-term failure. The growth in the 1960s of vast public sector housing tower blocks (or high-rise, to use US terminology) was perceived widely as a successful, because it helped deal with problems of over-crowding and deprivation. Decades later, views have changed considerably. Tower blocks are viewed widely as failures. Many are being demolished or are in a state of disrepair – epitomes of urban deprivation and complex social problems. The Sydney Opera House is an example of the reverse. Its creation was bogged down in budget and design wrangling, and even appeared in a well-respected book on expensive planning disasters (Hall 1982), but has since become one of the most famous and iconic buildings in the world, attracting visitors from throughout the globe (Bovens and 't Hart 1996).

Factoring-in spatial context

Space is defined here not in terms of geography but, rather, in terms of different jurisdictions (countries, regions and so on), each with its own distinctive political system, political tradition, policy style, dominant values, policy sector profiles and socio-economic conditions. Hence, a process, programme or policy considered successful in one spatial context is not guaranteed to be considered a success elsewhere. A study by Saharso (2007) of the right to wear Islamic headscarves in public institutions in the Netherlands and Germany illustrates that such a right is broadly successful in the Netherlands with its tradition of multicultural citizenship. In Germany, however, with its mono-cultural tradition, eight states have banned the wearing of headscarves. It seems – at least in terms of the perceptions of policy-makers – that a policy of accommodation can succeed in the Netherlands, but not in many German states. The spatial dimension of success is particularly pertinent to inter- and intra-country comparative studies. A good example is the process of national grant distribution in federal and quasi-federal states and, in particular, the process of fiscal equalization, which results in richer and more densely populated states subsidizing poorer and more sparsely populated areas (see OECD 2007). What is a fiscal success for one state, province or region is often fiscal failure for others, as evidenced by 'givers' lobbying and campaigning for the return of *their* money.

A broader example of the spatial dimension of success is the nature of the EU. One of its main legal instruments is the directive (sometimes known as 'soft law'), where EU goals are set and national autonomy is enabled in order to achieve these goals. Directives cover the entire spectrum of EU competences, including directives on drinking water standards, equal employment opportunities for men and women, food additives, product liability and data privacy. In essence, there is an acknowledgement here that what works in one country will not necessarily work in another. As Falkner *et al.* (2005: 1) recognize in their detailed study of EU soft law: 'one-size-fits-all solutions are often neither politically feasible nor normatively desirable'.

The importance of the above discussion is that the success or otherwise of policies cannot easily be separated from their contexts. To say that a policy is successful in itself, especially if it is also promoted as a solution in other jurisdictions, requires a judgement that completely downgrades the importance of a conducive context. Correspondingly, to say that policy and context go hand-in-hand to the extent that they are necessary conditions for success, implies that successful policy cannot be transferred to other realms unless there is near identical context to cultivate it. These issues will be revisited in the Conclusion to the book.

Weighing-up conflict between different outcomes in processes, programmes and politics

An issue that emerged in Chapter 3 is how we evaluate the results of differing successes in the process, programme and political spheres. For example, what if a policy is broadly a success in programmatic terms but not in political terms, because of the way the policy is portrayed in the media or by its opponents? In Sweden, a new carbon fuel tax on passenger cars proved to be cost-effective, but suffered because of it unpopularity (Jagers and Hammar 2009). A different example comes from the UK. Official crime statistics reveal that the number of crimes committed is falling but, paradoxically, the general public feel they the figures are getting worse. The disparity here between successful programme outcomes and the more failure-oriented political outcome of government agendas needing to cope with this seemingly intractable issue can be explained, in part, by a rise in the rise in violent crime associated with alcohol (Barber 2007; Office for National Statistics 2008: 125–6). It can also be explained by low confidence in the criminal justice system, with 63 per cent feeling that the system was 'not very' or 'not at all' effective at crime reduction (Office for National Statistics 2008: 133–4). The overlap and contradictions between outcomes in the different realms will be dealt with in later chapters (particularly the Conclusion). The important point for present purposes is to recognize the existence of significant methodological difficulties in weighing up the relative importance of differing combinations of successes and failures in the spheres of processes, programmes and politics. Once again, judgements are inescapable, if we wish to navigate our way through the complexities of policy success.

Practical advice for those seeking to assess whether a policy is successful

Chapter 3 of this book helped provide the starting point for those seeking to examine policies and their outcomes. It divided policy into process, programmes and politics, while detailing specific 'success' criteria within each. Chapter 4 has complemented the analysis by providing a framework that allows

Table 4.1   *Types of evidence sources used to assess whether a policy is successful*

Dimensions	Evidence
Process	o Legislative records, executive minutes, absence of legal challenges, absence of procedural challenges (e.g., ombudsman), absence of significant criticism from stakeholders o Analysis of legislative process, using legislative records, including identification of amendments and analysis of legislative voting patterns o Analysis of support from ministers, stakeholders, especially interest groups, media, public opinion o Government statements and reports, academic and practitioner conferences, interest group reports, think tank reports, media news and commentary, identification of similarities between legislation and that in other jurisdictions, identification of form and content of cross-jurisdictional meetings/visits by politicians and/or public servants
Programme	o Internal programme/policy evaluation, external evaluation (e.g., legislative committee reports, audit reports), review by stakeholders, absence of critical reports in media (including professional journals). o Internal programme/policy evaluation, external evaluation (e.g., legislative committee reports, audit reports), review by stakeholders, absence of critical reports in media (including professional journals) o Internal efficiency evaluations, external audit reports/assessments, absence of critical media reports o Party political speeches and press releases, legislative debates, legislative committee reports, ministerial briefings, interest group and other stakeholders' speeches/press releases/reports, think tank reports, media commentary
Political	o Opinion polls, both in relation to particular policy and government popularity, election results, media commentary

Source: Adapted from Marsh and McConnell (2010a).

us to capture the reality that most policies are characterized by a combination of success and failure. Categories of success, durable success, conflicted success, precarious success and failure were explored in detail, indicating something of a sliding scale. In some senses, assessing policies might seem a fairly straightforward task from thereon. All we would need to do, armed with the framework, is turn to the types of sources mentioned in Table 4.1, such as departmental evaluations, legislative inquiries, official statistics and much more. We would gather and interpret the information therein in order to help us locate policy outcomes in a particular category, such as durable programme success or political failure. However, the current chapter also seems to have thrown a 'spanner in the works'. Assessing policies is riddled with ambiguities, information deficits, and value conflicts, rendering it necessary for judgements and difficult choices to be made. Analysts might also want to evaluate for many different reasons, such as providing a means for confirming success or failure, to a genuine attempt to ascertain whether a policy has succeeded.

I do not want to pre-empt motives; hence, it is not feasible to provide a template that says, in effect: here is how you must assess a policy and here is how you reconcile all these complexity issues. However, I do want to provide, in Appendix 4.1, a ten-point framework offering guidance on issues to think about and the consequences of the different choices that analysts will have to make as they work through one or more of the criteria for process, programme and political success. Even if analysts agree with the criteria I have given, they might adopt different positions in relation to how we know that these criteria are fulfilled. For example, one of the criteria for programme success is producing a desired outcome. How do we know that such a condition exists? Do we examine indicators to see whether they have improved from a prior state of affairs? Or do we judge whether the benefits outweigh the costs? The Appendix does not provide the answers to such questions, because perceptions will vary to the point that the same phenomenon can generate claims to success and counter-claims of failure. As Fischer (1995: 1) suggests: 'Whether one seeks to document the accomplishments of government or to criticize its failures, there is almost always a study available to help make the point.'

Therefore, the intent is not to prescribe but, rather, to help analysts think through the consequences of their choices, in relation to matters such as the reference points for success and how they will weigh-up different outcomes when there is conflict between them. Many of the choices can be made prior to commencing an assessment, but will often have to be revisited in the course of the evaluation.

Appendix 4.1

A ten-point framework to help guide researchers in assessing the success or otherwise of a policy

QUESTION 1: DO YOU WANT TO ASSESS PROCESS, PROGRAMMES AND/OR POLICIES?

A. Process

(Comment: Good, on its own, if all you want to do is assess the policy-making process. However, process is rarely enough on its own to assess a policy. It tells us only about the process of policy-making, but not about the programme and political consequences. You might need to venture into assessing programmes as well, and possibly politics.)

B. Programmes

(Comment: Good, on its own, if all you want to do is assess the merits or otherwise of a policy and its impact. However, if you want also to consider the programme's broader impact on the government and its mode of governing, you will need to venture into a political assessment as well. If you want to think about the roots of any outcomes, you will also need to think about policy-making and so you will also need some assessment of process.)

C. Politics

(Comment: Good, on its own, if all you are you interested is in the political consequences of a policy – impact on government reputation, agenda control and governance trajectory. However, there is always the danger that you are accused of emphasizing politics and ignoring the programme itself and its impact. Hence, it is likely that you will need some form of programme assessment as well. Doing so might help legitimate your final assessment.)

QUESTION 2: WHAT TIME PERIOD DO YOU WANT TO ASSESS?

A. Short-term

(Comment: Such an assessment is usually retrospective and, therefore, substantial evidence is likely to be available. As a consequence, it is the easiest form to defend. However, a short-term assessment might neglect problems that emerged over the longer term, or are still being stored up for the future. Considering the longer-term might capture these issues, but you should be prepared for criticism that you are either downgrading initial achievements, or speculating about outcomes that are still to happen.)

B. Long-term

(Comment: If evaluation is conducted retrospectively, evidence is likely to be available and, hence, a legitimate assessment is possible. However, a long-term assessment on its own is vulnerable to criticism that it has not captured the outcomes in different phases of policy implementation. This is less of a problem for retrospective evaluations. However, if the long-term includes time periods still to happen, the assessment is open to criticism that it is little more than speculation.)

QUESTION 3: WHAT BENCHMARK WILL YOU USE TO ASCERTAIN SUCCESS?

A. Government objectives

(Comment: Good, if this is all you want to do. This is generally the most straightforward approach, and one that is easiest to defend because you cannot be accused of ignoring what government set out to achieve. However, there is a danger that you are failing to capture other policy outcomes, such as whether the government's goals were reasonable in the first place, or whether the policy has produced broader outcomes that are not captured simply by government objectives. You might need to consider appraising the policy-making process to understand how and why policy decisions were made. You might also need to consider replacing or supplementing government objectives with another success reference point. If you want to consider the broader impact of the policy or government's reputation, agenda control and general governance strategy, you will also need to assess the political dimensions of policy.)

B. Benefit to target group

(Comment: This is a good approach, if you want to consider the impact on the very people the policy is meant to benefit. However, assessment based around this criterion can be open to criticism that it is failing to take into account other outcomes of policy. Therefore, you might want to consider supplementing the analysis with other reference points to make a stronger case; for example, before-and-after, comparison with another jurisdiction.)

C. Before-and-after

(Comment: A historical comparison can be a very good way of highlighting whether the policy has made any significant difference compared with a previous state of affairs. However, you need to be able to defend against accusations that the change over time is due to something other than the policy impact. One of the best ways to do so is supplement with other benchmarks; for example, original government objectives, benefit to target group.)

D. Policy domain criteria

(Comment: Most policy domains have certain criteria that are highly valued by government and non-governmental actors; for example, controlling inflation (economy), national security (defence). Assessing against such criteria can be a very good way of ascertaining whether a policy has fulfilled one of its key, cross-party goals. However, the very fact that government and opponents agree on the value of certain criteria is liable to mean they will disagree on another aspects, such as the means of achieving it, or whether it really has been achieved. Therefore, if you want to assess a policy against policy domain criteria, you will probably need to capture disagreement by also using other measures; for example, before-and-after, balance sheet, and who supports the policy.)

E. Who supports the policy

(Comment: This is only useful to capture support for policies, if combined with other success criteria. It is a very weak form of assessment and is usually the last line of defence when all else fails. It needs to be used as an adjunct to other criteria; for example, government objectives, before-and-after, benefit to target group.)

F. Another jurisdiction

(Comment: This can often be a good way of examining whether a policy has made any significant difference compared with a broadly similar jurisdiction elsewhere. However, this reference point on its own is rarely sufficient to capture the impact of a policy. It usually needs to be supplemented by others; for example, benefit to target group, before-and-after.)

G. Balance sheet

(Comment: This can be an attractive reference point tht appeals to commonsense instincts. However, the issue of whether benefits outweigh costs is highly subjective, no matter the amount of data produced for each. Additional benchmarks will help produce a more robust and defensible assessment; for example, government objectives, before-and-after.)

H. Newness and innovation

(Comment: This can be useful for assessing whether a policy is breaking free from traditional ways of tackling a problem. However, you are likely to be open to accusations that this is a 'soft' form of assessment. Newness and innovation do not necessarily mean that things have got any better. You are liable to need 'harder' criteria for assessment; for example, government objectives, benefit to target group, before-and-after.)

I. Ethics, morality and the law

(Comment: This can be a useful means of assessing a policy against core societal principles and values. However, you are liable to come against others who argue the opposite. Hence, you might need to use other criteria such as government objectives or benefit to target group. The danger in doing so, however, is that you undermine your own analysis by diluting your argument and getting into the intricacies of whether or not the policy has 'worked'. You will need to make a judgement about which approach is most likely to meet your purposes.)

QUESTION 4: ARE YOU CONFIDENT THAT SUFFICIENT AND CREDIBLE INFORMATION IS AVAILABLE IN ORDER TO REACH A CONCLUSION?

A. Broadly, yes

(Comment: This is clearly beneficial for a legitimate assessment. However, be careful that you are not missing vital data or perspectives that are not already publicly available, or can be obtained through primary research.)

B. Broadly, no

(Comment: You might be recognizing that not all policy outcomes – especially in the political realm, but also in the process and programme realms – can easily be captured by primary and secondary research. However, you should ensure that the shortage of data/information is not a product of inadequate research on your part.)

QUESTION 5: ARE YOU CONFIDENT THAT YOU CAN ISOLATE THE POLICY OUTCOMES FROM ALL OTHER INFLUENCES ON THESE OUTCOMES?

A. Yes

(Comment: You are likely to have detailed statistical analysis to support your case. This will contribute to the legitimacy of any assessment. However, be careful. The task is a very difficult one, even for the most rigorous statistical analyst. You should ensure that you have not produced an analysis that is statistically sound but does not capture real-life policy dynamics and outcomes.)

B. No

(Comment: This is not a major problem. Very few assessments can 'isolate' policy in this way. However, you should double-check that you cannot do more. Also, make sure that you are able to defend yourself from criticism on this issue.)

QUESTION 6: TO THE BEST OF YOUR KNOWLEDGE AND/OR INSTINCTS, DO YOU CONSIDER A HIDDEN AGENDA TO BE AT WORK?

A. Yes

(Comment: You might have a point. Hidden agendas tend to be political to enhance reputations, to help control the agenda in a surreptitious way and/or steer a governance strategy in a desired direction, whether continuity or change. However, you should also be careful. You will need to defend yourself against accusations that you have no proof and that you are being politically biased, or that you yourself are indulging in 'politics' when you should be sticking to the 'facts'.)

B. No

(Comment: You might have a point. The goals of many policies are a matter of public record. However, be careful that you are not ignoring deeper policy motives, especially in the political realm, but also in process and programmatic ones.)

QUESTION 7: DOES THE SPHERE OF POLICY YOU ARE ASSESSING (PROCESS, PROGRAMME, POLITICS) HAVE MORE THAN ONE GOAL?

A. Yes

(Comment: You are likely to be correct in your assumption. Many policies have multiple goals. Nevertheless, in order to make final judgements about policy success, you will need to make a judgement about which goals or goals are most important in terms of needing to be achieved, and/or make a judgement about which is most important when achievement of one conflicts directly with achieving another. Regardless of the fact that your judgement is the product of complex policy, you might need to defend yourself against criticism that you are being selective and/or biased in your findings.)

B. No

(Comment: You might be right. Some policies do have only one objective. However, you should ensure that you are not missing other objectives, or small sub-objectives.)

QUESTION 8: ARE THERE ANY UNINTENDED CONSEQUENCES, INCLUDING SUCCESS BEING GREATER THAN PLANNED?

A. Yes

(Comment: This is quite possible. Therefore, you will need to weigh up how significant the unintended aspects are, and whether they add to or negate the policy goals. However, you should be prepared to defend yourself from criticism that you are neglecting 'core' policy aims and achievements.)

B. No

(Comment: This is quite possible, but you should double-check to make sure.)

QUESTION 9: DOES THE POLICY FALL SHORT OF MEETING THE TARGETS THAT WERE SET?

A. Yes

(Comment: This is highly likely. You are probably recognizing a reality of public policy. However, after double-checking your information, you need to weigh up how significant are the shortfalls in your assessment of success strength, or failure. Depending on your judgement, you might need to defend yourself against accusations that you are either being 'too negative' because your have given priority to the shortfalls, or are biased or over-optimistic because you have emphasized achievements.)

B. No

(Comment: This is uncommon, but does make the assessment job easier. However, an absence of shortfalls is rare. Double-check that you are not being misled, either by official sources or by weaknesses in your own research.)

QUESTION 10: ARE YOU ASSESSING MORE THAN ONE POLICY REALM (PROCESS, PROGRAMMES AND POLITICS)?

A. Yes

(Comment: You are likely to be capturing much of the complexities of public policy. However, you are also likely to have a difficult choice to make in terms of which realm should contribute most towards your final assessment. Whichever you choose, you should be prepared for criticism that you are being balanced and politicized because you are empathizing one factor (or one achievement) over another.)

B. No

(Comment: Good, if this is what you set out to do. However, you should consider why you have this narrow focus. If you are required to do so, this is valid. If you are not required to do so but want to understand whether a policy has been successful, you might need to consider appraising the policy-making process to understand how and why a policy decision was made. You might also need to consider replacing or supplementing government objectives with another reference point. If you want to consider the broader impact of the policy on government's reputation, agenda control and general governance strategy, you will also need to assess the political dimensions of policy.)

Chapter 5

Framing Success: Claims, Counter-Claims and Agenda Impact

One of the central themes of this book is that success is, to some extent, constructed. I cannot envisage success being nothing but an objective fact, simply because perceptions will vary on the desirability or otherwise of a government's ways of producing policy, its programmes, values and political trajectory. The importance of perceptions of success permeated the literature review in Chapter 1. Disagreements about what constituted success cut across writings from those on public value to policy improvement and Machiavellian politics.

Claims to success are not always articulated in the same way as I have presented the different forms of success in this book. Policy actors do not generally think in the kinds of typologies used in academic texts, and certainly not with regard to a phenomenon – policy success – that is rarely written about. Furthermore, some aspects of success are not viable for actors, especially governments, to proclaim (such as a pre-election budget helping bring votes for the governing party). Claims of policy success are part of language, with actors interpreting the world and communicating as they see it. In doing so, they adopt different bases for (measures of) success. Indeed, much of the difference between the criteria I have given for success (Chapter 2) and the political rhetoric of success is due to differing views not on what might be a broad characteristic of successful policy (for example, programmes that produce positive outcomes), but on how we know that the condition is met (for example, a positive outcome could be the benefits outweighing the costs, or it could be that outcomes are better than before).

The purpose of this chapter is to examine the constructed aspect of success, drawing out and developing issues raised in earlier chapters. The chapter is structured as follows. First, it deals briefly with the matter of who claims policy success. Second, it dissects an important aspect of the discourse surrounding policy success (and, indeed, failure) by examining what is actually claimed, in terms of types of success, time frame, scale, and measures by which success is assumed. Third and finally, the chapter identifies a number of agenda-setting functions that claims to success can perform or, at least, are intended to perform. These include maintaining social order, silencing critics and paving the way for further reform.

Who claims policy success?

Amid the complexity of public policies and the multiple impacts they have on society, there are many claims that policy has been successful. As Box 5.1 indicates, the word 'success' itself might be used by policy actors, but other statements such as 'policy is working' or 'we did what we set out to do' carry similar positive affirmations. The main sources of claims that a policy has been successful are governments and politicians, government agencies, quasi non-governmental organizations, political parties, media, interest groups, voluntary organizations, consultants, academics, and citizens. While claims of success will tend to emanate from those in and around government and its supporters (although they can emerge from any source), counter-claims will tend to emanate from outside government, particularly among opposition parties, media, voluntary organizations and interest groups.

Liberal democracies are the fuel for claims and counter-claims. Liberal democratic political systems are founded on principles of plurality and openness. Such principles manifest themselves in periodic elections, separation of powers, free media, freedom of speech, and so on. With occasional exceptions, a range of actors and institutions involved in policy processes can make almost any claim they wish. They can criticize government, support it, support the *status quo*, propose policy change and, importantly, they can lay claim to a policy being successful (or unsuccessful). There are many arenas in which claims of success can be made. They include:

- *legislative arenas*: legislative chambers (speeches, replies to questions), committee reports and discussions
- *executive arenas*: presentations to cabinet, speeches, press releases, on- and off- the-record briefings, reports and papers, departmental websites
- *party political arenas*: election platforms, conferences, websites, policy papers, intra-party policy debates, intra-party leadership contests
- *governmental departmental and agency arenas*: annual reports, subject specific reports and papers, evaluation reviews, websites, staff speeches at conferences and forums
- *quasi-governmental arenas*: committees of inquiry, audit committees, consultants' reviews, inter-governmental forums
- *media arenas*: news stories, editorials, opinion pieces, websites, blogs and electronic forums
- *voluntary and private sectors*: reports, papers, websites, speeches, media briefings press releases, conferences.

Box 5.1   Typical statements articulating policy success

'We achieved our goal'
'We hit our target'
'Our policy is working'
'We did what we set out to do'
'We met our objective'
'We got the results we wanted'
'Things are better than before'
"Our policy is the right one'
'The policy is successful'

The analysis now needs to dig deeper in order to make sense of what is being claimed.

Unravelling the discourse of claims to success (and failure)

Deconstructing language is not an exact science. It is beset by perennial problems of observer bias, the analyst's interpretation of others' interpretation (the double hermeneutic), as well as deeper issues of locating language within situational contexts of culture, power and social control (Fischer 2003; Gee 2005). However, given the broader public policy aims of this book in introducing readers to the concept of policy success, a degree of parsimony seems justified. In this regard, a number of strands emerge in political discourse that pertain to the very nature of success.

The multiple bases of success claims and counter-claims

Claims to policy success contain assumptions about what success actually is. We might call them benchmarks, standards, measures or bases, but they amount to the same thing: explicit or implicit assumptions about what constitutes success. As will be shown, they have mirror images in counter-claims of 'failure'.

The issues here relate directly to the discussion in Chapter 3, which provided a framework for understanding the complex relationship between success and failure and, in particular, the fact that many policies reside somewhere in between these extremes. The framework rested on categories of policy success, durable success, conflicted success, precarious success and failure. Importantly, policy-makers – at least, publicly – do not simply accept the 'realities' of how successful or otherwise a policy has been. Indeed, they might not even know. As Dye (2005: 332) argues:

> Does the government generally know what it is doing? Generally speaking, no ... [E]ven if programs and policies are well organized, efficiently operated, adequately financed, and generally supported by major interest groups, we may still want to ask, So what? Do they work? Do these programs have any beneficial effects on society? Are the effects immediate or long range? ... Unfortunately, governments have done very little to answer these more basic questions.

This knowledge gap, plus the imperatives of creating positive impressions of capacities to govern and commitment to espoused values, means that policy-makers will tend towards framing policies as far they realistically can towards the 'success' end of the spectrum, while critics and opponents will tend towards framing policies as far as they reasonably can towards 'failure'. These are tendencies, rather than iron laws. Governments do admit failure in the face of the inevitable. In 1991, for example, UK Environment Secretary Michael Heseltine admitted publicly that the controversial poll tax had failed as a means of financing local government. Opponents can also rally around government, especially in times of national emergencies, to support governments' policy responses. For example, in the early stages of the global financial crisis in 2008, opposition parties throughout the western world offered strong bipartisan support for government rescue packages. Nevertheless, the broad pattern of adversary politics is that governments govern and oppositions oppose. Even up until the final days of precarious successes, governments have a habit of portraying policies – at least, in public – as highly successful.

Crucially, as indicated, claims to success might use an evolving mix of what actually constitutes success. Success (and, indeed, failure) is always used with reference to a particular measure or standard, from original goals through to ethical priorities. Protagonists have substantial freedom to pick and choose from these different measures (based on genuine beliefs and/or pragmatic tactics) in order to put forward their argument. A number of bases for claims are common (see Table 5.1). There is some overlap between them, and different bases can be used in different time periods to frame and promote the success or otherwise of particular policies. Nevertheless, they are distinctive enough to be categories in their own right. Table 5.2 provides a mirror image in terms of framing failure in relation to these same reference points.

The first basis, and the one most in line with the formalities of policy processes, is *original intentions*. Supporters can point to an objective (even if it was only one of many) and emphasize its attainment, or critics can point to a

Table 5.1 *The multiple bases of claims that policy is successful*

Basis of claim	Typical statements	Hypothetical example
Original objectives	We achieved what we set out to achieve.	We said that hospital waiting lists would be cut by 50 per cent, and that is precisely what we have done. The facts speak for themselves.
Benefit to target group	Look at the positive impact on people's lives.	Our low interest policy has eased the mortgage burden for homeowners.
Before-and-after	Look how much things have improved.	Inflation is down from 5 per cent to 3 per cent.
Policy domain criteria	We all know how important X is, and we are doing just this.	Maintaining national security is paramount, and we will not jeopardize it by releasing our prior intelligence on this matter.
Who supports the policy	The policy must be working because it has the support of Y.	Our education reform must be doing something right when it has the support of parents' groups throughout the country.
Another jurisdiction	We are doing much better than Z.	Our policies have attracted more inward investment than our neighbours and competitors.
Balance sheet	The benefits outweigh the costs.	Building a new airport and reaping the benefits in terms of tourism and trade is a price worth paying for the small environmental impact created.
Newness and innovation	We have put a new framework in place.	We have put in place a new system to ensure that patient waiting times decrease.
Ethics, morality and the law	It is the 'right' thing to do.	Casualties are an unfortunate cost of war, but it right that we commit our troops to protect a country struggling to establish democracy.

different objective and demonstrate that it was not met. The discussion of public value in Chapter 1 indicates that public organizations typically pursue many, and often conflicting, values. Hence, differential points of reference are neither uncommon nor difficult to comprehend. For example, reforms to a public rail network could be portrayed by government as a 'success' because targets were met when 95 per cent of trains ran on time (the reference point being original objectives) and that this was an improvement on the old figure of 90 per cent (the reference point being a before-and-after comparison). However, opponents could say the reforms were a failure by using different reference points, such as customers getting a bad deal (non-benefit to target group) and because of increased ticket prices (costs outweigh benefits in the balance sheet).

Second, a claim to success can be based on the *benefit to a target group*. One of George W. Bush's constant justifications for military intervention in Iraq was that it freed the Iraqi people from the tyranny of Saddam Hussein. The fact that both Saddam Hussein and his regime no longer exist is indisputable and, hence, opponents have used many other standards to criticize the 'success' of the invasion. The Stop the War Coalition, for example, has defined the occupation as an abject failure, and used many counterpoints of reference, including the argument that the war is illegal (it breaches ethical and moral codes) and has actually worsened the plight of the very people it was meant to help (non-benefit to target group).

A third basis for claiming success is a prior state of affairs and whether things are better or worse than previously. In effect, this is a *before-and-after* comparison in order to offer support or to criticize. British Prime Minister Harold Macmillan's famous statement in a speech on 20 July 1957 that 'most of our people have never had it so good' (these words, entering mythology as 'you've never had it so good') is a classic example of claiming success based on improvement from a prior state of affairs. Decades later, the Labour Party's 1997 slogan and adopted pop song, *Things Can Only Get Better*, was, in effect, an invitation to judge prospective success under Labour in comparison to a gradual decline in life under successive Conservative governments.

Fourth, a claim can be made with reference to *criteria that are particular to that policy domain or policy issue*. In other words, some types of outcomes are highly valued by the dominant values in that policy sector; for example, secrecy (intelligence sector), efficiency (budgeting) and control of inflation (macro economy). For instance, Jean-Claude Trichet (2004), President of the European Central Bank (ECB) indicates what is important to the ECB:

> the ECB's monetary policy has been successful in keeping inflation and inflation expectations under control, even in the face of exceptional uncertainty and a number of substantial, mainly upward, price shocks hitting the euro area economy.

Table 5.2 *The multiple bases of claims that policy has failed*

Basis of claim	Typical statements	Hypothetical example
Original objectives	You did not achieve what you set out to achieve.	You said that hospital waiting lists would be cut by 50 per cent and you have not done so. The facts speak for themselves.
Damage to target group	The policy has damaged the very people the policy was meant to help.	Your interest rate policy has actually increased the mortgage burden for homeowners.
Before and after	Things have got worse.	Inflation is up from 3 per cent to 5 per cent.
Policy domain criteria	We all know how important X is, and you are failing to deal with it.	Maintaining national security is paramount, and you have jeopardized it by releasing intelligence on this matter.
Who opposes the policy	The policy must be wrong because it is opposed by Y.	Your education reform must be wrong, when it is opposed by parents' groups throughout the country.
Another jurisdiction	We are doing much worse than Z.	Your policies have attracted less inward investment than our neighbours and competitors.
Balance sheet	The costs outweigh the benefits.	The environmental damage caused by building a new airport is much greater than any benefits in terms of tourism and trade.
Anachronism	You are producing a tired, old response to the problem.	Your system for reducing patient waiting times is basically no different than what has been done in the past.
Ethics, morality and the law	It is the 'wrong' thing to do.	It is wrong to send men and women into battle and possible death.

A hypothetical example with which to illustrate the contestability of policy domain criteria is the related instance of a government minister justifying intervening in currency markets to prop up the nation's currency, on the grounds that currency stability is vital to successful economic policy. Such claims can, of course, be countered by others contesting within that particular criterion and/or with reference to other criteria. For example, intervention to prop up a currency could be criticized on the grounds that it is not in the national interest to use taxpayers' money to prop up a currency (in effect, the 'nation' is the target group that is being disadvantaged) and it is better to let the free market dictate currency levels (in effect, this argument contests what suitable policy domain criteria actually are).

Fifth, protagonists might claim policy success or failure by referring to *who supports/commends or opposes/criticizes it*. An example from the process aspect of policy relates to the proposal in 1986 to introduce a community charge (poll tax) and uniform business rate to fund local government in Scotland. When faced with strong criticism of the proposals, Scottish Secretary Malcolm Rifkind stated to the House of Commons, in justification for pressing ahead with the reforms:

> It is interesting to note that those who have welcomed the proposals for the community charge and the Government's other proposals are the ratepayers' associations in Scotland, which represents industry, the Chamber of Commerce, which represents small businesses and the CBI in Scotland, which represents industry. These organisations have all given a full welcome to the Governments' proposals. As they represent pretty well all the ratepayers of Scotland, that is something from which we can take great satisfaction.

> (*Quoted in McConnell 1995: 150–1*)

In a broadly similar vein, an evaluation report commissioned by the Canadian Public Service Commission into a programme for the recruitment of policy leaders concluded that:

> The most notable testimony to the success of the RPL Program is that its clients, i.e., senior government managers and policy groups within the federal departments and agencies, believe that the RPL Program is a very successful mechanism for recruiting highly-qualified policy specialists.

> (*Corporate Research Associates Inc.*
> *and Kelly Sears Consulting Group 2008*)

Sixth, success might be claimed by making *comparison to another jurisdiction*, and whether current domestic policy is better or worse than elsewhere. Federal and devolved systems lend themselves especially to such comparisons, but so do modern public sectors worldwide with the emphasis on policy performance indicators and league tables. If one jurisdiction performs better than another, there are strong political, and sometimes financial, incentives for policy-makers to claim success relative to how others are doing. For example, a trawl through the websites of local councils in England to examine their reactions to school performance tables, reveals many statements such as 'we have some of the best schools in the country' and 'we came in Xth place of Y number of schools'. Comparisons might also be beyond the level of the nation state. Canadian Finance Minister Jim Flaherty (2007) states: 'Canada quite simply is considered to have one of the most well-developed private pension and retirement saving systems in the world. We consider our pension system an economic as well as a social policy success.'

Seventh, a further basis for claiming success might be a *balance sheet* approach, assessing the policy in terms of whether the benefits outweigh the costs. Edelstein (2008: 7), in his study of military occupations, adopts this model, arguing that: 'Judgements of success and failure in military occupations are based on whether the occupying power accomplished its goals and at what cost.' He argues, therefore, that the post-World War II victories over Japan and Germany can be considered successes, because of the transformation of each country from a bitter adversary to a reliable ally.

Eighth, a reference point for success might be the claim that something *new, fresh or innovative* has been put in place. As Michael Barber, former Head of the Prime Minster's Delivery Unit under Tony Blair stated in his summation of achievements:

> The entire strategic framework for the public services has been radically changed for the better ... five-year strategic planning, three-year funding settlements, the publication of targets and results, and the independence of the Office of National Statistics have entirely changed the rules of the policy game.
>
> (*Barber 2007: 268*)

Ninth, and finally, judgements of success or otherwise can be based on *ethics and morality*, concerning (for example) equity, justice, adherence to the law and human rights. In other words, no matter what the policy evidence might reveal, claims of success (and failure) rest on the argument that the policy is successful because it promotes these values (or is unsuccessful because it damages them). Gerald Ford, in pardoning Richard Nixon, stated that 'in my own conscience it was the right thing to do'. Tony Blair argued that it was 'morally right' to send troops to Iraq. Australian Prime Minster Kevin Rudd's symbolic 'sorry' for the forced removal of generations of indigenous children from their families was, in his own words, 'aimed at righting past wrongs'. Claims for policy success are often justified with reference to achieving a higher moral or ethical purpose.

Appendix 5.1 to this chapter provides an example of a 2008 debate in the UK House of Commons on the Labour Government's fiscal rules. The Government minister Stephen Timms defended the government's record as successful, and the opposition spokesman said that it had failed. The Appendix is not intended to be a definitive piece of discourse analysis on the debate. Rather, in the tradition of Roe (1994), it is intended to get a sense of the government's main claim to success and the opposition's main line of criticism. Defence and criticism covered several criteria. However, I would argue that the main story produced by the minister was based primarily on before-and-after criteria. Therefore, his main line of argument was that things had got much better when compared with 1997 (before-and-after), because of an innovative approach (newness and innovation) and sound fiscal rules (policy domain criteria). By contrast, the opposition spokesperson David Gauke barely focused on the record over time. Rather, his main focus was that the government was doing worse than elsewhere (comparison to other jurisdictions), because of outmoded thinking (anachronistic) and failure to adopt principles crucial to fiscal stability (policy domain criteria). The framework, adopted in a rudimentary way for this case, has the potential to be applied in greater detail to other claims of success and counter-claims of failure.

Narratives of success

Claims of policy success are further complicated. Not only are there multiple bases or reference points for success, but also they embody narratives that vary from one claim or speech act to another. These narratives convey not only assumptions about the realm of success, but also the time frame that it covers and the scale of achievement.

The first narrative relates to the *realm of success*; that is, programme, process or political. Success in terms of programmes might be claimed on one or more of the bases mentioned (and summarized in Figure 5.1), ranging from meeting programme objectives through to conformance with ethical principles. However, the claim to success might also refer to issues of process, in terms of how an issue is dealt with. A government might say, for example, that 'we explored all options and weighed up the costs and benefits', or 'we made sure that stakeholders were involved in decision-making'. A much more sensitive claim is to political success. Government's usually tread warily in articulating the achieving of political goals, in case they are accused of partisanship rather than adhering to constitutional conventions of acting in the public interest. However, claims of political success permeate political discourse and include statements such as 'we succeeded in getting our message across', 'we stood firm and held our nerve' and 'we will build on the successes we have already achieved'.

The second narrative relates to the *time frame for success*. Claims can be made for past success, for progress to date or even success to come. Progress to date might refer to successes in comparison with the record of previous governments or within the particular term of a government. In the UK, Olympics Minister Tessa Jowell (see Box 5.2) provides an example of the former in her assessment of London's progress towards meeting the targets it set for changes in social attitudes, promoted by London's hosting of the Games in 2012. The claim has three main bases (original objectives, before-and-after, benefit to target group), with the temporal dimension clearly flagged. In effect, the message equates to 'we have succeeded to date and we are on track for success in the future'. In fact, in some policy areas, claims to success can be heavily future-oriented. For example, US Vice President Dick Cheney stated in 2005 that: 'We will succeed in Iraq, just like we did in Afghanistan. We will stand up a new government under an Iraqi-drafted constitution. We will defeat that insurgency, and, in fact, it will be an enormous success story' (CNN International 2005).

The third narrative relates to the *scale of the success*. As Figure 5.1 indicates, the 'lowest' point on the scale relates to fairly modest claims relating to a problem being fixed. For instance, a government minister might say that a loophole in legislation has been closed, or that more money has been allocated to allow a much-needed new hospital to be built. As we move further up the scale to the governmental level, the claim to success can be for the department, agency or even the entire regime that was responsible for fixing the problem. For example, one Bulgarian newspaper states that:

> The release and return to Bulgaria of the six Bulgarian medics imprisoned for eight years in Libya on HIV-infection charges is a big foreign policy success of the Bulgarian state and Bulgarian diplomacy, Prime Minister Sergei Stanishev said at the annual conference of the heads of this country's diplomatic representations abroad July 25. Stanishev said that the return of the medics to Bulgaria was an illustration of Bulgaria's EU membership, and shows the meaning of European solidarity and support.
>
> (*Sofia Echo* 25 July 2007)

Claims for success can be grander still, pointing to societal transformation in people's lives (they are healthier, happier, better educated and so on) or to core beliefs and the directions in which society is headed. For example, José Manuel Barroso (2007), President of the European Commission, stated that: 'The

European Union has helped to bring back freedom and democracy to all European countries. In that we have succeeded.' In 1938, when British Prime Minister Neville Chamberlain made his infamous 'peace for our time' speech and waved the Munich Agreement allowing Adolf Hitler and his regime to expand into the Sudetenland of Czechoslovakia, he presented it as document for peace that would allow people to sleep soundly in their beds.

The agenda impact of claims to success

Claims of policy success are part of the fabric political life. Political language is not only a system of communicating complex realities, emotions and desires in a simple and accessible way, but is also bound up with power, whether, for

---

Box 5.2   Example of claim to success based on achievements to date: Tessa Jowell, UK Olympics Minister, and London's hosting of the Olympic Games in 2012

'Let our legacy be judged on what we promised. Two pledges. First, we said the Olympics would change a generation of young people through sport. No more plucky-loser mentality, no more armchair sporting culture.'

'We started with school sport on a programme of transformation that will take a decade to fully achieve. Ninety per cent of children now take part in two hours of school sport a week, a dramatic increase from 25 per cent in 2002.'

'We also said we would transform the heart of east London, not just with outstanding new sports facilities but also new housing and new transport links and an Olympic Park that would become a sporting, cultural and commercial centre. We said this, and we meant it.'

'There are five sports venues in the Olympic Park that will remain after the Games. The Olympic Stadium, the Velodrome, the Aquatics Centre, Eton Manor football, hockey and tennis pitches and the Handball Arena, which is set to become a multi-use indoor sports arena. These will reap dividends long after the London Games are a distant memory. And none of this would have happened without the Olympics.'

Source: Adapted from Jowell (2009).

example, we subscribe to language as manifestation of political pluralism, or language as dominated by the ideological hegemony of a ruling class. There are very few, if any, political analysts today who refute the contention that language is closely connected to power. As Epstein (2008: 3–4) argues in her book on the 'power of words' in relation to the gradual birth of anti-whaling discourse in the latter part of the twentieth century: 'discursive power is not a fungible entity, yet it has very real effects ... social relations are both simultaneously the locus of power and the site for the production of meaning'. The argumentative turn and the growth of narrative policy analysis certainly seems to indicate an increased fascination with, and recognition of the importance of the power of language (Edelman 1977; Roe 1994; Schön and Rein 1994; Yanow 2000; Stone 2002; Fischer 2003; Hajer and Wagennar 2003).

The agenda-setting purposes or functions that claims to success perform are contingent on which conceptual approach we take. A pluralist approach, for example, would view claims to success (and failure) as open discourse from multiple interests that prevents any particular interests and value statements from dominating undemocratically – at least, for too long. By contrast, a neo-Marxist approach might emphasize the ways in which claims to success (and failure) help perpetuate the democratic shell that props up capitalist relations of production. The broad policy success framework put forward in Chapters 2 and 3 does not align itself with any particular explanatory or normative model of society. Its value is heuristic. Different perspectives can emphasize the importance of some factors over others.

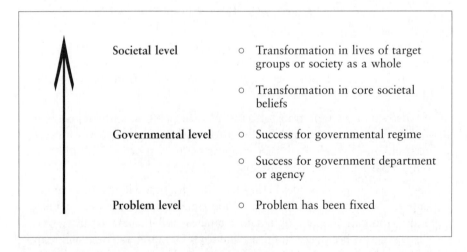

Figure 5.1   *Size matters: a scale of claims to success*

Communicating achievements

Government has many different 'tools' at its disposal, and one of these is information (Hood and Margetts 2007). The extent to which achievements are 'real' or simply 'constructed' in order to impress is a matter dealt with in Chapters 2 and 3. Nevertheless, government can disseminate its achievements in many different ways. The most direct is clear statements of policy success. They might appear in press conferences, press releases, TV and radio interviews; response to parliamentary questions; websites, publicity leaflets and strategic plans. For example, New Zealand Minister of Finance Michael Cullen (2005), stated in a speech to the Wellington Chamber of Commerce that:

> I am confident that history will judge Budget 2005 as an important further step towards putting New Zealand back in the top half of the OECD. That is the goal that the Labour-led government adopted early in our first term of office, and although it is what is known in business as a 'stretch-target' we have made considerable progress towards it. We are performing very well on relative measures of social well-being, personal security and educational standards. And we are starting to regain the ground we lost during the last quarter of last century in terms of economic performance and incomes ... What this means is that we have succeeded in halting the slide relative to the OECD average and have pulled back some territory.

The issue of who takes credit for success follows on. Often, this will be explicit. For example, Paula Lehtomäki (2007), Finish Minister for Foreign Trade and Development, stated in a speech that:

> High levels of investment in research and development and close cooperation between the Government, academia and business sector in the area of R&D are key features of the Finnish model. Our public R&D spending ranks among the highest in the world, and Finland of today is best described as an innovation and knowledge economy ... This success is not a coincidence, but the result of conscious policy decisions and consistent work by the Government in cooperation with academia and business.

Conveying achievement is one of the most elementary, and perhaps obvious, functions of a claim to policy success.

Ordering and stabilization

There are many definitions of public policy but few are liable to disagree with Peters (1986: 4), who suggests that: 'Stated most simply, public policy is the sum of government activities, whether acting directly or through agents, as it has an influence on the life of citizens'. Yet, beneath this simple definition there is immense complexity, as well as diversity of views that vie for influence and will readily criticize governments, their policies and the consequences of those policies. For example, supporters of the free market in the tradition of Friedman, Hayek and others would see 'the sum of government activities' to be bureaucratic, wasteful and unresponsive impediments to a greater society founded on free markets with little government intervention, save for the protection of private property rights. Correspondingly, others following in the socialist tradition of (for example) Hobson, Laski and the Webbs, would consider the sum of government activities to be a means of promoting social equality and insulating citizens from the vagaries of the free market. Debates about the role of government and its policies can often be vitriolic. Statements of policy success are an attempt to bring order to chaos, and to bring an authoritative stabilization of policy claims and counter-claims.

Legitimation

Claims that a particular programme has been successful can also confer – or, at least, be an attempt to confer – legitimacy. Such legitimacy might attach itself to a number of different targets. The most obvious is the programme itself. If a national government claims that a funding formula for local authorities is successful because it takes into account both population numbers and per capita demand for services, the implication is that the policy has 'worked' and does not need to be terminated or fundamentally reviewed. In other words, the pro-gramme is assumed to be a legitimate response to a societal problem. The next to benefit, at least in terms of intent, is the sponsor of the programme that is 'working'. It could, for example, be an individual departmental minister, or even a prime minister, premier, president or chancellor. Legitimation might even be conferred on government itself, its capacity to govern and the direction in which it is headed. If a policy is deemed successful, it can help legitimate the broader governance agenda of which it is a small part. For example, a successful experiment in citizen participation in planning decisions might be portrayed as a vindication of a broader 'new politics' agenda to bring government closer to the people.

Deflection of criticism

The other side of the legitimation coin is that claims to success are attempts to deflect criticism. Such claims are agenda-setting tools and can be part of the 'mobilization of bias' (Bachrach and Baratz 1970); that is, the defences and defenders of the *status quo* against those actors and forces that seek to criticize or topple them. Claims of success are policy stories of heroes, ascendancy and triumphs (Stone 2002). Policy stories are part of the discourse embedded in policy processes. Not only are they rallying points around which supporters and advocates can coalesce, but also they challenge critics and detractors to produce effective counter-stories. For example, Singapore's highly influential Minister Mentor, Lee Kuan Yew, said of Singapore's Institutes of Technical Education:

> I think it's one of the success stories of Singapore that we're able to uplift the academically less advantaged ... and use their other skills, hands-on skills and ability to improvise, to give them that added value so that they can make a contribution to life, to society and to make a good living.

> (*ChannelNewsAsia.Com 2008*)

The positive language of success can make it very difficult for effective counter-stories to emerge. Lee Kuan Yew's statement speaks of states of affairs that few people see as highly undesirable ('uplifting the academically disadvantaged', 'giving them added value', making a 'good living'). Hence, counter-stories would need to retain the same goals, but focus on evidence proving that those who are academically disadvantaged are not actually being helped to the extent suggested. In other words, the counter-story would need to focus on a claim of 'non-benefit to target group'. In the guided democracy of Singapore, such stories can struggle to emerge.

Furthermore, one of the most common implications of a statement of policy success is that critics should 'stop criticizing'. Canadian Conservative MP Dean Del Mastro stated in the House of Commons in defence of his government's handling of the issue of hospital waiting times:

> Mr. Speaker, yesterday the member for Brampton-Springdale stood in the House and falsely accused this government of failing to reduce health care wait times since taking office four short months ago. As usual, the Liberals' opposition is merely an indictment of their own time in government. This government is committed to wait times guarantees. A guarantee is a guarantee and this government has demonstrated that we honour our commitment to Canadians. As the member for Brampton-Springdale knows, wait times doubled during the 13 years of Liberal government in this country. The opposition should refrain from being so critical. This government has accomplished more in 130 days than the previous government did in 13 long years.

> (*Hansard 2006*)

Justifying continuity

Claims of policy success might be followed by an explicit statement on what will or should happen next, such as 'we need to build on this success'. However, implicit signals of 'more of the same' can be just as important. For example, South Korean Deputy Foreign Minister Lee Soo Hyuck stated with regard to engaging in nuclear talks with North Korea, the United States, China, Russia and Japan and South Korea that the 'policy has been successful so far. The recent rise of [support for reunification] in South Korea is very natural after the collapse of the Cold War ... but we are not pursuing this path blindly ... We are using it tactically and strategically' (*Washington Post* 2003). The implication here is that a statement of 'success' paves the way for a continuation of the strategy of engagement.

Opening a window for reform

Claims to policy success can be building blocks for reform. They can provide legitimacy for further reform, as the 'next stage' or 'second wave', in the host jurisdiction or even beyond. For example, Jeb Bush, Governor of Florida, stated in relation to his 'One Florida' educational policy that it had succeeded in increasing the number of minorities enrolled at college and that the policy: 'can be a model for other states because its goal is to transcend the increasingly tired debate about affirmative action. We intend to prove that government can be race-neutral in its decision-making without turning a blind eye to equal opportunity' (*New York Times* 15 September 2000). Aspirations for success, and avoidance of failure, can also lead to the language of success being used in order to provoke a deeper paradigmatic change. UK Prime Minister Gordon Brown (2009) stated in a speech on climate change that:

> the security of our planet and our humanity is at stake. Success will require two major shifts in how we think – as policy makers, as campaigners, as consumers, as producers, as a society. The first is to think not in political or economic cycles; not just in terms of years or even decade-long programmes and initiatives. But to think in terms of epochs and eras – and how our stewardship will be judged not by tomorrow's newspapers but by tomorrow's children. And the second is to think anew about how we judge success as a society. For sixty years we have measured our progress by economic gains and social justice. Now we know that the progress and even the survival of the only world we have depends on decisive action to protect that world. In the end, without environmental stewardship, there can be no sustainable prosperity and no sustainable social justice.

Closing a window for change

Claims to policy success can bring finality and closure to a policy. They can amount to a claim that 'the job is done', with implications that aspiring policy alternatives and their advocates should proceed no further. Commitments to withdraw troops sent overseas are a good example. Statements such as 'mission accomplished' and 'we did what we set out to do' help legitimate policy termination and close down political space for those who might argue otherwise.

Conclusion

Claims of policy success and counter-claims of failure are integral to the political discourse of plural societies. They embody the powers and aspirations of those seeking to make and defend public policy, as well as those seeking to challenge policy-making process, programmes and political trajectories. Political language displays remarkably invention, with governments and their supporters twisting and turning to defend policies that many consider to be unworkable and indefensible, or opponents magnifying small failings in what many consider to be otherwise sensible policies. No matter the 'successes' that might exist – such as government doing what it set out to do, or programmes creating benefit for some interests – the discourse of success and failure is fluid. However, the contest is by no means equal. Governments possess the powers, authority, legitimacy and support of political office, and for claims of policy success to be influential in stabilizing conflicts, steering agendas and more. Political scientists know, of course, that such dominance is not absolute, and that government, policy monopolies or advocacy collations of interests can fragment and lose their supremacy. However, governments and policy-makers have substantial power to steer policy evaluation processes in directions consistent with definitions of success that fit with their governance priorities. Such issues will be developed from Chapter 7 onwards. Meanwhile, the analysis turns in Chapter 6 to comprehending strategies for policy-making success.

Appendix 5.1

Framing success and framing failure: 2008 House of Commons Debate on the UK Labour government's fiscal rules

DEFENCE OF GOVERNMENT RECORD BY STEPHEN TIMMS, FINANCIAL SECRETARY TO THE TREASURY

Before-and-after comparison (things have got better)

> 'The fiscal rules are a key element of the framework introduced in 1997 for long-term macroeconomic stability, which has ushered in the longest period of success in the economy that we have ever seen in the UK. Before it was introduced, fiscal policy frequently amplified, rather than dampened, the fluctuations of the economic cycle, and fiscal policy decisions were made against vague and shifting objectives. We all vividly remember the consequences of that: 3 million unemployed, twice; 15 per cent interest rates; and record levels of repossessions and bankruptcies.'

> 'Today's global economic challenges are certainly unprecedented, but the framework has made a big contribution to growth and stability in the UK economy over the economic cycle that began in 1997, with inflation and interest rates over the past 10 years averaging around half what they were in the previous two decades. The International Monetary Fund said recently that "for over a decade, the United Kingdom has sustained low inflation and rapid economic growth – an exceptional achievement ... the fruit of strong policies and policy frameworks, which provide a strong foundation to weather global challenges". '

> 'During the economic cycle that started in 1996–97, net borrowing has averaged 1 per cent, compared with more than 3 per cent in the previous economic cycle under the Conservative Government.'

> 'The framework has improved transparency and increased the regularity of fiscal reporting. Fiscal policy has supported monetary policy, helping to smooth the path of the economy, which represents a break from the pro-cyclical fiscal policy of the past; and the golden rule has played an important part in breaking the bias against capital investment that so damaged public services. My hon. Friend the Member for South Derbyshire (Mr Todd) made that important point earlier. Public sector investment is over three times higher as a share of the economy than it was in 1997–98, having risen from 0.6 per cent of GDP then to 2 per cent this year.'

> 'Discipline through the framework saw net debt cut over the economic cycle that began in 1997–98 from 43.2 per cent of GDP at the end of 1996–97 to 36.5 per cent in 2006–07.'

Innovation

> 'The framework introduced in 1997 therefore marked a genuinely radical change. The code for fiscal stability, underpinned by legislation, sets out the

principles for fiscal management enunciated by my right hon. Friend the Chief Secretary to the Treasury earlier in the debate, along with new reporting requirements and the role of the National Audit Office in the independent audit of key assumptions behind the forecasts. It promotes openness, transparency and accountability, just as the framework for monetary policy did after the Bank of England Act 1998.'

Comparison with other jurisdictions (we are doing better than elsewhere)

'The fiscal framework has served our economy well. Net debt is lower as a percentage of gross domestic product in the UK than in all the other G7 countries except Canada, and in the euro area.'

Policy domain criteria (we are responsible and meeting the requirements in this field)

'It is absolutely right to focus on sustainable investment and prudent levels of debt, and we remain committed to that, and to the other fiscal policy objectives that we have pursued consistently since 1997. The objectives are: in the short term, to support monetary policy and smooth the path of the economy; and, over the medium term, to ensure sound public finances and fairness.'

Benefit to target group (we are assisting those who have difficulty helping themselves)

'That gives us the flexibility to support the economy through the current economic shocks, in particular through the automatic stabilisers and the targeted support that we have introduced for the least well off; so borrowing can rise this year to support families and businesses.'

Balance sheet (benefits outweighing costs)

'We will not run risks with the public finances. The pre-Budget report will set out how we are striking the right balance between supporting the economy and taking the necessary decisions to ensure that the Government live within their means.'

Before-and-after comparison + comparison to other jurisdictions benefit to target group + policy domain criteria

'We are certainly a great deal better placed to weather these shocks than we were in the 1970s, the 1980s or the early 1990s. There are five reasons for that … First, Bank of England independence has given us interest rates and inflation well below the double-digit levels that we saw in earlier decades. Secondly, our labour market is the most flexible in Europe, with employment remaining high and more than half a million job vacancies. Wage pressures are subdued, thanks in no small part to our decisions on public sector pay. Thirdly, Britain remains one of the best places in which to do business and is a magnet for overseas investment. There was more foreign direct investment in this country last year than in any other country in the world except the United States. Fourthly, thanks to decisions made since 1997, public debt remains low by historical and international standards. This means that we can provide targeted support to those who need it most, and protect investment in our infrastructure. That investment was sacrificed in previous downturns, but it will in truth underpin our future growth, which is why we need to maintain it. Fifthly, we have taken the long-term decisions to boost competitiveness – on energy, planning, transport, housing, science, skills and digital technology. However, there is no ground for complacency. Britain unquestionably faces great challenges. But we are facing them from a very strong foundation.'

CRITICISM OF GOVERNMENT RECORD BY DAVID GAUKE, SHADOW TREASURY SPOKESPERSON

Before-and-after comparison (things have got worse over time) + comparison with other jurisdictions (we are doing worse than others) + policy domain criteria (government is not meeting the requirements of this field)

'What of the then Chancellor's proposals? In 1997, he described the rules as providing a new discipline, openness and accountability. However, if they provide a new discipline, why do we have the highest borrowing figures for any major economy apart from Hungary, Egypt and Pakistan? If the rules provide financial discipline, why, according to the Institute for Fiscal Studies, have 19 out of 21 comparable industrial country Governments done more than the UK Government to improve their structural budget balances, and why have 16 of them done more to reduce their debt burdens? What sort of financial discipline is it that allows consistent borrowing in good years, leaving us nothing spare in the bad years? The International Monetary Fund, the European Commission, the OECD and just about every independent commentator advised the Government that their fiscal policy was reckless, and yet the fiscal rules did nothing to prevent that from happening.'

Policy domain criteria (government is not meeting the requirements of this field)

'To return to the fiscal rules, so fiddled have they been, to use the word that the hon. Member for Great Grimsby used, that the IFS has said that they "are now regarded by most informed observers with scepticism at best and cynicism at worst". I challenge the Minister to name a single reputable commentator who now believes that the rules are taken seriously or, indeed, anyone who has taken them seriously for the past three years. Even the credibility of the Treasury's fiscal forecasts has been badly tarnished. For seven consecutive years, the Treasury has made over-optimistic Budget forecasts, underestimating the size of the Government's deficit and overestimating how quickly it would shrink, as the hon. Member for South Derbyshire has pointed out.'

'A balanced Budget was always round the corner. In 2003, the Budget would be back in balance by 2005. In 2004, that date was 2007; in 2006, it was 2008; in 2007, it was 2009; and in 2008, it was 2011. I predict that in 2009 the date of the balanced Budget will be moved on again from 2011. However, at least then the Government will have the defence that there is an economic slow-down. The previous years were the good years. If the rules allowed the date to be moved in the good years, there is something flawed in the rules. As Robert

Chote of the IFS has put it, given that record of forecasting, the Treasury has engaged in a "sustained display of conviction forecasting". '

Anachronistic (existing policy is outdated)

'We must do better. It is time for a new approach that is not based on subjective dating of the economic cycle. As the Treasury Committee has consistently said, we must be forward looking, with a Government who concentrate on bringing down debt rather than evading their own rules.'

Did not meet objectives (government did not do what it set out to do)

'The fiscal rules have failed and, in many respects, they sum up the Prime Minister. At first, they appeared a bit complex and rather technical, but worthy, prudent and reassuring. Then came the realisation that the complexity and technical details were there more to baffle and confuse than to assist. Finally, there came the recognition that the fiscal rules – perhaps like the Prime Minister – were not as worthy, prudent or reassuring as was once thought, and that they were in fact entirely ineffective in achieving their objective.'

(*Source*: All quotes extracted from HC Debates 7 October 2008, cols: 181–91. Parliamentary material is reproduced with the permission of the Controller of HMSO on behalf of Parliament).

Chapter 6

Strategies for Policy-Making Success: Understanding Opportunities and Risks

Public policy-makers want to be successful in achieving their goals. Rational choice theory would place motivations and preferences at the core of any understanding of policy (Mueller 2003; Hindmoor 2006). However, as Chapter 1 argued in its discussion of Machiavellian politics and political survival, one does not need to be a rational choice theorist to recognize that strategy and calculation can be an important driver of political behaviour. Additionally, it seems reasonable to suggest that policy-makers seek some form of 'success'. After all, what policy-maker would want to fail, except as an interim measure in the pursuit of a longer-term success? Yet, where public policy becomes particularly complicated is that, for policy-makers, there are often conflicting goals to pursue (process, programme and political). Either consciously or unconsciously, policy-makers must engage in a difficult balancing act, striving to achieve success in these three spheres, but often making trade-offs between them.

In the field of policy analysis, no framework presently exists that would help us map out the types of choices faced by policy-makers, as well identifying the opportunities and risks involved in pursuing particular strategies. This chapter goes some way to filling the gap. Its underlying rationale is explanatory rather than normative. It maps outs a number of strategies (such as deal-making, using evidence and engaging in deliberative practices with stakeholders) that policy-makers can use in order to strive for policy success, outlining the basic strengths and weaknesses of each. It then identifies a number of contextual factors (such as degree of issue politicization, degree of urgency and the extent to which electoral and reputational issues are at stake) that point towards contexts that make some strategies more feasible or riskier than others. It also provides a framework that allows analysts to map individual cases against the prevailing context, followed by short case studies of policy-making episodes that led to policy success (gun control in Australia) and policy failure (the poll tax in the UK).

Strategies for policy-making success

A crucial starting point is to recognize that strategic choices are not simply the product of the intent of political agents. They operate with contexts (as will be examined later in the chapter) that can be both enabling and constraining. In essence, different strategies can be more or less risky, depending on the context. A persistent theme is that short-term success 'fixes' (such as rushing through legislation or marshalling evidence to legitimate a course of action) have the capacity to rebound at a later date. It should be noted that the strategies might overlap and, indeed, go hand-in-hand, but there is enough differentiation to treat them separately for purposes of analysis.

Striking a deal

Log-rolling, horse-trading and other forms of bargaining in order to produce an agreement that (at least, to some degree) satisfies a range of interests is part of the nature of liberal democracy (Susskind 2006). The putting together of deals is studied by political scientists and economists, examining coalition-building (Riker 1962; Laver and Schofield 1998), veto players (Tsebelis 2002), game theoretic choices (Scharpf 1997) and incremental bargaining (Braybrooke and Lindblom 1970). Striking a deal is often needed for process success. In other words, if a government has a policy vision of what it wants to do (for example, to install a new piece of legislation, or a new regulation or a new directive), it often needs some kind of supportive alliance (albeit that the nature of this alliance, such as the support of the 'median voter' or 'minimum winning coalition', is debated). Striking a deal can help fulfil all the categories for process success. It can:

- help preserve government goals and policy instruments – for example, Germany's post-unification deal with the EU for free movement of labour to be suspended for seven years (see Jacoby 2005)
- confer legitimacy on the policy – for example, bills agreed by each chamber in a bi-cameral legislature
- help build a coalition of interests that is likely to sustain through the implementation and evaluation phases – for example, Sweden's post-war corporatist agreements
- at times, symbolize innovation and influence – for example, grand coalitions to tackle extraordinary national challenges.

In some countries, such as Belgium and Switzerland, obtaining a broad policy-making consensus or agreement is paramount, even to the point that it might at times override problems solving and/or use of evidence (see, for example, Sager and Risi 2009). Put crudely, process success and political success have priority over programme success. In most liberal democracies, however, 'striking a deal' is a more pragmatic exercise. It provides policy-makers with legitimation (process success) in the pursuit of successful programmes, and a flow of policy in the government's desired direction. For example, when Jacques Chirac's centre-right government attempted to push through controversial legislation in 2004 to ban the wearing of conspicuous religious symbols in French state schools, it made a last minute concession to the Socialists by agreeing to an amendment that the legislation would be reviewed after one year (see Box 3.1, p. 000). Also, in 2007, the UK government managed successfully to pass the Corporate Manslaughter and Corporate Homicide Bill after making concessions to penal reformers that the legislation would cover deaths in custody.

Despite such apparent benefits, agreements are not a guarantor of success. Agreements can prove rather fragile, with the potential to splinter and even backfire. Italy's 'Martelli' law in the early 1990s, to control immigration, came about as a result of complex and changing alliances in a five-party coalition government. The end result was a law that could scarcely be implemented amid its lack of clarity and contradictions (Adolino and Blake 2001: 134–6). Common causes of agreements to prove much more vulnerable to collapse than policy-makers anticipated are:

- changing circumstances that alter the views of players – for example, the collapse in the latter half of the 1970s of Labour's Social Contract with trades unions in the context of economic crisis and Britain's near bankruptcy
- players do not behave the way that policy-makers thought they would behave – for example, Hitler's notorious breaking of the Munich Agreement
- different interpretations on what the agreement was about – for example, Fortna (2004) in her work on peace agreements shows that deals often collapse at a later date.

It is easy to see why 'striking a deal' is a common feature of policy processes. It has the potential to allow government legitimately to achieve its broad aim of introducing policy/legislation, as well as producing workable policy and maintaining the broad trajectory of government. However, it is not a panacea. Short-term deals can generate long-term programme and political vulnerabilities that can get lost in the flurry of deal-making.

Using warm, fuzzy, ambiguous language

This strategy is often used alongside 'strike a deal'. Potentially, policy-making is a minefield for policy-makers. They might know what they want (often to achieve the endorsement of a particular policy with the minimum of fuss and resistance), but they can be faced with multiple stakeholders who not only want to be heard, but also want their views and suggestions taken on board in the final policy decision. However, the very nature of pluralistic polities is that it is virtually impossible to please everyone. For example, if government wants to withhold from local communities the names and addresses of sex offenders who live in the area, then many local residents are likely to feel aggrieved because they consider their children to be at risk from an unknown enemy. Or, if government wants to approve a new housing development on a greenfield site, doing so is unlikely to meet the approval of local environmental campaigners opposed to the erosion of public land.

In many instances, it is possible for executives, especially in parliamentary systems, simply to use their executive powers to drive through their preferred policy option. However, this use of 'executive muscle' (which will be examined shortly) has its own pitfalls. Besides, as a general rule, policy legitimacy is easier when there is broad or tentative agreement between stakeholders, rather than division. Here, therefore, we come to the essence of this strategy: political language and the symbols it evokes (Edelman 1977; Stone 2002; Poole 2007). What has been known variously as the 'argumentative turn' or 'discursive turn' has proved fruitful for public policy analysis ever since the late 1980s (Majone 1989; Fischer and Forester 1993; Fischer 2003). The particular issue of relevance to this book is the use of 'positive' language that means different things to different people, allowing different interests to coalesce, each feeling that policy decisions will incorporate at least some of their proposals. Words such as 'democracy', 'community empowerment', 'service improvement' and 'defending the national interest' can be the 'glue' that sticks different interests together. For example, the phrase 'ever closer union among the people's of Europe' was a key phrase in the preamble to the 1957 EEC treaty, which, over the years, allowed diverse national and institutional interests to coalesce, each interpreting this commitment in accordance with its own vision. Furthermore, much of the language of public services reform in the past few decades is based on phrases such as 'performance improvement', 'smarter services' and 'citizen empowerment'. Such discourse is powerful in drawing in a range of interests, from free-market sympathizers to state interventionists. After all, who really wants 'performance degeneration', 'dumber services' and 'disempowered citizens'?

Stone (2002: 157) goes further and argues that: 'a type of policy analysis that does not make room for ambiguity in politics can be of little use in the real world'. Ambiguity allows different interests, multiple motivations and expectations to coalesce, making collective action possible. The simple implication is that successful policy processes require language that disparate interests can engage with and support. However, strategic use of ambiguity in political language at the policy-making phase also has pitfalls. Two are particularly important.

First, it can mean that a quest for process success in getting a policy approved is simply storing up problems of programmatic and/or political failure. In their study of youth justice policy at the federal level in Canada, Campbell *et al.* (2001) argue that the government's use of the language of 'balance' (between those in favour of rehabilitation and those in favour of punishment) facilitated the building of populist policies and an apparent consensus among diverse interests, yet it produced legislation that was vague, ambiguous and contradictory. In essence, programme success struggled, despite broad process success. Second, galvanizing language at the policy process stage might not be matched in implementation, despite the wishes of government. For example, Smith and Kern (2009), in their study of the 2001 Fourth National Environmental Policy Plan in the Netherlands, found that the policy formation process adopted a 'transitions' storyline that was sufficient to build a coalition of actors who interpreted this story in a way that had relevance to their own agendas and networks. In programme terms, however, continuity dominated over change, largely because of the power of market forces and infrastructure institutions that drive the energy sector. This example illustrates the capacity for success at the process stage to lean towards failure in the programme implementation stage.

Overall, ambiguous language can help smooth the pathway to process success, but the short-term confluence of multiple meanings and expectations contains the seeds for conflict to arise in the programme and political spheres. Ambiguity in language can be both a blessing and a curse for policy-makers in their quest for policy success.

Using evidence

Evidence-based policy making has become commonplace for many western governments (Davies *et al.* 2000; Parsons 2002; Head 2008). Indeed, it has become something of a 'gold standard' in terms of public policy-making. The implication is that using evidence to inform policy-making is the safest way to ensure policy success. For example, David Blunkett, Labour cabinet minister in the Blair government, stated that it is: 'self-evident that decisions on Government policy ought to be informed by sound evidence' (cited in Parsons 2002: 46). Australian Prime Minister Kevin Rudd stated that: 'the Government's agenda for the public service is to ensure a robust, evidence-based policy making process. Policy design and policy evaluation should be driven by analysis of all the available options, and not by ideology' (Prime Minister of Australia 2008).

The corollary of such statements is that evidence-based policy modernizes and depoliticizes policy-making because it filters out decision-making biases and the inordinate power of special interests. This point was made by Lasswell (1956: 15) when he wrote of the 'policy sciences of democracy' and the ways in which research and evidence can improve both policy-making and democracy. Essentially, use of evidence by government seems to tick the boxes of process success. Doing so makes it more difficult for government policy making to be knocked off course by the presentation of credible, alternative evidence. Also, it adds legitimacy by virtue of its status as a form of rational decision-making. Furthermore, evidence is something 'tangible' that can aid coalition-building, as well as symbolizing rigour and advancement. The implication of process success carved from 'rationality' is that it leads also to effective programmes and political stability.

There is little doubt that an evidence-based process can be, and has been, used with the intent of achieving programmatic and political goals. Evidence-based policy interventions do not come much bigger that the Coalition invasion of Iraq. Despite subsequent failures, legitimation for the incursion was based on Saddam Hussein's possessing of 'weapons of mass destruction'. A less high profile example is the UK Home Office's 'What Works' initiative in the probation service, which legitimized reforms because of the emphasis on evidence and technicality, allowing government to move towards a centralized service. In effect, from the perspective of central government, process success contributed to programme success, which in turn spilled over into political success in steering the government down an evidence-based agenda over which it had a dominant agenda-setting role (Robinson 2001).

There is, of course, another side to the coin. As the Iraq example illustrates, use of evidence is not a guaranteed route to success. The clues come in the many critiques of evidence-based policy-making – particularly the existence of multiple evidence bases, the inescapable need for interpretation and judgement, and dominant agendas filtering in certain types of evidence and filtering out others (Davies *et al.* 2000; Parsons 2002; Bovens *et al.* 2006; Head 2008). Therefore, use of evidence in the policy-making phase can flounder, particularly because selective framing and presentation of evidence can lead to accusations of bias and serious questions being raised over the legitimacy of policy-making. For example, Hughes (2007) argues that the Australian Federal Government's evidence-based Illicit Drug Diversion Initiative was little more than a legitimating framework that allowed the government to cherry-pick the evidence that suited its 'Tough on Drugs' strategy. A further implication of the critique of evidence-based policy-making is that it does not guarantee either programme success or political success. Flyvbjerg *et al.* (2003), in their study of public sector mega projects such as the Channel Tunnel and the Øresund bridge between Denmark and Sweden, found that the viability for the projects rested in constructing and inflating 'evidence' in order to ensure the feasibility of the projects. Common implementation problems included cost overruns of

50–100 per cent, and user demand between 20–100 per cent less than was projected (Flyvbjerg *et al.* 2003: 44–5).

This latter example illustrates the more general argument that evidence-based strategies are little more than power in disguise. The power to use evidence in order to frame policy-making as 'rational' has considerable potential to ensure (particularly) short-term process success as well as longer-term programme and political success, but it carries no special weight in its ability to do so. As with all strategies for success and all exercises of power, risks of counter-reactions and mobilization are unlikely to ever disappear, and might even rapidly make their way up the political agenda.

Deliberating

Even although the idea that policy-makers should speak to and engage with ordinary citizens and stakeholders is rooted in a modern liberal tradition stretching from John Stuart Mill and his focus on the educative benefits of participation, such thinking has only come alive in recent decades. Many analysts and policy-makers have turned to deliberation as a means of tackling declining public trust, democratic deficits, legitimacy gaps, divided societies and so forth (see, for example, Schneider and Ingram 1997; Hajer and Wagenaar 2003; Gutmann and Thompson 2004; Dryzek 2006b; Fischer 2009). Definitions of deliberation abound. However, a definition that captures the spirit of much of the contemporary turn towards deliberative democracy is provided by Gastil and Levine. They suggest that:

> Advocates of deliberation presume that it is worthwhile for diverse groups of citizens – not just experts and professional politicians – to discuss public issues. Civic discussions, moreover, should have an impact on something important – usually law or public policy but sometimes mass behavior, public knowledge and attitudes, or cultural practices. Even in a representative democracy, direct, participatory democracy plays an important role in emphasising and furthering public discussion, dialogue, or deliberation and thereby addressing public problems in ways that respect diverse interests and values.
>
> (*Gastil and Levine 2005: 3*)

Put crudely, according to its proponents, deliberation produces better public policy. If we translate this into the terminology of this book, then the argument is that policy-makers who engage in deliberation might do so with a view to achieving different types of success. Process success is an important one. In theory, according to Gutmann and Thompson (2004), policies produced under conditions of deliberation are valued because they are based on reasoning and mutual respect among the various interests involved. In 2003, Perth (Western Australia) held its Dialogue with the City initiative, drawing together roughly 1,100 citizens, public servants, interest representatives and others to deliberate the future development of the city in light of projected population expansion and high economic growth. As Hartz-Karp (2005) suggests, the process of engagement was highly successful in drawing ordinary citizens into policy-making, even to the point where they defended the government's strategy in the face of criticism and scaremongering. Despite some scepticism of the benefits of the Dialogue initiative (for example, Maginn 2007), it seems reasonable to label the case as a 'durable' policy process success.

In theory, process success through deliberation can also lead to programme success. Schneider and Ingram (1997) in their influential work on policy design argue that building deliberation into policy design helps avoid failures caused by pathologies such as political manipulation, and the creation of 'deserving' and 'undeserving' target groups. Sintomer and de Maillard (2007), in their study of France's innovative twenty-year policy initiative to revitalize impoverished urban areas, argue that deliberation has helped ensure some degree of success in the meeting of two main programme goals: greater efficiency (for example, through better demand management and encouraging labour market flexibility), and a deepening of democracy (for example, through greater scrutiny of local politicians).

More generally, political success in line with that detailed in Chapters 2 and 3 might also flow from deliberation. It eases the business of governing because it prevents continual backlashes, and it helps government maintain broad policy trajectories without damage to its legitimating framework. In essence, deliberation can be 'good politics'.

Needless to say, there are counter-arguments (see, for example, Shapiro 1999; Stokes 2003; Pincione and Tesón 2006). Deliberation is not the golden key to policy success. Deliberation can actually delegitimize policy processes, because it raises expectations that cannot be met. Deliberation can also produce programme failure, because policies try to accommodate too many diverse interests. Deliberation can also rebound politically. In essence, it can create a form of gridlock, where government is barely able to change course or introduce new initiatives because it is held back by the need to accommodate diverse interests, or by disgruntled deliberators who thought they had real influence but did not. Noh and Tumin (2008) argue, in their case study of Singapore's shift towards public deliberation and engagement (manifested particularly in the issues of building a controversial casino and ministerial pay), that the conversion is 'pseudo' and that there is a danger of creating a greater divide between government and civil society. As with all recipes for policy success, deliberation has many attractions, but also many pitfalls. Process success through deliberation does not assure programme and political success.

Joining it up

An additional strategy in the quest for success is to create a sense of unity among all the actors and institutions involved in policy-making, through what is known as a joined-up government, whole-of-government, integrated or holistic government approach (6 *et al.* 2002; Ling 2002: Pollitt 2003; Bogdanor 2005). In many respects, such approaches are rooted in putting back together what the years of new public management (NPM) took apart (Christensen and Lægreid 2007: 10–11). While NPM focused on disaggregation, devolution of powers and single purpose organizations, joined-up government emphasizes unity and coordination within and across institutions. The trend is found especially (although not exclusively) in the UK, Australia and New Zealand. Pollitt (2003: 35) describes joined-up government as:

> the aspiration to achieve horizontally and vertically co-ordinated thinking and action. Through this coordination it is hoped that a number of benefits can be achieved. First, situations in which different policies undermine each other can be eliminated. Second, better use can be made of scarce resources. Third, synergies may be created through the bringing together of different key stakeholders in a particular policy field or network. Fourth, it becomes possible to offer citizens seamless rather than fragmented access to a set of related services.

Examples of joined-up initiatives are:

- London's preparation for the 2012 Olympic Games
- Denmark's transition to e-government
- Singapore's approach to coping with an ageing population
- New Zealand's strategy for tackling climate change.

It can be argued that whole-of-government initiatives have the potential to bring four particular aspects of process success. They have the capacity to:

- preserve government goals and policy instruments in instances where government sets policy goals and parameters, allowing whole-of-government discussions to flesh out the practicalities
- confer legitimacy on the policy because all relevant stakeholders have actively been involved in the policy-making phase
- build a sustainable coalition, because the process entrenches debate and dialogue, facilitating collective ownership of the agreements reached
- symbolize innovation because it creates the appearance of a modernist, integrated approach to policy problems and solutions, rather than those of a previous era, emphasizing cost efficiency and quasi-markets.

In theory, such process successes also have capacity – and, indeed, are intended – to create programme success, as well as political success in enhancing government's reputation and maintaining its strategic direction. The UK and US governments' work in the latter half of the 1990s to tackle the impending Y2k problem, was a resounding programmatic success because of a coordinated approach that had zero tolerance for systems failing to be Y2k compliant (Quigley 2008) although, ironically, many policy actors refused to give political credit on the grounds that the problem was 'much ado about nothing'.

Whole-of-government and joined-up government approaches have not escaped criticism (for example, 6 *et al.* 2002; Ling 2002; Page 2005; Davies 2009). They are accused of being old-style planning by another name, being over ambitious in assuming that they can eradicate bureaucratic silos and cultures, creating confusion over who is accountable and being a recipe for inaction. However, let us translate these problems specifically into 'success' pitfalls.

First, whole-of-government approaches to policy-making can create varying risks of programme failure. There is a danger of so many complex inputs and agreements being reached at the policy design stage that the reality of policy implementation is ambiguity over the deal that was brokered. There is also the danger that the original policy-making goals remain, but that the programmatic arrangements are diluted to the point that the goals are not realistically achievable. May *et al.* (2009), in their study of the Department of Homeland Security (DHS) – an integrated multi-agency initiative post 9/11 – demonstrate that the creation of the DHS came up against the 'conservative' forces of the various policy sub-systems such as natural disaster preparedness and techno-logical hazards. The authors conclude by recognizing:

> the evident difficulty of coordinating actions among multiple subsys-tems that have different agendas, constituencies, and political con-cerns. Though governmental reorganizations seek to achieve such coordination, our findings about the impacts of the DHS underscore the limits of structural reforms as mechanisms for altering institutional alignments within disparate subsystems.
>
> (*May et al. 2009: 190*)

If Hurricane Katrina was a test case for the new DHS, it seems that it presided over many failures (Cooper and Block 2006). In effect, a joined-up strategy rebounded on government, resulting in large departures from both programme and political goals.

Second, political success of joined-up initiatives is not assured, despite the symbolic benefits of coordinated thinking and action. One of the main criticisms of joined-up approaches is that there are no clear lines of accountability when things go wrong. Hence, there is potential for confusion over who is responsible, as well as buck-passing. The post-Katrina blame game is an exemplar, with continual buck-passing and blaming between local, city, state and federal government (Boin *et al*. 2010).

'Joining it up' is pervasive in many modern public sectors but it can be double-edged, in a similar vein to the use of ambiguity in political language. Joined-up government can bring policy success, especially because it can bring legitimation to policy-making process, coherence to programme implementation and stability in terms of governance. However, it also has the capacity temporarily to mask conflicts and generate new ones. As a recipe for success, joined-up government is bittersweet.

Using executive muscle

Using executive powers to push aside critics and make sure that broader deliberation is curtailed, or even absent, is a further way of attempting to ensure success in terms of meeting goals by means of a bill becoming law or a policy decision being taken. Use of executive muscle is, all things being equal, easier for government in majoritarian systems such as France, the UK and Greece, where power is concentrated in the hands of the executive (relative to consensus democracies such as Switzerland, the Netherlands and Germany). Such concentration is considered to provide strong, stable and effective government. Use of executive muscle fits neatly into the concept of 'mobilization of bias' (Bachrach and Baratz 1970), where elites can utilize and adapt existing procedures in order to filter out grievances and objections. For example, executive prerogative can be used to:

- speed up the entire passage of legislation, perhaps framing the issue in 'crisis' terms
- limit the time for debate, once the scrutiny process has started: in Parliamentary terms, the guillotine (formally, an allocation of time motion) is an agenda-setting device used to limit the time remaining for debate
- create a new procedure or norm (or even revive an antiquated one), in order to limit debate
- cajole or threaten potentially recalcitrant legislators.

Such tactics are often used to ensure process success; that is, government operates within constitutional rules in order to get the legislation or policy decision it wants. There are many examples of process success from government's point of view. This is the case particularly in parliamentary and majoritarian systems, based on the fusion of executive/legislature and disciplined parties, where the executive can keep most backbenchers in line by holding power over their promotion prospects and undermining any specialisms they might wish to purse at the expense of party unity (Judge 1981, 1999). However, such powers are not absolute or certain in the results they produce. There are pitfalls of using executive muscle.

First, a strong executive move might not actually work because the opposition is in a stronger position than was assumed. Hence, proposed legislation or policy does not obtain approval; that is, there is a process failure. In 2001, during the Tampa crisis when a Norwegian ship carrying 438 refugees was bound for Australian waters, Prime Minster John Howard tried to block the ship by rushing through the Border Protection Bill. However, he was unable to get the support of the Labor opposition, who described the refugee issue as a 'serious problem', as opposed to crisis or national catastrophe (see Marr and Wilkinson 2004). An amended version was, in fact, passed some four weeks later. This is an example of executive muscle drawing on the rhetoric of crisis to ensure process success (but failing), as well as a second attempt (which succeeded). More broadly, the strength of opposition to executive power might even come from within the ranks of the governing party. Cowley (2005), in his examination of how the Blair government 'mislaid its majority', is a fascinating wake-up call for any political executive who assumes that party discipline is guaranteed. Even in France, where the National Assembly has been presumed to be one of the weakest legislatures in the western world, French MPs (deputies) in recent years have been proving increasingly independent-minded (Kerrouche 2006).

Second, a strong executive push for process success can create the risk of programme failure, and even political failure. Swift passage of policies with little or no deliberation might not be the best formula for programme success. It is generally recognized that careful deliberation of policy proposals can 'improve' policies from the executive's point of view. In other words, potential implementation problems can be flagged-up and dealt with at an early stage through minor refinements in programme proposals. Such reforms might not necessarily be what critics want (they might want the entire proposal to be dropped), but they can prove invaluable for government. However, executive muscle often dominates scrutiny during the policy process. In its extreme, the results for government can be catastrophic. The 1987 legislation for Scotland that produced the hugely controversial poll tax passed easily through the Westminster parliament without a single Conservative MP or peer voting against it (McConnell 1995). Constitutionally, the process was legitimate, but a *per capita* tax where rich and poor alike paid essentially the same level of tax stored up programme and political failures that were unprecedented in modern British history (Burns 1992; Butler *et al.* 1994). This is an example *par excellence* of executive muscle being used to ensure process success from government's point of view, but leading, in the longer-term, to programme and political failure (see pp. 151–3, for a detailed study of the case).

Third, use of executive muscle might lead political elites into new territory where they stretch their executive power and legality to their limits – and perhaps beyond. The Bush administration's creation of the Guantanamo Bay Prison camp to intern terrorist suspects never managed to escape from strong criticism that its creation and operation were illegal under international law. In essence, a desire for programme success (isolating the suspected terrorists where they could do no harm) and political success (pursuing the War on Terror) was hampered though by, not least, precarious process success. Finally, cajoling and threatening potential dissenters can simply sow the seeds of political failure later on. Many political leaders have won short-term battles to enact legislation, but lost longer-term support within their party.

Overall, therefore, using executive muscle can be a tempting proposition for policy elites, be it prime ministers or chief executives, but risks involved (as will be discussed shortly) need to be carefully judged. Using executive muscle to ensure success at the process stage can store up problems in the form of ill-thought out programmes and political backfire on the reputation, agendas and trajectory of government.

Inwards transferring of ideas and practices from other jurisdictions

An additional strategy that can be adopted in an attempt to ensure successful policy-making is to import best practice or policies from other jurisdictions. Doing so has the potential to be particularly beneficial, when, as (Rose 2005: 2) argues: 'past experience is no longer adequate ... [and] policymakers must start searching for a measure that works'. Three particular forms of importation can be considered.

The first is 'policy transfer' from other countries, or even from a different region within the same country (Rose 1993, 2005: Evans 2004; Dolowitz *et al.* 1999; Dolowitz and Marsh 2000; Levi-Faur and Vigoda-Gadot 2004; Cairney 2009; Evans 2009). Many different aspects of policy can be transferred, as opposed to transfer being all-or-nothing. As Dolowitz and Marsh (2000) suggest, transfer might involve policy goals, policy content, policy instruments, policy programmes, institutions, ideologies, ideas and attitudes. Well-known examples of policy transfer include the influence of Australia's higher education reforms on student funding in the UK (Pierson 2003), the influence of US welfare-to-work programmes on the UK's 'New Deal' for young people (Dolowitz *et al.* 1999) and the growth world-wide of tobacco controls on consumption and dispersal (Studlar 2004; Cairney 2009). A particular form of policy transfer commonly found in modern public sectors is the utilizing of 'best practice' policy-making based on standards originating elsewhere. This can take the form of:

- codes of conduct identified by professional organizations – for example, in the fields of public accountancy and planning
- good practice guidelines issued by a 'higher' level of government to 'lower' levels of government – for example, conducting public consultation, building systems of e-governance
- good practice drawn from the experiences of the same policy sector but in another jurisdiction – for example, one locality employing a new water regulatory framework based on a similar scheme already having been produced in another locality.

A policy transfer strategy drawing on experiences in other jurisdictions has potential to bring process success. It can help preserve (and perhaps even inform) policy goals and instruments, and/or bring legitimacy, because it symbolizes a policy that has been 'tried and tested'. When Japan reformed its higher education system in 2004 and reconfigured public universities as quasi-independent corporations, one of the main legitimating factors was the UK's new public management style reforms and, in particular, the Next Steps agentification of the civil service and many aspects of British higher education (Goldfinch 2006). Success for government in term of policy transfer can also be programmatic. The assumption is that inward transfer will produce better, more workable programmes. The Ecotrans employment programme in the environmental sector was successfully transferred from Denmark to Germany, because it created employment opportunities for the unemployed, facilitated sustainable development goals and led to a better understanding of the needs of small and medium size enterprises (SMEs) (Ladi 2004). Political success can also accrue, because transfer can validate and provide the programmatic basis for policies broadly desired by government in terms of the direction it is pursuing. Moynihan (2005), in his study of the gradual diffusion of new public management-style Managing for Results (MFR) reforms at the state level in the US, found that:

> For elected officials the symbolic benefits of MFR are more important than the instrumental benefits. The symbolic benefits are based on the ability to communicate to a variety of audiences that government is being run in a rational, efficient, and results-oriented manner and that bureaucrats are being held accountable for their performance. As elected officials and appointees convince audiences of these claims, they are more likely to accrue benefits that are important to them: a

positive public image in the media, improved re-election chances, and a greater capacity to implement the programs that they want.

(Moynihan 2005: 227–8)

However, importing ideas and policies from other jurisdictions is not infallible. Dolowitz and Marsh (2000) identify three pathologies that can lead to failure. First, there is 'uninformed transfer', where the 'borrower' lacks sufficient or credible information. For example, Sharman (2008), in his study of anti-money laundering policies, examines the change from the mid-1980s when no country had anti-money laundering schemes (AMLs), to the position some two decades later when 170 countries had adopted very similar schemes. As Sharman demonstrates, most of the schemes have had very little effect in meeting the goals of disrupting criminal financing and its underlying sources. In essence, a policy transferred by coercion (blacklisting), supplemented by mimicry (social expectations for action) and competition (the risk of not acting), meant that more and more countries adopted very similar AMLs, without awareness of their overwhelming lack of effectiveness. As Andreas argues, this is an example of 'politically successful policy failure' (quoted in Sharman 2008: 636). To use the language deployed in Chapter 3, this is an example of 'good politics but bad policy'.

Second, there is 'incomplete transfer', where key components of the original success are not transferred. A good example is the case of the Child Support Agency (CSA) in the UK and its origins in the Child Support Enforcement System in the US (Dolowitz and Marsh 2000). One of the reasons for failure in the UK was that the transfer process left out something that was crucial to its role in the US; that is, the courts had a role as an 'escape valve' for the agency and individuals. In the UK, however, the CSA had supremacy and the courts and the Department of Social Security had no role at all.

Third, there is 'inappropriate transfer', where the original policy or practice 'works' because of the prevailing context (for example, economic, political and ideological) but there is insufficient attention paid to the context into which it is being imported. In the earlier example of successful transfer from Denmark to Germany, the same project was transferred unsuccessfully to Piraeus in Athens. The reasons for failure were contextual. Environmental issues in Greece were of low socio-economic interest, local autonomy was limited in a centralized public sector, and organizational mandates overlapped, making it difficult to ascertain responsibility (Ladi 2004).

Overall, as Rose (1993: ix) argues: 'Borrowing a program that is effective elsewhere is no guarantee of success. Understanding under what circumstances and to what extent programs effective elsewhere will work here is an essential element in lesson-drawing.'

Innovating

Innovation symbolizes modernization and progress (Considine *et al.* 2009; Fagerberg *et al.* 2009). When US President Franklin D. Roosevelt used radio addresses ('fireside chats') for the first time to communicate with ordinary voters, doing so symbolized a new form of politics, engaging ordinary people in policy debate and influence. When the Wilson government adopted the 'white heat of technology' as Britain's agenda for change in the 1960s, it symbolized a future based on dynamism and scientific rationality rather than stagnation and class interests (for example, see Sandbrook 2006). New ideas in the modern world of the twenty-first century seem to be unfolding at a rate far beyond previous generations; the Internet, global positioning systems and satellite communications to name but a few. In many policy sectors such as health and defence, and across issues such as information provision and communication, we find the development of norms that new policy ideas will harness 'blue sky' thinking and the latest technology.

It seems that new and cutting-edge initiatives have the capacity to bring process success. They can certainly confer legitimacy on policy-making; one aspect of process success. When US President John F. Kennedy spoke in 1961 of landing a man on the Moon within the decade, the promise of this breathtaking feat helped galvanize support to invest significant resources in the Apollo space programme. Innovation can also help conserve the policy goals of government, precisely because it has been able to draw on new ways of thinking and working. At least in principle, YouTube is a gift for governments who seek new ways of drawing citizens, particularly young people, into the political process (see Leadbetter 2008). Innovation can also be a point around which sustainable coalitions can be built. In the field of disaster management, the growth of new technologies, such as interoperable communications and global position systems, has helped create planning synergies between different branches of the emergency services (see Pine 2007). Once again, the assumption is that programmatic success will follow. In the latter case, the assumption is that process success translates into programme success. In the event of a disaster, rapid and accurate communications within and between organizations is a key programmatic goal of disaster management.

Political success can also be a goal of innovation. In the twentieth century, one of the key proposals put forward by Mitrany (1966), and others who supported post-war peace in Europe and throughout the world, was based on technical cooperation among former and potential adversaries. The argument was that achieving this goal would have a spillover effect and create longer-term political stability. In more recent years, many inter-country collaborations (such as the International Space Station with 11 collaborators including the US, Russia and Japan; and several scientific and industrial collaborations between North Korea and South Korea) have been built around technological projects that are either 'new' in technology terms and/or framed as 'new' in the sense that mere collaboration is innovative. Indeed, as the Korean example suggests, political success might be the prime goal of some innovations.

As with all strategies for success, there are potential pitfalls. Innovation does not necessarily bring legitimacy to a policy option at the policy-making stage. Another way of framing innovation is 'high risk' or 'the latest fad'. However, the toughest pitfalls are programmatic and political. Just because an innovatively-driven process success has produced a cutting-edge policy, this does not mean that it will actually work well in practice. For example, Gauld and Goldfinch (2006), in their study of the failure of public sector IT infrastructures in New Zealand, argue that two of the principal reasons for the pervasiveness of failure is an obsession with the latest technology ('it's state of the art so it must work') and a management eagerness to embrace the latest fads. Such failures are not always confined to the bureaucratic arena, but can manifest themselves in the political arena. New advances in science and technology, supported by government (such as genetically modified foods, mobile phones masts, human DNA cloning and police use of tasers), can prove politically difficult because government has to cope with negative publicity that recurs on the political agenda.

As with all the strategies identified, there is a double edge to innovation. Policy-makers reaching out to other jurisdictions might, at times, achieve process, programmes and political success. To coin a phrase, however, overstretching the mark can run the risk of failure.

Placing success strategies in their context: helping explain feasibilities and risks

Mapping the contexts

The analysis now needs to move beyond the simple pros and cons of different strategies. Important questions that arise include: which strategies are riskier or more feasible than others, and under what circumstances? Appendix 6.1 to this chapter deals directly with these issues. Its starting point is identifying five variables, derived from a wide variety of public policy literature, that provide the 'context' to strategy. They are:

- degree of issue politicization
- degree of urgency
- degree to which electoral/reputational issues are at stake
- strength of pressures for policy-making consensus
- strength of likely opposition to government.

Context is fundamental. A strategy that is viable and likely to succeed in one set of circumstances is at a high risk of failure in another. The variables take into account the nature of the issue itself, timing and broader political context. The framework can be used by analysts to help explain (at least, partially) policy-making strategies under uncertainty. However, before discussing the variables in detail, some important qualifying points need to be made in terms of the use and limits of the Appendix and the framework.

First, success strategies can be grouped to help capture much of the political dynamics surrounding policy-making. One group can be called 'alliance-building' factors, because their roles (in part) are aimed at a building some kind of agreement, even a temporary or uneasy one, among policy-makers, This category refers to the strategies of striking a deal; using warm, fuzzy, ambiguous language; using evidence, deliberating and using a joined-up approach. The sum of this approach fits well with those traditions within the policy sciences that focus on the policy and broader political benefits of bargaining, negotiation, deliberation, expertise and pluralism. The second group is a group of one: 'executive muscle'. This tradition sees policy-making strength in terms of decisive leadership, unafraid to use its power and authority to promote the values and policies in which it believes. The third category, and a slightly trickier one, can be called 'horizon-expanding' factors, because it refers to solutions that are innovative and/or transferred from other jurisdictions.

Second, the interaction and degrees of synergy and conflict between the variables is crucial. No framework can adequately capture the essence of political interplay, even when some factors are weighted above others. Therefore, the rule of 'all things being equal' applies when exploring each of the variables. In reality, policy issues will straddle several variables. Sometimes these might be broadly compatible in the sense of being conducive either to an alliance-building, executive muscle or to a horizon-expanding approach. For example, the issue of where to site a new nuclear reactor fits into categories of high politicization, reputational issues likely to be at stake, strong pressures for consensus and high levels of opposition to any decision. All such characteristics point towards consensus, deliberation and evidence being major features of the policy process. However, particularly interesting issues arise when an issue cuts across at least two of these categories. For example, the decision to go to war is a highly politicized issue (such issues, as will be argued, are conducive to alliance-building strategies) but it is also an urgent one (by contrast, conducive to the use of 'executive muscle').

Third, political prediction is not an exact science. As Shapiro and Bedi (2007b: 12) point out in their book on political contingency: 'The study of politics is fraught with the vicissitudes of nagging counterfactuals, un-generalizable conclusions, and unexpected events.' The implication, in terms of policy success, is that the explanatory power of Appendix 6.1 has limitations. For instance, there might be circumstances when a high-risk strategy pays off.

Equally, a low-risk strategy might backfire, particularly when we factor in pathologies of risk-taking, including overconfidence and judgement biases, (Janis and Mann 1977; Slovic *et al.* 2000). Risks are judgements about the likelihood and consequences of particular outcomes, rather than scientific predictions (Slovic 2000; Althaus 2008).

Fourth, the five variables amount essentially to issues of 'structure' in debates on the relationship between 'structure' and 'agency' in shaping political events. Hence, political contextual factors do not take into account the personalities and styles of individual leaders and decision-makers, or non-personality issues such as length of policy experience or specific policy expertise. Leadership typologies are many but one is example is:

- *crusaders* who challenge constraints, are less likely to rely on information, and have a focus on expanding their power and influence

- *strategists* who are also prepared to challenge constraints but are more open to information and seek to avoid limiting their flexibility where possible

- *pragmatists* who are respectful of constraints, but closed to information and have a preference for steering policy down their own preferred pathways where this is viable

- *opportunists* who are also respectful of constraints, open to information and driven by a need for bargaining and deal making.

(*Hermann et al. 2001*)

One implication is that leaders vary in their comfort with and capacity to take risks. Some leaders might be more adept at taking risks than others and, hence, certain success strategies are more feasible for them. The further implication is that some types of leaders will prefer to operate on a low-risk basis.

The foregoing qualifications are designed to inject a dose of realism into our ability to explain the course of strategies for success. The framework does not offer a 'magic bullet' to explain the pursuance of any particular strategy. Rather, it should be used simply to help inform analysis of policy-making strategies and the extent (or otherwise) to which they stored up problems for the future. Each of the variables can be discussed in turn

Issue politicization

Some issues are more politicized than others. Some constitute 'low politics', where debates tend to be confined to administrative arenas and small groups of experts. Examples might include motor vehicle registration, patents, drinking water regulations and food standards. Other issues are of strong political saliency, perhaps even able to divide political parties and competing interest groups. Examples include human embryo research, student funding, same-sex marriage and major constitutional reform.

The inference from the Appendix is that, all things being equal, the greater the degree of politicization surrounding a particular policy issue, the greater the risk that executive muscle and horizon-expanding solutions will backfire and lead towards process, programme and political failure. They are liable to attract considerable criticism for the use of illegitimate 'strong arm' or risky tactics, produce programmes with insufficient consideration given to implementation, and result in a political backlash further down the line. Hence, alliance-building strategies are the most feasible as the level of politicization increases. The reason is that policy-making will be considered more legitimate (whether it is informed, for example, by evidence or the product of 'joined-up' thinking), will be more likely to have resolved implementation issues, and will be less liable to rebound on programme implementation or the broad governance agenda. For example, if a fairly tolerant liberal regime such as the Netherlands or Sweden sought to introduce capital punishment, such would be the controversy generated that its only realistic hope of doing so would be after much public dialogue and use of evidence on the death penalty as an effective deterrent. Whatever the final programme and political outcomes, they are liable to be better than if the government simply rushed a bill through the legislature and whipped elected representatives into line.

Urgency

Issues are subject to various time pressures for a policy response. In some instances, time constraints are low, and so there are likely to be no significant pressures to produce policy decisions. Examples might include planning, consumer protection, legal aid and school curriculums. In other cases, there might be strong time pressures to produce a policy decision and, hence, policy-makers are under pressure to proceed rapidly. Crisis situations typify (Boin *et al.* 2005; Drennan and McConnell 2007). Examples include dealing with hostage taking, infrastructure damage, terrorist bombings and water contamination. The broader implication is that the greater the urgency to deal with a problem, the greater the risk that alliance-building strategies (such as deliberation with stakeholders or use of evidence) will delay decision-making and lead to process, programme and political failure. Conversely, the greater the urgency to deal with a problem, the likelihood of process, programme and political success is increased when strong executive power is used and new or innovative solutions are adopted. If, for example, a highly contagious and lethal virus emerged unexpectedly and was transmitted by travellers around the world, the delay through public deliberation and waiting for 'evidence' would be fatal. Conditions of urgency, especially under crisis conditions where there is a high level of threat and high uncertainty, legitimates the centralization of power ('t Hart *et al.* 1993) and renders lack of evidence not particularly problematic: the precautionary principle applies (see Drennan and McConnell 2007: 74–8).

Electoral and reputational issues

Many analysts, particularly (but not exclusively) rational choice theorists, would weight the logic of political survival ahead of any other influence (see Chapter 1). Therefore, some important issues emerge in terms of the extent to which electoral prospects or government leadership reputations are at stake. In some instances, the policy decision is likely to impinge on the views of the electorate or the reputation of leaders. For example, a popular leader with strong support in opinion polls and high levels of support within his or her party is less likely to be troubled by an issue than a 'weak' leader whose reputation and party's electoral prospects hinge on an issue. Of course, it depends on what the issue is, although even the 'strong' leader is better placed to cope with issues of high political saliency. Broadly, however, the greater the reputational and electoral issues at stake, the greater the risk that executive power and horizon-expanding solutions will backfire and lead to process, programme and political failure. Policy alliances are likely to be unsustainable, programmes are liable to be ill-thought out and government is likely to be seen as dictatorial and out-of-touch. Therefore, as electoral and reputational stakes increase, alliance-building strategies such as deal-making and use of joined-up working are more feasible, because they can help dampen criticism and create the appearance, at least, of pursuing policy in the public interest rather than a private one.

Pressures for policy-making consensus

Another important issue is the extent of pressure for government to produce widespread agreement for a policy among a range of stakeholders. In some cases, expectations are low, but often there are quite substantial expectations of reaching an agreement and to do otherwise would be to risk inaction; for example, social democratic bargaining, peace negotiations and constitutional reform. Put simply, the greater the pressures for consensus, the greater the risk that executive power and 'quick fix' solutions will backfire and lead to process, programme and political failure. Therefore, as pressures for consensus increase, the most feasible options are alliance-based ones such as deal-making, deliberation, use of ambiguous language and evidence-based strategies. For example, any sustainable resolution to a civil war is liable to come about through negotiation rather than top-down imposition by a political executive.

Strength of likely opposition to government

Opposition can come from weak or strong coalitions, or convergence of oppositional interests. Opposition can have strong potential to disrupt or even veto the entire policy-making process, whether it is an episode of farmers and agricultural reform or doctors and health care reform. The risk implication is that, the greater the strength of likely opposition to government, its policy solutions and direction, the greater the risk that executive power and 'quick fix' solutions will backfire and lead to process, programme and political failure. In other words, proposals might be defeated; concerns about the logistics of programme implementation are pushed aside, leaving programmes unworkable; and government is seen as arrogant and out-of-touch. Hence, the greater the strength of likely opposition to government, its policy solutions and direction, the likelihood of process, programme and political success is increased when consensus, deliberative or evidence-based strategies are adopted. Doing so is more likely to preserve government's basic proposals (perhaps with minor concessions), refine programme implementation and defuse criticism of government. It is little wonder, for example, that French adoption and implementation of Common Agricultural Policy reforms have been based heavily on negotiations with farmers.

An overview of feasible and risky strategies

Having mapped out different policy contexts and the types of policy-making strategies that are most prone to producing failure or most likely to lead to success, broader observations can be made about low-risk, medium-risk and high-risk strategies. It is important to stress that risk calculations by decision-makers, whether done consciously or unconsciously, involve politics, not just programmes or processes. As Althaus (2008) demonstrates – in her impressive study of political risks in Australia, the UK and the US – political risk calculation (particularly in terms of electoral implications) is part of the very essence of policy-making in western democracies. Drawing on the works of Douglas (1992) and Douglas and Wildavsky (1982), emphasizing the importance of cultural context to risk, she argues that the broader political implications are such that policy-makers put proposed policies through political filters, weighing up the risk and benefits, with a particular 'emphasis on image over substance' being significant in the calculation of political risk (Althaus 2008: 56). It is also important to remember that assessment of risk involves judgements rather than facts. In her survey of one hundred (mostly senior) policy actors in Australia, 'good nose or gut instinct' was the most common way of figuring out the risks involved (Althaus 2008: 90).

Most feasible (low-risk) strategies for policy success

As Appendix 6.1 indicates, all strategies can be feasible if the context is conducive. The many and varied strategies that exist would not have emerged over the years if they had not been of use to policy-makers. However, many policy contexts do not offer 'idealized' conditions for policy-makers, such as low political saliency, low opposition and no time constraints. Therefore, beyond these 'ideal' realms, a generalization can be made that low-risk policy-making strategies are generally those of alliance-building. Picking just a few of the success criteria to illustrate, alliance-building can help facilitate:

- *process success* – allowing government to engage in debate and negotia-tion, while preserving its original goals through the power to frame evidence in particular ways and use upbeat but ambiguous language to integrate disparate interests
- *programme success* – enabling implementation in line with objectives because many potential implementation problems have been dealt with at the deliberative and consultative stage
- *political success* – giving substantial agenda-setting power to government and authoritative interpretation of consultation procedures and outcomes can allow it to sustain its capacity to govern by mobilizing wicked issues down the political agenda.

As Appendix 6.1 also indicates, a major exception to the generally low-risk nature of a alliance-building strategy is an issue that is very urgent. In such cases – which are often instances of scandals, fiascoes, crises or disasters – the need for swift intervention by those in positions of political intervention opens a window for use of strong executive power to be deployed. To do otherwise (through a slow process alliance-building process of waiting for 'evidence', engaging in deliberation and so on) is to run the risk of producing programmatic and political delays, leading to an ineffective response and impressions of excessive caution and lack of decisiveness.

Mixed feasibility (medium-risk) strategies for policy success

All strategies have, depending on context, the capacity to tread a fine line between being potentially feasible but potentially risky. They are neither com-fortable options nor foolish ones. Use of strong executive power falls into this category when the issue has one or more of the characteristics of being reasonably politicized, with moderate electoral/reputational issues at stake, some pressures for policy consensus and the likelihood of moderate opposition. Details are provided in Appendix 6.1. They indicate that executive power can be enough to galvanize supporters, fend off critics and cut a pathway through difficult issues. The outcome can be process, programme and political success. Government can get its way through constitutionally legitimate policy-making, feasible programmes, and maintaining political stability and direction. However, outcomes can equally turn in the opposite direction. Using executive power in such circumstances to push through preferred policies can lead to unworkable programmes and a reputation for being an out-of-touch, uncaring government.

Horizon-expanding solutions (innovative policy solutions and inwards transfer from other jurisdictions) can also, depending on context, be finely balanced in their ability to produce success or failure. In contexts of high politicization, extreme urgency, reputations being on the line, strong pressures for consensus and high levels of opposition to government, novel solutions might be enough for policy-makers to preserve their goals, produce practical programmes and wrong-foot opponents, while helping garner support. However, the outcomes could tip the other way. Novel solutions can lead to serious criticisms of a policy's legitimacy, framing the solution as 'too risky' or 'suitable for somewhere else but not suitable for here'. It might also produce solutions that struggle to be implemented because policy-makers were too enamoured with the ideas at the expense of considering the practical realities of implementation. In political terms, it can also damage election prospects and leadership reputation because it is seen as another sign of too much force and too little listening.

Alliance-building strategies rarely constitute medium-level risks. They only time they do so is when there are quite sharp, but not critical, time constraints. Building alliances through means such as joined-up working and deal-making is certainly feasible, if time constraints allow, and doing so can help add legitimacy to policy decisions. However, time constraints can get the better of alliance-building, leading to decisions that store up problems further down the line in terms of programme feasibility and governance strategies.

Low feasibility (high-risk) strategies for policy success

Strong use of executive powers is generally the most likely to result in policy failure, unless the issue is very urgent and can be located at the low end of the scales of politicization, reputational/electoral stakes, pressures for consensus and level of likely conflict. Taking a few success criteria as illustrative, we find that an executive muscle strategy generally poses high risk in terms of:

- *process failure* – stirring-up opponents and even drawing in dissidents from within government's own ranks, leading to failure to produce a sufficient coalition of support and leading, in turn, to a derailing of the policy process

- *programme failure* – leading to unsuccessful implementation, because strong and enforceable rules/regulations/law have not received sufficient prior scrutiny to 'solve' logistical problems
- *political failure* – destabilizing government's capacity to govern by creating a programme with so many implementation problems that it keeps rebounding on the government's agenda, often at the expense of other issues.

Two short cases can now be used to examine how this framework can be used in practice to help explain two very different policy-making episodes. The first is an example of policy-makers 'getting it right' and the second is an example of 'getting it wrong'.

Case Study 1

Gun control reform in Australia after the 1996 Port Arthur massacre: mapping policy-making contexts to explain a case of policy-makers 'getting it right'

On 28 April 1996, Martin Bryant went on a shooting spree in the Port Arthur historical site in Tasmania (see Norberry *et al.* 1996; Mouzos 1999; Prasser 2006b; Chapman *et al.* 2009). He killed 35 people, ranging from the ages of 3 to 72 years. The case shocked Australia. Within a three-week period, gun laws were reformed, driven by the Commonwealth government under Prime Minister John Howard. The centrepiece was the prohibition of certain types of firearms, particularly semi-automatic rifles/shotguns and pump action shotguns, supplemented by a 'buy back scheme' of roughly 600,000 weapons. In broad terms, the reforms constitute process, programme and political success. The process was successful because the government did what it set out to do, and with overwhelming support. The controls themselves have endured with no more mass shootings since (in contrast to 13 in the 18 previous years) and Howard is long-remembered as a 'hero' in taking swift action at a time of national tragedy.

Table 6.1   *Port Arthur: mapping the policy-making context*

Contextual issue	Strength of context	Lowest-risk strategy	Medium-risk category	High-risk strategy
Degree of issue politicization	High	Alliance-building	Horizon-expanding	Executive muscle
Degree of urgency	High	Executive muscle	Horizon-expanding	Alliance-building
Degree to which electoral and reputational issues at stake	Medium	Alliance-building; Horizon-expanding	Executive muscle	None
Strength of pressure for policy-making consensus	Low	Any	None	None
Strength of likely opposition to government	Low	Any	None	None

Table 6.1 rates the policy context of this case against the criteria in Appendix 6.1. Justification for each rating is as follows.

Degree of issue politicization: The issue was highly politicized. Gun control issues in Australia were not routinely an issue of high politics, but there had been some previous community concerns after several smaller-scale shootings. A National Committee on Violence had been set up in 1987, but little reform was produced and many recommendations were never implemented. Controls were left to the six states and two territories, and there was no national uniformity or nationwide legislation. The Port Arthur shooting was a focusing event to bring a long-standing issue to the top of the Commonwealth agenda. The issue immediately became highly politicized, with Australian citizens looking to their national government to deal with this controversial issue.

Degree of urgency: Crises and disasters typically produce pressures on key political decision-makers to ensure that a similar incident does not happen again. This case was no exception. The Prime Minister was under pressure to act swiftly and calm public fears.

Degree to which electoral and reputational issues are at stake: The government was a relatively new one (only six weeks into office), and so it was in something of a 'honeymoon period'. Had this not been the case, the reputation of the new Prime Minister might have been on the line. However, it seems reasonable to describe the potential impact on John Howard's reputation as moderate. He had enough political sympathy to quell severe leadership concerns; he had been landed with a difficult issue that was obviously not his fault, although he still needed to prove that he was capable of dealing with a national emergency.

Strength of pressure for policy-making consensus: The pressures were low. Public concerns were focused on finding a quick solution, rather than spending time getting agreement from the pro- and anti-gun control lobbies.

Strength of likely opposition to government: The level of opposition was likely to be low. Polls immediately afterwards showed about 80 per cent public support for tightening gun controls. If not for the tragedy, opposition to gun control might have been stronger. There was (and still is) a fairly small but strong pro-gun lobby in Australia. Also, the coalition government included the National Party – traditionally a rural and farming-based party, supportive of limited gun controls. Furthermore, two states (Tasmania and Queensland) were against tighter controls. However, the impetus of the crisis and collective grief was enough to destabilize the power of the pro-gun lobby.

In sum, the context of Port Arthur seems initially to present a mixed picture. The high level of urgency points towards strong executive powers as the most feasible option, but the intense level of politicization points towards an alliance-building strategy. The moderate pressure on the reputation of the Prime Minister and his new coalition government suggests alliance-building and horizon-expanding strategies as being the most feasible. However, now that we know something of the details of the case, a credible explanation can be constructed.

The critical issue here is the nature of the tragedy. It was the result of deliberate attack from a non-politically motivated source, rather than the product of government failings or an attack on its policies. Typically, under such circumstances, there is a 'rallying around' government effect, because it is doing its best under difficult circumstances. Therefore, the strong sense of urgency to 'do something about gun control' was enough to quell much the adversarial debate that would typically take place around the issue. The dampening of controversy makes feasible an executive-driven strategy, supplemented at the margins by fairly swift alliance-building. This is precisely what happened. After some initial prevarication, particularly on the part of the state of Tasmania (dealt with by the Commonwealth's threat of financial penalties), all levels of government supported tighter gun controls at a meeting of the Australasian Policy Ministers' Council on 10 May 1996. Of course, successful pursuit of a 'logical' strategy does not guarantee success but, in this episode, it is not difficult to see why it did.

Case Study 2

The poll tax in Britain: mapping policy-making contexts to explain a case of policy-makers 'getting it wrong'

Local taxation has always been a controversial issue in Britain (see Butler *et al.* 1994; McConnell 1995, 1999). Until the mid-1980s, the main system that had existed for almost 400 years, was a property-based system known as 'the rates'. A modern version had existed since 1929. Properties were intended to be valued and re-valued every five years (although, in practice, the time spans were longer), with each local authority applying a rate poundage in order to determine how much each individual householder paid. Roughly 17 per cent paid partial rates or were exempt, because of low incomes; and roughly 49 per cent paid no rates at all, because they were non-householders. Essentially, the system was a tax on the property-owning middle classes. Despite several inquiries throughout the years, all struggling with issues of equity and practicality, alternative systems (such as a local income tax, local sales tax and poll tax) were considered to be even less feasible. Reforms always amounted to marginal refinements, rather than replacement with a new system.

The situation changed in 1985. In response to a property revaluation in Scotland, which particularly hit the Conservative middle classes, the Thatcher government made a commitment to abolish the rating system. A carefully managed search for an alternative led to the only option that fitted with the parameters set by government: a poll tax. After a consultation exercise with only one option (the poll tax, formally called the 'community charge'), separate legislation was processed for Scotland, (where it was introduced in 1989) and England (where it was introduced in 1990). The poll tax was essentially a *per capita* tax, based on the assumption that everyone used local services and, therefore, everyone should pay the same. There were some rebates for those on low incomes but everyone, even the unemployed, was required to pay a minimum of 20 per cent. The political essence of the tax was a move from a tax based on ability to pay, to a tax based on usage of services. Put crudely, it shifted the tax burden from the middle classes towards the working classes.

The poll tax was the most controversial policy in modern British history. It was widely proclaimed as a policy disaster. Despite many warnings during the policy-making stages that it would be unworkable, it proved in programmatic terms to be just. Millions of non-payers, high levels of non-collection and huge administration burdens meant that the tax was not viable as a source of local government revenue. Politically it also proved unviable – prompting demonstrations, riots and civil disobedience. The Conservative Party slumped in opinion polls and the tax was a key factor in the resignation of the Prime Minister Margaret Thatcher in 1990. Within a matter of months, a commitment had been made by her successor, John Major, to a new Council Tax. It is a property-based tax and essentially a modified version of the old rating system.

Table 6.2 maps the policy context of this case against the criteria in Appendix 6.1. Justification for each rating is as follows.

Degree of issue politicization: Local taxation had always been an issue of high political saliency. The annual setting of rate poundage levels, plus periodic revaluations, generated considerable controversy over what constituted a 'fair' system. The Labour party had always been more sympathetic to the rating system than the Conservatives, who had tried (and failed) to find a workable replacement – most recently in a Green Paper (1981) and a White Paper (1983).

Degree of urgency: In temporal terms, the issue can be graded as 'medium'. A backlash against the Conservatives from their own natural base of support, as a consequence of the April 1984 property revaluation in Scotland, placed pressure on the Prime Minister and the Scottish Secretary to find an alternative system. A review in Whitehall was already under way (one of many down the years) and, with the Scottish Conservative conference scheduled in May, there was pressure on the Conservatives to offer some hope to the party and its supporters.

Degree to which electoral and reputational issues at stake: Again, this issue can be rated as medium. In UK terms, the problem was localized in Scotland (there was no revaluation in England). It could certainly have spilled over to the UK level in damaging the government's ability to preside over the Union of Scotland, Wales and Northern Ireland, but the issue barely received a mention in UK newspapers such as the *Times*, the *Daily Telegraph* and the *Guardian*.

Strength of pressures for policy-making consensus: Such is the contestability of local tax issues that pressures for a widely-supported solution are high. This was one reason why the 1983 White Paper concluded that the rating system was here to stay for the foreseeable future; that is, there was no agreed alternative.

Strength of likely opposition to government: Opposition was likely to be very high. The Chancellor Nigel Lawson had predicted that the tax would be unworkable, and a wider range of professional and political bodies had predicted substantial opposition.

Table 6.2   *Local taxation and the rating system in the UK (1985): mapping the policy-making context*

Contextual issue	Strength of context	Lowest-risk strategy	Medium-risk category	High-risk strategy
Degree of issue politicization	High	Alliance-building	Horizon-expanding	Executive muscle
Degree of urgency	Medium	Executive Muscle	Horizon-expanding	Alliance-building
Degree to which electoral and reputational issues at stake	Medium	Alliance-building	Executive muscle	None
Strength of pressure for policy-making consensus	High	Alliance-building	Horizon-expanding	Executive muscle
Strength of likely opposition to government	High	Alliance-building	Horizon-expanding	Executive muscle

In sum, when mapped against the five contextual factors, all but one point to the most feasible strategy as being an alliance-building one. Those familiar with the history of local taxation in Britain will be unsurprised at this suggestion. Programmatic and political feasibility had been a constant barrier to reform. The only factor pointing towards a strong executive strategy is the medium level of urgency. However, even if it was rated 'high', the matter of urgency was very different from the Port Arthur case. The local tax 'problem' was essentially a party political one – of more interest to the Conservative party and its supporters (especially in Scotland) than to the rest of Britain. Contextual 'logic' points towards an executive-driven proposal for a poll tax as being exceptionally high-risk. Contextually, there is little or nothing in its favour.

Why, under such circumstances, would the government pursue such proposals? The proposals fitted with the government's logic of continually reforming (some would argue, undermining) local government in order to make it more accountable. This strategy, in turn, fitted with the broader thrust of 'Thatcherism', and its attempts to reduce the role of the public sector and make it more efficient and accountable. Mrs Thatcher herself argued that people would grow to accept the tax and see it as fair.

In this light, it is plausible to argue that the Thatcher government sought to achieve 'political' success through a flagship policy/programme that epitomized its broader neo-liberal governance strategy, and that an executive-driven policy process was the way to do so. However, the outcome exemplifies high-risk executive-driven policy, sweeping aside criticism and concerns in its aspirations for process, programme and political success, but generating programmatic and political vulnerabilities further down the line.

Conclusion

One final but important dose of realism is needed to conclude this chapter. As illustrated by the two case studies (gun control in Australia and the poll tax in the UK), policies do not always fit neatly into particular contexts, allowing us to say with certainty that any particular strategy is high-risk, medium-risk or low-risk. Notwithstanding points made earlier, governments often adopt multiple strategies. So for example, the potential pitfalls of executive power can be diluted through use of ambiguous language or consultation exercises in order to build some form of policy-making alliance. Nevertheless, I consider the framework presented in this chapter to be an important step in helping us think about policy-making strategies and the contextual factors that can work for and against them. Any answers we have do not have the precision of 'hard science', but they can at least be informed judgements. This is a step beyond where we are at the moment in terms of understanding strategies for policy-making success, and quite consistent with the 'art' of policy analysis (Wildavsky 1987).

Appendix 6.1

Differing contexts and the feasibility of strategies for policy-making success

Degree of politicization		*Most feasible* (low-risk)	*Some feasibility, but caution needed* (medium-risk)	*Least feasible* (high-risk)
	Low	• EXECUTIVE MUSCLE • ALLIANCE-BUILDING • HORIZON-EXPANDING When an issue is of low political saliency, many different success strategies are quite feasible and none carry risks of any significance.	None	None
	Medium	• ALLIANCE-BUILDING • HORIZON-EXPANDING When an issue becomes more politicized, there is a greater need for government to use an alliance-building and/or horizon-expanding strategy. Both can help preserve government's goals as much as possible, enhance policy-making legitimacy and build a sustainable coalition.	• EXECUTIVE MUSCLE There is moderate risk that policy-making proposals pushed forcefully by government thwart aspirations for success in the realms of: **Programmes:** A danger of putting in place a programme that confronts implementation problems because there is little consideration of multiple stakeholder views or possible alternative solutions; **Politics:** Government is considered heavy-handed and too keen to foist its own solution.	None
	High	• ALLIANCE-BUILDING For intensely political issues, there is a pressing need for an alliance-building strategy to help preserve government's goals as much as possible, in order to help diminish political tensions and cultivate an impression of	• HORIZON-EXPANDING There is a moderate risk that bringing in horizon-expanding solutions creates problems with regard to: **Programmes:** Adoption of a programme that has been untried in the local context;	• EXECUTIVE MUSCLE The danger of using strong executive power to push through proposals on intensely political issues is the high risk of compromising success in terms of: **Process:** A widespread view that

Degree of urgency	Feasible strategies			
Low	• EXECUTIVE MUSCLE • ALLIANCE-BUILDING • HORIZON-EXPANDING When time is plentiful, many different strategies are feasible for policy success, carrying minimal intrinsic risks.	non-partisanship. Politics: Concerns over government's capacity to govern because it is resorting to ideas and policies from elsewhere, or adopting new, 'faddish' solutions.	policy lacks legitimacy because it has been pushed through with little dialogue; Programmes: Creating programmes that are not workable because implementation issues have not been properly resolved through prior dialogue; Politics: Creating the impression of an arrogant government.	None
Medium	• EXECUTIVE MUSCLE • HORIZON-EXPANDING When there is a reasonably urgent but not critical time period needed for a decision, the most feasible strategies involve a reasonably strong push from the executive. Horizon-expanding solutions are also often feasible. There is enough time to research their likely impact as novel solutions to a fairly pressing problem.	• ALLIANCE-BUILDING There is some risk particularly to two forms of success: Programmes: Government has spent too long in dialogue and building an alliance, so that the policy solution has been overtaken by the speed at which the issue is developing; Politics: Government is considered weak because it is taking too long to find a solution to an urgent issue.	None	None
High	• EXECUTIVE MUSCLE Issues where time is of the essence require swift executive action to cut through debate and the range of possible policy solutions.	• HORIZON-EXPANDING Such solutions might be feasible amid the rush to find a solution to a highly pressing problem, but they pose moderate risks in terms of: Programmes: The measures have not	• ALLIANCE-BUILDING Urgent issues are not the time for the slower process of building alliances. There is the danger of success being compromised in all realms. Process: Takes too long waiting for	

Degree to which electoral and reputational issues at stake	Appropriate strategies	Risks	
Low	• EXECUTIVE MUSCLE • HORIZON-EXPANDING • ALLIANCE-BUILDING When an issue has little or no implication for government's reputation and electoral prospects, many different success strategies are quite feasible and none carry risks of any significance.	None	None
Medium	• ALLIANCE-BUILDING • HORIZON-EXPANDING When an issue has fairly strong but not critical potential to enhance or diminish government's reputation/electoral prospects, there is a greater need to use an alliance-building and/or horizon-expanding strategy. Both can help avoid alienating stakeholders and government's natural supporters.	• EXECUTIVE MUSCLE There is a moderate risk that using executive powers to push through a proposal is a barrier to success in the realms of: Programmes: A danger of putting in place a programme that might confront implementation problems because political priorities have dominated over consideration of multiple stakeholder views or possible alternative solutions; Politics: Government is considered to be putting its own political interests above the public interest.	None
High	• ALLIANCE-BUILDING For an issue where government's reputation and electoral prospects hinges on this critical issue, there is a	• HORIZON-EXPANDING There is a moderate risk that bringing in horizon-expanding solutions creates problems with regard to: been well-thought through, and hence expectations of them might be unrealistic; Politics: Government is considered reckless in proposing an untried and untested solution.	• EXECUTIVE MUSCLE The main risks of the executive pushing through a proposal when its reputation and electoral prospects are 'evidence'; Programmes: The policy solution is too late to produce realistic goals; Politics: Delay damages reputation. Government is seen as not treating the issue with the level of urgency that is needed.

Strength of pressures for policy-making consensus			
(continued)	pressing need for an alliance-building strategy to emphasize the public interest, dampen criticism and galvanize supporters.	**Programmes:** Danger of an 'imported' quick fix' solution, with goals that will be difficult to achieve; **Politics:** Concerns over government's capacity to govern. It is considered out-of-touch and willing to bring in solutions that might be suitable elsewhere, but not necessarily for the present context.	on the line, are: **Process:** It has not built up an alliance capable of sustaining the policy; **Programme:** The programme is at high risk of failure because its feasibility has been given little consideration, overwhelmed by the broader politics of the issue; **Politics:** Government is seen as dictatorial and out-of-touch.
Low	• EXECUTIVE MUSCLE • ALLIANCE-BUILDING • HORIZON-EXPANDING When there are no significant pressures for government to reach a consensus, many different success strategies are quite feasible and none carry risks of any significance. Government can even opt for an alliance-building approach without any significant risks. Just because there are no process pressures for consensus does not mean that there are no benefits in terms of producing workable programmes or cultivating good government image.	None	None
Medium	• ALLIANCE-BUILDING • HORIZON-EXPANDING When there are fairly substantial pressures for consensus, there is a greater need for government to use an alliance-building and/or horizon-expanding strategy. Both can help build support/agreement and deflect criticism.	• EXECUTIVE MUSCLE There is a moderate risk that a strong executive pushing through policy proposals will damage success aspirations in terms of: **Programmes:** A danger that consensus pressures are given little attention at the policy-making stage might cause implementation problems because	None

Strength of Likely Opposition to Government				
	High	• ALLIANCE-BUILDING For an issue where there are very strong pressures for consensus among relevant stakeholders, there is strong need for an alliance-building strategy to demonstrate, if not achieve, it.	stakeholders involved in implementation have not had their concerns heard and/or might try to circumvent implementation rule; **Politics:** Government is criticized for 'not being willing to listen'. • HORIZON-EXPANDING There is a moderate risk that bringing in horizon-expanding solutions will be a barrier to achieving success in the realms of: **Process:** Solutions might be too new or novel to generate a strong and sustainable consensus; **Programmes:** Danger that the pressure for consensus was for good reasons, and that listening to concerns would have helped deal with potential implementation problems; **Politics:** Government is criticized for being too radical in its solutions and not prepared to listen to opinions that offer more mainstream solutions to the problem.	• EXECUTIVE MUSCLE The main risks of the government pushing through its proposal in the face of very strong calls for consensus, are: **Process:** It has not built-up a coalition capable of sustaining the policy; **Programmes:** The programme is at high risk of failure because potential implementation difficulties and concerns have been pushed aside; **Politics:** Government accused of partisanship and unwillingness to listen at a time when unity is needed.
	Low	• EXECUTIVE MUSCLE • ALLIANCE-BUILDING • HORIZON-EXPANDING When there is likely to be little or no opposition, government has a broad range of success strategies available, all being quite feasible and without any significant risks.	None	None
	Medium	• ALLIANCE-BUILDING • HORIZON-EXPANDING When likely opposition to government	• EXECUTIVE MUSCLE There is a moderate risk that a strong executive-driven strategy will be a	

159

	is considered to be reasonably strong, the most feasible approach is for government to use an alliance-building and/or horizon-expanding strategy. Both can help build support/agreement and deflect potential critics.	barrier to success aspirations in terms of: **Programmes**: A danger of 'quick fix' solutions, with goals that will be difficult to achieve; **Politics**: Government is criticized for refusing to pay heed to genuine concerns.	
High	• ALLIANCE-BUILDING For an issue where there is likely to be high levels of opposition to government, the lowest-risk and most feasible strategy is an alliance-building one. It can help give the impression that government is prepared to listen to potential critics, and perhaps even take on board some of their views, while still maintaining the main thrust of what it seeks to do.	• HORIZON-EXPANDING There is a moderate risk that bringing in horizon-expanding solutions creates problems with regard to: **Programmes**: Danger of adopting a programme that has been unfamiliar and untried in the local context; **Politics**: Government might prove divisive in adopting unfamiliar measures. Some support might accrue but further opposition may emerge.	• EXECUTIVE MUSCLE The main risks of the government pushing through a proposal in the face of high levels of opposition are: **Process**: Proposals might be defeated; **Programme**: The programme is at high risk of failure because its feasibility has been given little consideration, overwhelmed by government's desire to push through its solution to the problem; **Politics**: Government is seen as arrogant and out of touch with significant societal opinion.

Chapter 7

Strategies for Evaluating Success: Understanding Pay-Offs and Pitfalls

The logic of societies based on plural politics is that policy programmes are examined to assess if they are 'working'. If they are, then government seems to have been successful in achieving its goals. If not, programmes are refined through a process of adjustment and learning. This is the classic logic of the policy-cycle, fitting with the aspirations of Lasswell (1956) and others in the early post-war and cold war periods, as well as (even today) the public face of public policies. Policy-makers speak regularly of processes of examination and reflection, based on the language of rationality, accountability and democracy.

This traditional or quasi-constitutional approach is manifested in an approach to policy evaluation that Bovens *et al.* (2006) describe as 'rationalistic evaluation'. It is based on the assumption that the role of evaluation is gathering 'the facts' in as comprehensive and unbiased manner as is reasonably possible. Adherents to such an approach tend to focus on evaluation tools and techniques – such as cost-benefit analysis, user surveys and the benefits of various statistical packages – in order to analyze performance data (Gupta 2001; Davidson 2005; Weimer and Vining 2005; Miller and Robbins 2007). Most of this literature sees 'politics' are residing in the policy making arenas of legislatures and executives, and not a matter to consider for the analyst or evaluator, who needs to adhere to 'apolitical' professional standards such as analytical integrity and responsibility (Weimer and Vining 2005).

This chapter takes a very different approach to policy evaluation. It begins from the simple point that evaluations do not just 'happen'. They have to be instigated or commissioned at some point. Hence, evaluating policies to ascertain their success, or otherwise, is a political act (Taylor and Balloch 2005b). It is political because there are multiple and often conflicting evaluation formats, tools, methods and approaches in existence – each liable to produce different (sometimes staggeringly different) results. Choosing one particular configuration of these over others requires a political judgement, by virtually any definition of politics.

Such judgements are crucial, investing considerable power with policy-makers and other strategic elites who have the authority to take authoritative decisions to set the evaluation process in motion. A series of sub-decisions typically follows, most residing in the constitutional/legal/political authority to do so. These pertain to the type of evaluation, its scope, who will undertake the evaluation, timescale and funding, tools and techniques to be used, whether to intervene in the course of the evaluation, how to disseminate the report, and how to interpret and respond to the report. Such decisions set the agenda for how others within the political system will conduct the evaluation. As will be discussed, policy-makers are not all-powerful in doing so, but these strategic choices permeate evaluations of how 'successful' or otherwise policies have been. Indeed, I would argue that they politicize and substantially mould the evaluations, rendering the supposedly apolitical evaluator playing a significant role in direct contrast to that anticipated by much of the rationalist-type evaluation literature.

In this context, and in a similar vein to Chapter 6, this chapter maps out a range of strategies that decision-makers use, consciously or consciously, in taking key decisions over the nature and parameters of policy evaluations to ascertain success, or otherwise. Its focus is principally on ex post evaluation (conducted during or after implementation and focusing on results) as opposed to ex ante evaluation (conducted at the policy-making stage and focusing on anticipated outcomes), although the boundaries between them are often blurred because the former can inform future policies. The aim of the chapter is to help understand evaluation processes, rather than recommending any particular strategic approach.

At the heart of the analysis is a framework based on policy-makers keeping a 'tight grip' on evaluations, a 'loose grip' or an intermediate 'relaxed grip' position. This chapter concentrates on, and examines the pros and cons of, the tight- and loose-grip approaches from a policy-makers' point of view, before examining in detail a number of contextual factors (such as issue politicization and degree of urgency) that make some strategies more viable than others. It should be noted that the chapter concentrates simply on the tight- and loose-grip strategies. The basic elements of a relaxed-grip approach are outlined in Table 7.2. Concentrating on divergent approaches is partly for reasons of space. However, as will be argued later, the relaxed grip is a diluted version of both the tight- and loose-grip strategies, exhibiting many of the strategic advantages and disadvantages of both. It is not necessary to repeat them for the benefit of completeness. The chapter concludes by suggesting which strategies will tend to be more feasible (and less risky) for policy-makers, as well as those that carry higher risks. A case study application of the framework is provided through an examination of the 2002–06 Review of Public Administration in Northern Ireland.

One of the key arguments of the chapter is that policy evaluation strategies are linked inexorably with three main types of policy success: processes, programmatic and political (see Chapters 2 and 3). An evaluation might investigate and legitimate success in one or more of these spheres, but not in others. Some evaluations, for instance, are geared heavily towards producing political success (for example, proving that a policy is the 'right' one and that the direction of government is a legitimate one), but at the expense of programmatic success (for example, a wide-ranging review to determine whether or not a programme really did achieve what it set out to achieve).

What do policy-makers want to achieve from evaluations?

Understanding and explaining the desires of policy-makers is a journey without end. Philosophically, it would take us to the heart of different and highly contested ontological, epistemological and methodological issues (see Hay 2002; Marsh and Stoker 2002). For example, a behaviouralist approach would be likely to study, without preconception, as many cases as possible – preferably asking policy-makers what they wanted to achieve and then coding the results to observe trends. By contrast, a rational choice approach would assume that every policy-maker is driven by self-interest, and then seek to examine how this utility maximization manifested itself in different cases. The approach taken in this chapter is heuristic, rather than definitive. In other words, the purpose is to provide a framework to help our understanding (whatever our underlying approach to political analysis) of what policy-makers want to achieve from evaluations, rather than to say that they are always driven by X or Y.

Chapters 2 and 3 dissected policy successes and failures into multiple dimensions: process, programme and politics. A simplified adaption, as shown in Table 7.1, reveals a range of desired evaluation outcomes on the part of policy-makers. Three particularly interesting issues can be drawn out from the table.

First, policy-makers will generally want confirmation that their policies, more or less, are working. It would be unthinkable, for example, for a health authority chief executive to wish for a damning evaluation of a series of reforms that he or she had initiated based on conviction that the reforms were in the interests of local health provision. However, it should not be assumed that policy-makers will always seek programme success as the outcome of an evaluation. Policy-makers might actually seek a critical evaluation in order to give legitimacy to the reform or jettisoning of a troublesome policy. Many a university department has been closed after a review provided confirmation that the department was 'failing'.

Second, even policy-makers who desire an evaluation to be stamped 'success' will often be happy with – and, indeed, might want – some minor shortfalls to be highlighted. Not only might learning be a reason for doing so, but there are issues of legitimacy at stake. All things being equal, an evaluation that, in effect, produces a report of durable success with shortcomings in plain view is more legitimate than an appraisal that gives a programme a 100 per cent clean bill of health. Such an evaluation will help avoid accusations of a 'fix' or whitewash. Therefore, aspirations for programme success often require a helping hand from a successful and legitimate evaluation process.

Table 7.1   *Range of outcomes that policy-makers might want from policy evaluations*

	Success	*Durable success*	*Conflicted success*	*Precarious success*	*Failure*
Process	Wants to ensure that the evaluation process is seen as legitimate and robust. Prepared for and can tolerate some criticism that the evaluation process is biased towards achieving particular outcomes.		Does not particularly want, but is prepared to accept, tough and substantial criticism that the evaluation process is illegitimate; e.g., biased, politicized. Hopeful or confident that this is a price worth paying in order to obtain the desired outcomes in the programme and political spheres.	Does not want evaluation process to be seen as illegitimate but pragmatically is prepared to tolerate intense criticism if the evaluation validates programme and/or produces political success.	
Programme	Wants to ensure that the programme is evaluated as broadly resilient and successful. Minor shortcomings and failures are acceptable, and even beneficial, because the evaluation is less likely to be criticised as a 'fix' (a process failure).		Wants a searching and realistic evaluation. Prepared to accept that major reforms are necessary, if the programme is to be viable.	Wants to ensure that the programme is evaluated as broadly unsuccessful in order to reform or terminate a troublesome policy, but that there are enough clues in the evaluation in terms of the direction that reform or policy replacement should take.	
Politics	Wants the evaluation to enhance electoral prospects/reputation, keep the issue down or off the agenda and/or help sustain the broad direction of government policy. Mostly, this will involve an evaluation that validates programmatic success, but it might involve an evaluation of programmatic failure, if government is helped by using the evaluation to reform or terminate a very troublesome policy.		Does not particularly want, but is prepared to accept, tough political fallout from the evaluation. Hopeful or confident that the political damage is not fatal.	Does not want the evaluation to damage electoral prospects/reputation, push an issue to the top of the agenda or agenda, and/or help knock off course the broad direction of government policy. However, is prepared to tolerate such unsuccessful political outcomes, if it achieves its programme evaluation goals. This is likely to be either that a programme is evaluated as a failure, or evaluated as broadly resilient and successful.	

Third, criticisms that an evaluation is illegitimate because it is a quick fix, biased or an exercise in proving the success of a programme (these are accusations of process failure) will often be tolerated or coped with by policy-makers, because of the imperative to seek programme and/or political success. Therefore, allegations of 'biased' policy evaluations are not as damaging to policy-makers as the damage caused by an authoritative trashing of cherished programmes, and the political fallout that could ensue. Evaluations amounting to conflicted or even precarious process success can be tolerated by policy-makers if, in programmatic terms, the programmatic appraisal tilts much more towards their desired evaluation outcomes.

These issues and more will be dealt with through an examination of strategic tools to shape evaluations, as well as the contexts in which some strategies are riskier than others. Different approaches can be taken to each: tight-grip, loose-grip and relaxed-grip.

A tight-grip policy evaluation strategy

As the terminology implies, and as Table 7.2 indicates, a tight-grip strategy seeks to steer evaluations heavily towards producing particular outcomes. Kitts (2006), in his detailed study of US presidential national security commissions (Pearl Harbor, CIA, MX Missile, Iran-Contra, 9/11), provides a flavour of this strategic approach:

> an overarching political imperative is at work behind the scenes. Presidents have a preferred outcome and are willing to use the blue-ribbon option to help achieve that end ... The political pressure on commissions comes in different forms. In the five cases examined, political activity ran the gamut from careful screening of members to censored reports, from curiously defined mandates to secretive phone calls. From a president's perspective, it is a clear that a little planning goes a long way.
>
> (*Kitts 2006: 170*)

To use the terminology of this book, therefore, three types of successes are being sought here: programme success (keeping US foreign policy on track), political success (insulating the president from severe criticism from congress) and process success (doing so through the legitimacy of a blue-ribbon commission).

It should be noted that there is a normative element to saying that certain practices constitute 'tight-grip ones' (as opposed to relaxed-grip or loose-grip). Also, a tight-grip strategy might not necessarily involve use of every strategic tool that will be mentioned in this chapter. Nevertheless, for present purposes, it seems useful to deal with a range of instruments that can be used in an attempt to keep a tight rein on evaluations, getting a sense within each of their significance.

Keeping tight control of the format of evaluations

Inquiries, investigations, reviews and evaluations come in many shapes and forms often lacking clear definitional boundaries (Barker 1998; Prasser 2006b). Some are triggered automatically by legal requirement (such as accident investigation boards). Others are triggered by choice in response to specific circumstances such as crises or scandals (Peachment 2006). Yet others are part of the fabric of modern public governance, including the emergent norm of 'evidence-based policy-making' in many western democracies (Parsons 2002; Sanderson 2002). The vast majority involves a decision, either at the policy design stage and/or the implementation phase, to set up a particular type of evaluation. Types of evaluations include:

- internal departmental/agency investigations – for example, child protection cases, security breaches, internal reviews
- externally commissioned investigations from consultants, academics or acknowledged experts in the field
- ministerial reviews, working groups and task forces
- royal commissions – for example, 1991–06 Canadian Royal Commission on Aboriginal Peoples, 2004–05 Royal Commission to Enhance the Operation and Management of the Royal Malaysia Police
- presidential commissions – for example, Rogers Commission on Space Shuttle Challenger, 9/11 Commission
- public inquiries – for example, 2001–05 public inquiry in the UK into the mass murderer Harold Shipman, 2004–05 public inquiry in Australia into the teaching of literacy
- statutory non-public inquiries – for example, the 1996 inquiry by Lord Cullen into the shootings at Dunblane Primary School in Scotland
- legislative committee inquiries – for example, 2001 Finish Foreign Affairs Committee investigation into Finland's response to globalization, 2004 French parliamentary committee investigation of voluntary euthanasia
- audit investigations – for example,. by public audit offices such as the Audit Commission (UK) and Supreme Court of Audit of Greece
- performance reviews – for example, treasury reviews of efficiency and effectiveness, public value reviews, academic research assessment exercises.

The format of evaluations has repercussions for many of the other interventions to be discussed in this chapter. Nevertheless, it merits discussion in its own right.

Table 7.2   *Approaches of strategic decision-makers regarding policy evaluations*

	Tight-grip	Relaxed-grip	Loose-grip
Format of evaluation	A format that gives little or no leeway for evaluators to produce outcomes beyond what policy-makers want.	A format that gives a reasonable degree of discretion to evaluators, in being able to produce evaluation outcomes at odds with government wishes.	A format that gives substantial freedom for evaluators to produce evaluation outcomes, potentially in direct conflict with what policy-makers might want.
Parameters of investigation	Narrow Clear limits set on what can be evaluated – typically whether a programme has been implemented according to original goals.	Narrow Limits are set on what can be evaluated. However, evaluators have freedom to ask for a broadening of the scope of the evaluation beyond implementation only, or to move beyond the original scope, if they consider it relevant to do so.	Wide Extending not just to the policy, programme or event itself, but also to the role played by broader political, economic and social factors.
Who will conduct the evaluation	Either individuals (or at least the chair) who are known and sympathetic to the wishes of government, or respectable legal figures who will stick rigidly to the terms of reference.	A combination of individuals, some of whom are supportive of the wishes of government and some who are not.	Individuals who are not sympathetic to government and its aims.

Partly, this is related to the symbolism of choosing one format over another, whether it is the public inquiry or the internal investigation. It is also because certain ways of working tend to flow from certain formats. For example, public inquiries, by their nature, are open. They hold evidence sessions in public forums and will sometimes also deliberate in open forums (Prasser 2006b). By contrast, internal agency or departmental evaluations – again, by their nature – are conducted behind closed doors and their reports might not even be made public.

Strategic choices over the type of evaluation have a significant impact on evaluators. A tight-grip approach would involve a choice of format that gives little leeway for an evaluation report to be outside what policy-makers broadly want. For example, a 2006 review of general skilled migration categories commissioned by the Australian Department for Immigration and Multicultural and Indigenous Affairs was tasked only with assessing issues of

Funding and timescales	Either insufficient time or resources to produce credible and authoritative report, or considerable resources and considerable time, in order to 'take the heat' off the issue for months, and even years.	Some use of financial powers and reporting timescales, in order to influence the work of the investigation, although not to the point of overwhelming the work of the investigation.	Refusing to use funding and timescales (too much or too little of both) as a means of influencing the work of the investigation.
Tools, techniques and methods	Clear specification and limits placed on tools, techniques and methods.	Some specification by policy-makers, combined with some discretion by local evaluators.	Allowing substantial freedom for evaluators to choose which means are the most appropriate.
Attitude to the progression of the evaluation	Intervention during the course of the evaluation: e.g., discrediting the evaluation, refusing to testify before a committee.	Public display of allowing the evaluation to proceed unimpeded, but working behind the scenes to influence its investigation and report.	Allowing the evaluation to take its course, without intervention.
Disseminating the report	Refusing to publish, or publishing with heavy censorship.	Publishing with censorship of some parts, and/or some restrictions on its release; e.g., some parts of the report but not others.	Allowing full and widespread publication.
Responding to the report	Portraying the evaluation in best possible light from government's perspective: e.g., 'cherry picking' to legitimate programme and political success.	A balancing act, admitting that government got it right on some things and wrong on others.	Acceptance that 'government got it wrong'.

efficiency and effectiveness. Its terms of reference stated explicitly that it was 'excluding issues relating to the numbers selected through this process, which is subject to policy considerations' (Birrell *et al.* 2006: 7). Policy-makers might also seek a format that spills over and produces political success. The centrally determined evaluation for the UK government's youth justice projects was such that local evaluators needed to evaluate on the basis of a national template, designed to measure levels of compliance with targets. In creating hierarchies that filtered out critical commentary, and even the views of young people themselves, the Blair government's flagship policy was substantially insulated from criticism (Squires and Measor 2005).

All choices of evaluation format based on tight-control ideas are not guaranteed to produce the types of success that are often intended. One danger is in attracting serious accusations of cover-up; that is, accusations of process and even political failure. The British government's refusal to hold a public inquiry into the 2005 shooting in London of young Brazilian John Charles de Menezes has attracted sustained criticism that the Metropolitan Police has something to hide, despite two investigations by the Independent Police Complaints Commission, a coroner's inquest and a review by the Crown Prosecution Service.

Another danger of a format based on tight-grip principles is accusations of passing the buck and refusing to accept responsibility. In essence, trying to keep a tight control of the format of evaluations with particular goals in mind (usually programme and political ones) might actually produce the opposite effect, with accusations of illegitimate process being thrown in for good measure.

Narrowing the parameters of investigation

If the format of an evaluation can steer investigation broadly in a particular direction, the exploration is guided further by the specific scope given to evaluators. The power to decide the parameters of evaluation is crucial. To use an analogy, it is akin to building a rail track and sending evaluators on a journey of exploration, but there is only so much they can see and only so far they can travel. Committees of inquiry have terms of reference to specify which aspects of a policy and/or its context can be examined. So, for example, when in 2008 the National Audit Office of Finland conducted an investigation into the relocation of the Policy IT Management Agency to the Rovaniemi region, it was empowered only to examine the operational, financial and personnel impacts, plus the impact on the region. The wisdom, or otherwise, of the decision to relocate was a 'given'. Many policies have the parameters of their evaluation built into the design of the policy. The EU structural funds, for example, have elaborate systems of appraisal built into policy formation processes.

Keeping a tight grip on parameters results in a very restricted target of investigation. For example, the terms of the extensive 2002–06 Review of Public Administration in Northern Ireland excluded examination of the existing 11 government departments, on the grounds that that review was not to be used as a means of renegotiating the Good Friday Agreement by the 'back door' (Knox 2008). An analysis of this case later in the chapter provides further details and situates it within its risk context.

Those who are able to decide the scope or parameters of evaluation can exercise this power because they have the formal authority to do so. Often authority is backed up by the threat of sanctions, if evaluators fail to comply. Breaching the format of evaluations can result in financial disadvantage, legal penalties, job loss or reputational damage. Campbell-Smith (2008), in his mammoth study of the Audit Commission in the UK, examines the controversial push from government that the audit body should become an 'inspectorate' in order to implement New Labour's Best Value programme for performance improvement in local councils. After much internal debate, the Commission realized that not to conform with government wishes would mean that the work would go elsewhere, possibly to the National Audit Office, with the real possibility that the Audit Commission would cease to exist (Campbell-Smith 2008: 427–32).

More generally, strict parameters to an investigation can result in an evaluation that provides a quasi-constitutionally authoritative stamp of approval that a policy has worked, or that a particular type of reform is needed. Political success can also accrue because government reputation and direction can be maintained. Restricted evaluations can certainly be criticized as 'bad' process, although most policy-makers can live with criticism of process if they get the programme and political outcomes they want.

Needless to say, a restrictive approach can be rebound. It can bring accusations of a fix, or a smokescreen for the protection of reputations and policy trajectories. Political elites attempting to protect a programme from wide scrutiny can, at times, run the risk of doing so at their own political expense.

Choosing evaluators who are most likely to produce the desired outcomes

The issue of who will conduct an evaluation can be in terms of specific individuals and/or institutions. Many programmes have evaluations built into them by those bodies or agencies involved in running or providing the programme. In this regard, the issue of 'who will evaluate' is an organizational one. Organizations will typically have substantial discretion to decide who will be part of the evaluation team. However, there are many issues where strategic policy-makers have the opportunity to decide 'who' on a personal level; for example, who will chair an inquiry or commission of investigation, or who will sit on an evaluation team.

A crucial issue, therefore, is: should we expect evaluators to be chosen who are sympathetic to policy-makers and their goals, or should we expect evaluators to be chosen who are 'independent' and with no sympathies or allegiances to policy-makers? This question indicates a classic and difficult issue for political elites. The potential advantage of choosing evaluators who are sympathetic to policy aims and values is clear. They are likely to produce evaluation reports in line with the sympathies of policy-makers. When Ronald Reagan established a presidential commission to examine the administration's high profile and controversial MX missile defence system, potential members were sought out who held sympathies on the need for balance in the face of a Soviet threats, with Reagan personally vetoing Henry Kissinger as chair precisely because of his association with a policy of détente (Kitts 2006: 79–80).

The corollary is that evaluations in this mould produce authoritative judgements on programme success, with a spillover into political success as well.

However, such outcomes are not inevitable. In the first instance, the process of evaluation itself is open to criticism for being partisan. The Bush administration was heavily criticized for distorting much of the work of scientific evaluation committees though 'industry appointments' (McKee and Novotny 2003; Wagner and Steinzor 2006). Of course, there is always the possibility that an evaluation might not work out as intended. The chair of an inquiry might 'go native' and produce a critical report that is damaging to the programme itself and, possibly, even the reputation of government. The 1987 Fitzgerald inquiry into police corruption in Queensland, Australia interpreted its terms of reference much more widely and with greater vigour than was expected by the appointing government (Prasser 2006b: 60). The investigation, led by QC Tony Fitzgerald, resulted in the police commissioner being jailed, three ministers being sacked and the state premier being tried for perjury.

An important issue that needs to be addressed briefly here is the role of lawyers. They have overseen many inquiries and investigations. The issue is: does appointing lawyers fall into the category of keeping a tight grip on evaluations or keeping a loose grip? I would suggest the former. Rogue personalities aside, lawyers are liable to stick to the terms on which they have been appointed. Utter professionalism in law can be a political gift to policy-makers. To revisit the rail track analogy, they will stick to the route down which they have been directed, unless there is a valid legal reason why they need to question or depart from doing so. Legal systems are one of the bastions of modernism and, in terms of evaluations, apoliticism. Snider (2004), in examining the intersection of law and science, argues that:

> Both science and law are routinely presented to the public as dispute resolving mechanisms that eliminate ambiguity, that brook no come-back or resistance, that convey objective truth which only the immoral and criminal (in the case of law) or the uneducated and stupid (in the case of science) would question. In the real world, science and law are complex and multifaceted entities, full of competing individuals, institutions, discourses and truth claims. They are in no sense singular units. However, the point is that they retain sufficient legitimacy that they can be presented *as if* these contradictions and complexities did not exist. The assumptions hidden under each label, the intricacies of data collection in science or of what counts as evidence in law, and all the other inconsistencies and ambiguities that underlie any particular truth claim, are not generally known outside the world of experts.
>
> (*Snider 2004: 267*)

All things being equal, appointing lawyers to head evaluations has strong potential to confirm policy success, where this is sought. In other words, the process is liable to be seen as fair and legitimate (rather than unfair and partisan). When combined with narrow and strict terms of reference, it is likely to confirm what government wants it to confirm – that the policy is successful (or occasionally, unsuccessful). Some form of political success might also follow. An example is the Australian inquiry into alleged financial 'kickbacks' paid to Saddam Hussein's regime for wheat exports by the privatized AWB Limited (formerly the statutory Australian Wheat Board) and in breach of UN Sanctions. The inquiry, chaired by Terence Cole, QC, stuck diligently to its terms of reference, focusing purely on investigating the legality or otherwise of AWB Limited's dealings, rather than the broader policy environment, including government competence in dealing with early warning signs, or the wider 'light touch' regulatory framework, within which the organization operated (McConnell *et al.* 2008). The coalition government led by Prime Minister John Howard was able to claim a triple success: that the government did its job as well as it could (programme success); it was rightly exonerated (political success); and that, in singling out AWB Limited officials for further investigation, justice was done after a fair and impartial inquiry (process success).

Strategic use of funding and timescales

To put the issue simply, evaluators can either be given a great deal of time and a great deal of money with which to conduct their business, or little time and a little money. It is not always the case that the former is tightly controlled and the latter more open. Strategically, it is easier to think in terms of using funding and timing to keep a tight rein on the findings of the evaluation, or to do the opposite. Ways in which a tight rein can be kept are:

- ensuring that so little money is allocated to the evaluation that it does not have the resources to conduct a credible investigation
- tying the funding received by the evaluating organization into producing the type of evaluation report that is desired
- ensuring that so little time is allocated for evaluation that evaluators cannot produce credible research or report writing in the time available
- giving evaluators so much time that the political heat is taken off an issue, and the matter either never receives a critical evaluation or the report is published in a different climate where a critical evaluation has much less impact on programme and political success than might otherwise have been the case; Stutz (2008), in his study of 11 public inquiries in Canada, Israel and Northern Ireland, found that reports published sooner, rather than later, are more likely to produce policy action because they are considered by the same governments that commissioned them.

Success for government can follow from the close management of funding and timescales. Sanderson (2002) argues that the Blair government's evaluations of pilot programmes in many health and welfare initiatives left little time for the pilots to run and be evaluated, primarily because of the political pressures to deliver on electoral promises. The pilots and their evaluation, therefore, helped serve the purposes of keeping New Labour's governance agenda on track. There is a danger, however, that rushed evaluations are considered something of a sham (that is, bad process) although this might be tolerable for policy-makers, if it means keeping policies on track. There is also the possibility that, despite strategic use of funding and time allocation, the evaluation can still be damaging programmatically, and even politically. In 1999, the killing of Nigerian President Baré Maïnassara during a military coup resulted in a swift internal investigation, which described the event as an 'unfortunate incident' that required no further investigation. Human rights groups persisted for many years in seeking truth and justice in the form of an international inquiry.

Specifying tools, techniques and methods

Evaluation tools, techniques and methods are many and varied. Different combinations will lead evaluators down different pathways towards particular findings. Chapter 5 examined, in detail, nine different standards for claiming policy success, ranging from original objectives and whether things have improved, through to whether the benefits outweigh the costs and whether the policy is morally sound. The focus here is not on providing the 'best' approach; it is on highlighting the capacity of strategic policy choices to steer evaluations in many different directions, depending on the choice(s) made. It also alerts strategic policy-makers and decision-makers to some of the strengths and pitfalls of different types of approaches.

At a strategic level, the tools, techniques and methods that help shape evaluations are based on the following questions:

- What aspect of the policy is being evaluated? Is it simply the programme, or should there be any room for evaluation of the original process that produced the policy or the political repercussions?
- Is evaluation simply of policy outputs or performance, or should it include outcomes (the impact on society)?
- What time-frame should be evaluated? Is it short-term, medium-term, long-term?
- What is the reference point against which the policy should be evaluated? Is it against the original goals of the programme? Whether things are better than before (a before-and-after study)? Against a benchmark? Against pre-determined policy domain criteria (such as efficiency and

effectiveness)? Against the benefit for a target group? Against another jurisdiction? (See Chapter 5 for a full discussion of these issues.)

The permutations are endless. Nevertheless, some example will suffice of ways in which control over such factors can help control evaluation outcomes. Northcott and Llewellyn (2005), in their study of the UK's National Health Service (NHS) benchmarking systems, suggest that, despite the policy rhetoric of knowledge-sharing to encourage best practice, performance appraisal systems in reality are principally centralized political instruments to ensure adherence to policies and standards. Ambrose (2005), in his study of urban regeneration in Bristol, England, shows how the top-down specifying of measures for progress/success (to the exclusion of consulting residents for their views) are skewed towards producing particular outcomes. One measure of success, for example, was deemed to be rising rents and property prices. This benchmark produced results that might have been a success for some (owners and landlords), but not for others (aspiring homeowners and tenants).

There are also pitfalls to such a directive approach. Accusations of biased evaluations are common – although, as indicated previously, these are often tolerable for policy elites if they can obtain the desired (usually healthy) 'report card' on the programme, as well as keeping the general direction of government policy on its desired track. The more serious danger is longer-term backfire, because programmatic and political problems will not go away, despite having been subject to evaluation.

Intervening during the course of the evaluation

Strategically, it is possible for policy elites to make interventions during the evaluation period, particularly if the scrutiny process does not seem to be working out as anticipated. A tight-grip approach might involve undermining the legitimacy of the evaluation before it has reported. A visible means is refusing to testify, or agreeing to participate only under certain conditions. More covertly, a tight-grip approach might involve leaking discussions to show that there is division between evaluators. It might also involve discrediting the evaluators themselves, particularly the chair. A further tool is the setting up of another evaluation or alternative process, with the underlying implication that the first one is insufficient. It might even involve terminating the inquiry – such as in 1997, when the Canadian government took unprecedented action to cut short an inquiry into the role of Canadian forces in Somalia (d'Ombrain 1997).

From the perspective of policy-makers, there are advantages to an interventionist tactic. It can protect a programme from deep criticism, as well as protecting the veracity of the original policy ideas. In a sense, therefore, strategic interventions can protect the 'success' of the programme and the political reputation of the government that sponsored it. However, such theoretical advantages are not guaranteed to work in practice. Interfering during the course of an investigation can create the stench of political manipulation in policy processes, as well as storing up programme and political failures for the future. In other words, programme problems might not disappear (despite the discrediting of a critical evaluation), and there might still be serious challenges to the integrity of government. In Canada in 2008, Newfoundland and Labrador Premier Danny Wilson described a judicial inquiry into errors and delays in breast cancer results as a 'witch hunt' (cbcnews.ca 2008). For many months after, the issue kept resurfacing to challenge his political authority.

Restricting or blocking the release of the report

Next, is the issue of how to disseminate a report, especially one that is critical. Policy elites can censor some of the content, or refuse to make the report public. Or it can be released at a time when news is dominated by other events. Or the report can be released at a time of year when the nation is in holiday mode (for example, the controversial 1980 Black Report into health inequalities in the UK was released during the August Bank Holiday). A less covert form of shielding a report from the public gaze starts with the classic internal review, the findings of which will never be made public. In 2009 in Ireland, a maternity hospital refused to publish an external report, claiming it was intended only for internal management purposes.

Essentially, in shielding critical evaluations, the advantages are that the reputation of the policy and its policy sponsors can remain intact. The risk is political damage, especially if the contents of the report become known, perhaps through a leak. Therefore, restricting or blocking the release of reports run the risk of being perceived widely as bad process, and bad politics.

Spinning the report

When a report is produced, it might be anything from a wholehearted validation of policy success, to an unequivocal demonstration of policy failure. Most evaluations will be somewhere in between. To varying degrees, and depending on the scope evaluators have been given, criticism can focus on issues such as:

- shortfalls in meeting goals
- implementation problems
- failure to benefit those who were intended to benefit.

The responses of policy-makers to such criticism are a process of attributing 'meaning' to the report. The concept of policy narratives and policy stories also applies (Roe 1994; Stone 2002), and therefore policy-makers need to tell the 'story' of the report and where it leads. The criticisms can be framed in many different ways. If the report basically is at odds with what policy-makers had hoped for, varying responses are possible, sometimes in combination. A tight-grip strategy might involve one or more several tactics. Three factors in particular are worth highlighting

The first is a 'cherry picking' exercise. In other words, it is to select the bits from the report that are wanted, and frame what the report 'means' in a manner that fits with what had been hoped for. In Germany in 2008, a controversial government report into poverty and wealth in the country was reworked after proving unpalatable to some ministers. The revised report still showed that an eighth of Germans lived in poverty and another eighth were on the edge, although a government spokesman stated that the report was confirmation that 'Germany's welfare state works' (*Spiegel Online International* 2008).

A second tool is a discrediting of the evaluation, a practice that fits with much of the literature on public policy blame games and blame avoidance (Weaver 1986; Ellis 1994; Hood 2002). The language used can be measured or combative, but need not necessarily be so. Discrediting or playing down the significance can be attempted through:

- discrediting the motives or credentials of evaluators – for example, a report by academics at the Workplace Relations Centre at the University of Sydney produced data that contradicted the government's argument that low-skilled workers were better off as a consequence of flagship industrial relations reforms. Minister for Employment and Workplace Relations Joe Hockey described the authors of the report as 'former trade union officials who are parading as academics' and 'I'm not sure that this institution is known for academic rigour' (*Sydney Morning Herald* 2007)
- discrediting the tools, techniques or methods used – for example, stating that figures are out of date, stating that the evaluation was a narrow one that does not reflect the bigger picture
- discrediting the timing of the evaluation – for example, accusing it of being released at a time that will embarrass the government, or a time when it is likely to inflame an already difficult problem.

Potentially, for policy-makers there are several advantages to putting such interpretations on critical responses. Cherry picking and/or denigrating the evaluations lead to a successful defence of the 'success' of the policy by attributing its critics as biased, unfair or misleading, and/or by carefully selecting the bits most favourable to what is wanted. The disadvantage is vulnerability to accusations of 'spin' or being arrogant and out of touch. In essence, trying to protect and frame a policy programme as successful can rebound, because it generates enough speculation and criticism from a wider rage of influential policy actors that there is the danger of some degree of process failure, programme failure and political failure.

Finally, what if the report does actually meet with policy-makers' expectations? In such cases, policy-makers generally need do little more than praise the investigation to and frame it as the definitive evaluation. A desired evaluation, from the perspective of policy-makers, meets the various criteria of policy success. There is successful process (a legitimate report, heavily steered by government), a successful programme (validated by evaluators) and successful politics (because government policy can stay on the desired track). The only danger comes back to the perennial issue of subjectivity and success. Not everyone might agree. Critics could allege that the process was a fix. They might also label the programme a failure, despite what the evaluation suggests. And they might still seek to question the direction in which government is headed. Such differences are a reminder that success in meeting goals is usually only viewed as a success by those who support the original goals.

Strategy: a loose-grip approach to policy evaluations

As the terminology implies, and as Table 7.2 indicates, a loose-grip strategy does not seek to steer evaluations heavily towards producing particular findings. This approach is less constrained in comparison with a tight-grip approach, and can best be understood through an examination of the ways in which a loose-grip strategy manifests itself. Each component mirrors the tight-grip strategy. There is less space given to the intricacies of the loose-grip approach, simply because many of the introductory points have already been covered in the previous sections. Also, many of the advantages of a loose-grip approach are easy to understand in theory, and less easy to see in widespread practice among policy-makers.

Relaxing the format of the evaluation

The format of evaluations has repercussions for many of the other interventions and non-interventions to be discussed. Different formats bring symbolic benefits (such as openness in relation to public inquiries), but there are process issues in terms of how the evaluation is conducted (such as witnesses being questioned in public, or terms of reference being wide). A loose-grip approach to the evaluation format gives substantial autonomy to evaluators, and not necessarily at the expense of policy elites. An open evaluation can be a success in process terms, because the evaluation is considered credible, but also in programme terms, because it allows substantial independence to evaluators to examine programme goals and see whether they have been met. In February 2009, Victorian Premier John Brumby established a Royal Commission to examine the bushfires that devastated communities and led to over 200 deaths in Australia. Its terms of reference were as wide as they could possibly be, covering preparations, causes, responses and any other matters deemed appropriate by the Commission. The scale of the tragedy and the collective grief in Australia was such that anything less would have been politically unacceptable. Such approaches can help a government be successful in terms of its reputation with the electorate and in continuing on its broad strategic direction, without damaging accusations that it has 'fixed' the evaluation.

However, a more relaxed format can also rebound. It is less likely to do so in process terms, because choosing an evaluation format that is open and expansive is often considered good process. The problem for policy-makers is that, if they misjudge and opt for a format that backfires, 'success' is liable to be elusive, in both programmatic and political terms. Making misjudgements in setting up inquiries is perhaps easier than one might think. Sulitzeanu-Kenan (2010), in his study of 132 inquiry appointment decisions in the UK over the period 1984–2003, concludes that short-term blame avoidance issues are the key to understanding why political elites set up commissions of inquiry. Perhaps in some instances, therefore, policy elites anticipate that a wide-ranging investigation will ease short-term political pressures on them, while hoping in the longer-term that the report will not be damaging, or might be released in a political climate that is dominated by other issues. Yet, outcomes for government do not always fulfil such aspirations. The 1991 Spicer Commission in Canada (formally, the Citizen's Forum on Canada's Future) assisted the Mulroney government to deal, in the short term, with voter apathy and complex constitutional issues through what Tanguay (1999: 325–6) describes as: 'a kind of roving psychiatrist's couch created in the wake of the collapse of the Meech Lake Accord to probe the causes and consequences of voter angst in the country'. In the longer term, the report relayed much popular discontent with Mulroney, as well as fuelling the debate on independence for Quebec.

Allowing wide parameters for investigation

Here, evaluators are given a wide-ranging remit. Typically, doing so allows for an examination of what has/has not worked, but also the broader policy context and any other matters deemed relevant by the investigators. Broad parameters to an investigation are not always problematic for policy-makers. Indeed, they can bring success, because the process is seen as legitimate, the programme receives strong scrutiny to see if its goals have been met, and political reputations can benefit. However, a wide-ranging evaluation can backfire on those who approved it. The findings might suggest that the policy was flawed in the first place, and that the process that produced it was not fair and legitimate. Or, the report might be highly critical of existing policy. Potential negative political repercussion for government could follow. In 2001 in Walkerton, Ontario, Premier Mike Harris responded to a major water contamination disaster (in which seven people died and almost half the population of the town fell ill) by setting up a wider-ranging commission of investigation, chaired by Justice Dennis O'Connor. Its terms of reference were very wide, encompassing not only the local circumstances surrounding the contamination, but also the broader policy environment, as well as any other matters deemed relevant. The investigation and report were devastating, both programmatically (in terms of the neo-liberal light touch regulatory regime and spending cutbacks initiated by Harris) and politically (in terms of his reputation) (Snider 2004; Schwartz and McConnell 2009). In times of crisis and disaster, particularly because of pressure to set up an inquiry within 24–48 hours, policy elites might establish a wide-ranging inquiry in order to satisfy public concerns at a time of national stress and grief, without having the time or capacity to think through the longer-term repercussions of what kind of critical report might be produced.

Choosing evaluators who might be highly critical of government policy

The approach here is to throw caution to the winds and choose evaluators who are not 'on side'. In theory, doing so is liable to bring legitimacy to the process and lead to seemingly 'fair and reasonable' investigations. As argued previously, however, a lawyer chairing an inquiry with limited terms of reference is liable to bring more credibility and be less risky. The fact that examples of throwing caution to the winds are hard to find is telling. As Barker (1998) argues, in his study of policy inquiries in the UK:

> To take the risk of commissioning not a consultant or a 'tame academic' or other sympathetic or otherwise pliable expert to attempt to borrow some external authority, but rather a more plainly independent commission or panel which will take its own evidence and reach its own conclusions requires rather more nerve and is still quite a novelty.
>
> *(Barker 1998: 120)*

Refusing to mould the evaluation through use of funding and timescales

As was argued earlier, giving an investigation a great deal of time and a great deal of money does not necessarily equate with a loose-grip approach. To use the medical analogy deployed by Hogwood and Peters (1985), pathology can be a consequence of overeating as well as starvation. Many a policy investigation has been cast into the political wilderness by being given many years to report. In general terms, a loose grip is more likely to stop short of using issues of time or money (too much or too little) to mould the shape of the final evaluation. This rather apparently even-handed approach is, in fact, very common. For example, a series of inquiries in Australia included: government-business practices in Western Australia (almost two years, Aus$ 30.4 million); police corruption in Western Australia (almost two years, Aus$15 million); aboriginal deaths in custody (almost five years, Aus$30 million), building and construction industry (a year and a half, Aus$60 million) (Peachment 2006: 23; Prasser 2006b: 188). Such generosity is 'good process' and, in turn, 'good politics', because it gives the impression of thorough investigation, devoid of political interference. However, much depends in its interaction with other inquiry factors – particularly the terms of reference. Generosity in terms of time and money needs to be accompanied (at least) by wide terms of reference for it to be a loose-grip approach that is not steered heavily by political elites. Of course, even when considered in isolation, there is a danger for elites in allowing substantial time and resources for investigation. The end result could be a forensic, exhaustive critique of policies and their sponsors. In other words, aspirations for process success with a spillover into political success, might backfire and wreak programme, and even political, damage.

Allowing substantial freedom in evaluation tools, techniques and methods

As we know, there is enormous variety in the types and combinations of tools and techniques that can be applied to evaluate policies and their success, or otherwise. A loose-grip approach gives considerable freedom to evaluators to decide:

- whether to evaluate programmes and the processes that produced them, as well as the political repercussions
- whether to evaluate policy outputs or performance and/or to focus on the outcomes – that is, impact on society
- whether to focus on one or more of the short-term, medium-term and long-term impacts
- which particular reference point(s) will be used to evaluate the policy – for example, original goals of the programme, whether things are better than before, whether a benchmark has been achieved, whether the target group has benefited, whether the benefits outweigh the costs and so on.

A loose-grip approach would be more or less indifferent to such questions, leaving them to be resolved by evaluators. The advantage of doing so is that it confers a strong degree of legitimacy on the evaluation process as 'independent', and is liable to ask penetrating and searching questions about the rationale for, and success of, a programme. In theory, at least, there might be political pay-offs as well, especially if government is seeking to enhance its credentials as having a more evidence-based, depoliticized attitude to public services.

The disadvantages of such a strategy are not difficult to ascertain. As the top-down approach to policy implementation implies (see Hill and Hupe 2009, for a summary), an absence of strong, authoritative rules means that when policy-makers have strategic evaluation goals, a loose-grip approach would be counterproductive, because there are no strong rules to constrain evaluators (a type of street-level bureaucrat) and prevent them from producing evaluation reports that run counter to the wishes of policy elites. In other words, aspirations that a loose-grip approach will achieve process, programme and political success might produce failure in the latter two categories. Achieving process legitimacy is liable to be little consolation for a damning evaluation and serious political fallout.

Resisting temptation to intervene during the course of the evaluation

In essence, this tactic amounts to restraint from intervention in the hope that the evaluation will not be completely at odds with what is desired. A hands-off approach can be seen as good, legitimate process, as well as allowing for 'independent' programme evaluation, so cultivating the reputation of a government that is open to scrutiny and criticism. For many policy elites, such restraint is not difficult to achieve if they have restricted the evaluation in other ways, such as carefully limiting its terms of reference and appointing evaluators who will not stray from the mandate they have been given. The danger comes when they have not done so, and it seems that an 'independent' investigation is headed towards producing a report that does its job and is damning. Therefore, belated interventions can attract strong accusations of political interference in independent evaluation processes. In 2002, for example, Sir William Stubbs, Chair of the Qualifications and Curriculum Authority in England, alleged that Education Secretary Estelle Morris had interfered in an independent inquiry into A-level results by asking her officials to prepare for a re-grading of results (*Guardian* 2002). The implication was that she pre-empted and guided the findings of the inquiry. The veracity of this claim is of little concern, other than to illustrate that such accusations have the potential for a bandwagon of significant political criticism of government.

Restraint from interfering in evaluations has clear advantages from the perspective of policy elites, but there are also pitfalls. It can leave them at the mercy of critical reports and the alliances that form around a story of failure.

Allowing full and widespread dissemination of the report

Allowing reports to be made widely available is common practice, and can be seen as healthy and democratic process, with accruing political benefits for government, symbolized by its willingness to release evaluations that contain (at least some degree of) criticism of government. Furthermore, from the perspective of government, a critical evaluation is often less liable to attract unwanted publicity than a report that has been 'blocked' or 'refused' release. Therefore, openness and transparency can go a long way in cultivating the image of 'good process' but, unless the evaluation produces a strong element of what policy-makers want to hear (usually some form of durable success), then it is possible that the road is clear for an evaluation that affirms some form of programme, or even political, failure.

Resisting spin

Deciding what is and what is not 'spin' is a complex and difficult task. The notion of 'spin' as an undesirable feature of the rhetoric surrounding public policies has gained much currency among those who see it as a degenerative trend towards a form of political lying, simply for the purposes of promoting policies and attacking opponents (Franklin 2004; Farnsworth 2008). However, as Nicoll and Edwards (2004: 44) argue: 'rhetoric is involved in all descriptions of reality, and always has been, including those of policy'. Furthermore, 'to suggest that a policy discourse is "simply" spin or "empty" rhetoric implies that there is a more truthful or honest political discourse' (Nicoll and Edwards 2004: 45).

Therefore, if a strategic option for policy-makers is to resist spin, the implication is that an evaluation report possesses an authentic truth in terms of the message it is trying to convey, and that spin would somehow compromise this truth. This argument has some appeal, but is difficult to sustain wholeheart-edly. Even on the most basic of levels, evaluation reports contain many different findings that can be interpreted and prioritized in many different ways. Political actors are engaged not only in 'sensemaking' (trying make sense of what reports seem to be saying), but also 'meaning making' (articulating the 'meaning' to a broader audience).

We cannot hope to resolve such debates here, but what we can do is get a sense of strategy in the face of a report that produces a story or narrative that runs counter to what policy-makers had hoped for. A case in point might be a local council that finds itself responding to an external investigation into the management of its schools. In this hypothetical case, the chair of the investigation is critical of poor budgetary control and lack of appropriate training for head teachers, and the local parents' association concurs, because the report legitimizes what it had been arguing for many years. A loose-grip strategy would not offer any significant counter story. It would adopt a 'we got it wrong' stance, constituting a form of blame acceptance. Former Queensland Premier Peter Beattie made an art form of the *mea culpa* strategy, continually diffusing criticism on a series of issues throughout his premiership (Williams 2005). A *mea culpa* approach can be good politics because, as the blame management and public relations literature indicates, there is often a lot of sympathy, and even respect, for politicians who admit mistakes or misjudgements (Hood 2002; Brändström and Kuipers 2003; Hearit 2006). It can also be a 'good process' because it can indicate that the evaluation process was genuinely independent. However, the main risk here is of a trade-off. Process and political success can come at the expense of admitting programme failures. In the hypothetical example above, an admission of failure might be good politics (perhaps conflicted political success), but it does not negate what seems to be authoritative evidence and argument that schools are managed badly. Hence, for political success to be of the durable variety, it is likely that a commitment to reform will be needed.

Contexts in which some strategies are riskier than others

Mapping the contexts

No strategy to ensure success (whether is it trying to produce policy that is successful or trying to cultivate an evaluation that fits with the desires of policy-makers) is guaranteed to produce results. For example, policy-makers might feel they have a tight grip, but it is, in fact, much looser than they think. The Scarman Report into the 1981 Brixton riots in South London is arguably one such case, with its report being a landmark in recognizing problems of racial disadvantage in Britain. Lipsky and Olson (1977), in their work on riot commissions, also point to the problems once commissions have been let loose from the executive mantle. By a process of drift, they can develop their own organizational identities. Such outcomes are certainly possible, although their significance in becoming barriers to governmental aspirations for success will depend to a large extent on the broad strategic configuration of an evaluation which, in itself, can be shaped by contextual factors. The issue arises, therefore: under what conditions are some strategies likely to be more feasible or more risky than others? This question is crucial because, as was mentioned in Chapter 6, the context of risk is vital (Douglas 1992; Slovic 2000; Drennan and McConnell, 2007). Behaviour X might be high risk in context A, but low risk in context B. For example, a national strategy for evaluating schools is something that had become the norm in western democracies, but was strongly resisted at the school level in post-apartheid South Africa, with memories of apartheid inspections and heavy state surveillance (Jansen 2004).

Appendix 7.1 to this chapter is based on a minor variation on the variables used in Chapter 6, to help provide the context for policy-making success. It provides a heuristic framework that can be used to help explain why evaluations take the course that they do, focusing on a range of feasible options and the degrees of risk associated with them. It should be remembered that this is an exercise in judgement, rather than an exercise in science. Risks are judgements about outcomes, rather than predictions (Althaus 2008). Each of the variables can be dealt with in turn. The *ceteris paribus* rule should be noted. Each variable is treated in isolation and all other factors are constant. Let us now discuss the contextual variables in turn.

Issue politicization

Some issues are more politicized than others, and some might have more national political significance than others. The issue of where to locate a new bus stop, for example, is of low salience nationally and likely to be confined to a very localized policy sub-system. Correspondingly, the issue of where to site a new nuclear reactor is liable to generate interest and controversy, beyond the policy sub-system surrounding nuclear energy. The issue, in terms of present concerns, is the extent to which issue politicization affects the evaluation strategy. As Appendix 7.1 implies, the greater the degree of politics and political controversy surrounding an issue, the higher the risk of a loose-grip approach producing an explosive 'policy failure' report. The corresponding logic is that the greater the degree of politicization, the greater the realpolitik pressures to keep a tight grip on evaluations to ensure 'successful' outcomes. Although a tight-grip approach is not free from the risk of being accused of political manipulation, the risks to policy-makers of a report concluding a case of programme failure, and possibly political failure, is likely to be greater if an evaluation or inquiry is damning.

Urgency

The issue here is the length of time needed for a report to be produced. Conceivably, the time frame might be only a day or two in terms of crisis issues, where there are often immense pressures for a swift and provisional investigation into what went wrong. By contrast, there might be few or no time constraints. Generally, there is more pressure to have a successful and rigorous evaluation process than to produce a swift report. Therefore, some investigations can take many years. The Saville Inquiry into the events of 'Bloody Sunday' in Northern Ireland began in 1998, and has still to report at the time of writing in late 2009. The implication of Appendix 7.1 is that the greater the urgency of obtaining a report, the greater the risks of a loose-grip approach; there will simply not be sufficient time to gather information and produce a report when its mandate is very broad. Hence, urgency and the tight-grip approach are far more feasible matches.

Electoral and reputational issues

For some issues, evaluations and investigations can be critical in making or breaking the reputations of policies, leaders and electoral legitimacy. Policy-makers can typically ill-afford open, loose-grip investigations when the stakes are high. Hence, when a government's reputation and electoral legitimacy hinges on getting the stamp of approval for a particular policy decision, then the most expedient approach is likely to be the tight-grip approach. Certainly, there is no guarantee of success. There is vulnerability to accusations of political manipulation, and this is particularly likely to be the case when a government minister or official has stepped in to discredit an investigation. Nevertheless, as Althaus (2008) suggests, in her study of political risk, electoral calculations are not an irrational burden on policy-makers. Rather, they have a logic and drive of their own, often helping to explain why elites take the decisions they do.

Pressures for particular evaluation outcomes

The issue here is the extent of the pressures to produce an investigation or evaluation that gives the authoritative seal of approval to a particular policy, or (occasionally) to legitimate its failure. In reality, the issue is likely to overlap with some of the previous issues, but not completely so. It is useful to treat them separately, because pressures might come from other sources. Powerful stakeholders might seek positive evaluations of policies from which they gain rights and rewards. The stakeholders might be multiple, perhaps including government itself and bureaucrats, as part of a wider policy monopoly, advocacy coalition or policy community. High-profile manifesto policies and flag-ship policies would be relevant here, as would popular programmes of reform. Of course, policy-makers need not bow to such pressures. Nevertheless, the point remains that pressures for a particular evaluation outcome of policy success (or failure) can be considerable, and a loose grip on the evaluation is a risky proposition when there are powerful pressures for affirmation that current arrangements are working (or not). Once again, the most feasible strategy is a tight-group approach.

Strength of alliance likely to oppose strong steering by government

This refers to instances where there is likely to be substantial opposition to government strongly steering an evaluation to giving a clean bill of health to a policy or (occasionally) a diagnosis of failure. This particular variable is an exception to the others, because a tight-grip approach is high risk. In essence, under conditions where there is a strong alliance likely to oppose strong government steering, the most logical measure is to opt for legitimate process (relaxed grip) and hope, for example, that criticism of the programme and policy-makers is relatively minor, rather than running the risks of tightly controlled evaluation that attracts accusations of manipulation and does not end the smell of programme or political failure hanging over it.

Having mapped out these varying contexts, we now need to put them together and make broader suggestion about low-risk, medium-risk and high-risk strategies towards evaluation, bearing in mind continually the qualifier that risk is, to a large degree, about judgement rather than science.

An overview of feasible and risky strategies

Low risk for policy-makers in seeking their desired outcomes from evaluations

Taking into account the numerous factors that help make up 'context', it seems that the lowest risk for policy-makers is generally to keep a tight grip on evaluations and investigations. If an issue fits even one of the criteria of politicization, urgency, reputational significance and pressures to produce a 'successful' evaluation, then the most feasible approach is for strategic policy-makers to keep a tight grip on evaluations. There is one important exception (pp. 167–8), and there is also the issue of process. A tight-grip approach almost inevitably attracts criticism of a fix because of, for example, narrow terms of reference, or a chairperson being picked who is sympathetic to the views of government. So, accusations of process failure are liable to accompany this strategy – but I would argue that such approaches have become the norm in politics, to the extent that it is easier for governments to dismiss critics. Therefore, it seems that governments often trade process success for the stamp of programme success and the hope that political success that will accrue.

High risk for policy-makers in seeking their desired outcomes from evaluations

Examining the various contextual factors as detailed previously and summarized in Appendix 7.1, the highest-risk strategic policy choice in terms of evaluations is generally the loose-grip approach. In essence, it has the highest capacity to backfire. There might be some compensation, because open and wide-ranging evaluations are liable to attract process legitimacy. However, for policy elites, 'good' process (durable process success or, occasionally, conflicted success) is often a luxury they cannot afford when it is at the expense of knocking off course their cherished programmes or political goals. Evaluations that are set in motion with wider terms of reference and unsympathetic evaluators are liable to produce findings at odds with government aspirations. The one context where the loose-grip evaluation is not high risk is when there is a strong and powerful alliance waiting to pounce on government at the slightest suspicion of a whitewash.

Medium risk for policy-makers in seeking their desired outcomes from evaluations

Based on the contextual factors identified, a medium-risk approach is generally one that is just tight enough for policy elites to exercise control, but just loose enough to allow 'independent' evaluation; that is, a relaxed-grip approach The only context in which it is a highly feasible option is when there is likely to be very high opposition to government heavily steering the evaluation process, and a relaxed grip can help take (at least, initially) potentially fatal political pressure off the government. More broadly, a relaxed grip has the capacity to produce the best and worst of both worlds. Logically, it points to policy-makers needing to proceed with caution, if they adopt this strategy. Only an appraisal of each case can determine where the relaxed approach is liable to more or less risky. Let us now examine one particular case, illustrating that, 'logically', it was conducive to a 'tight grip' evaluation

Case Study

The 2002–06 review of public administration in Northern Ireland: mapping policy contexts to explain a 'tight-grip' strategy

Northern Ireland has always been a 'special case' in terms of the governance of the UK (see Knox and Carmichael 2006; Birrell 2008; Knox 2008, 2009). Since the imposition of Direct Rule from Westminster in 1973, the province had been governed by a variety of piecemeal and complex measures designed, arguably, to deal more with political sensitivities in Northern Ireland and the absence of any longer-term constitutional settlement, than any rationalistic assumptions about public service delivery. In the aftermath of the 1998 Belfast (Good Friday) agreement and the establishing of an elected assembly and executive, the system of six pre-existing government departments was expanded to ten (plus the Office of the First Minister and Deputy First Minister). The implication in this expanded configuration was that ministerial portfolios could be distributed in such a way as to balance political sensitivities and facilitate power-sharing. All parties who participated in the Belfast Agreement accepted that a review of public service delivery was needed. The review was established in June 2002. The broad role of the review was to examine the structures and effectiveness of public service delivery. The context of the review, when mapped against the criteria in Appendix 7.1 is summarized in Table 7.3.

Locating contexts in particular categories is a matter of informed judgement, rather than scientific precision. All the contexts below point towards the need for government(s) to tightly control the review.

Degree of issue politicization: Politics in Northern is strongly contested and a matter of high politics, demonstrating throughout the years that various protagonists favour force/violence and the ballot box.

Degree of urgency: The original deadline was for the review to report by the end of 2003, although the suspension of the Northern Ireland Assembly in October 2002 helped changed the time frame. Final decisions on outcomes were not announced until November 2005 and March 2006.

Degree to which electoral and reputational issues at stake: The Northern Ireland issue has never been a deciding factor in the electoral fortunes or reputation of British governments at Westminster although, within Northern Ireland, the role of the British government has been hotly defended and attacked by unionists and nationalists. The reputation and sustainability of the new Northern Ireland executive (until its suspension in 2002) depended on producing a review outcome that did not unravel the Good Friday agreement. The British government held a similar goal.

Strength of pressures to produce a particular evaluation outcome: Maintaining the power-sharing settlement was paramount for the British government, the Northern Ireland executive and all the main participating political parties.

Table 7.3   *Mapping the policy evaluation risk context of the Review of Public Administration in Northern Ireland*

Contextual issue	Strength of context	Lowest-risk strategy	Medium-risk strategy	High-risk strategy
Degree of issue politicization	High	Tight-grip	Relaxed-grip	Loose-grip
Degree of urgency	Low/medium	Tight-grip	Relaxed-grip	Loose-grip
Degree to which electoral and reputational issues at stake	High	Tight-grip	Relaxed-grip	Loose-grip
Strength of pressures for a particular policy evaluation outcome	High	Tight-grip	Relaxed-grip	Loose-grip
Strength of likely opposition to an evaluation outcome steered by government	Medium	Tight-grip	Loose-grip	Relaxed-grip

Strength of likely opposition to an evaluation outcome steered by government: The main opposition was from the small UK Unionist Party. The overall level of likely opposition was low.

In assessing the combined impact of all these factors, it should be noted that classifying evaluations as tight-grip, relaxed-grip or loose-grip is a matter of informed judgement, including weighing the synergy between the different variables and the importance of some in relation to others. Most features of the Review of Public Administration in Northern Ireland suggest that it is 'tight-grip', but the first three categories are crucial in capturing the main flow and dynamics of the review.

Format of evaluation: The review was led by ministers and senior civil servants, rather than a team of independent reviewers. Devolution was suspended in October 2002 and the final response, in 2005, was the responsibility of Secretary of State for Northern Ireland, Peter Hain.

Parameters of investigation: The carefully negotiated system of 11 government departments was crucial to power-sharing agreements in Northern Ireland. The 11 departments were excluded from the review, which focused on local government, non-departmental bodies and 'Next Steps' agencies. The key political settlement in the Belfast Agreement was insulated from scrutiny.

Who will conduct the evaluation?: The review was headed by civil servants in the Office of the Minister and Deputy First Minister, drawing on a variety of independent experts.

Funding and timescales: Funding surfeits or deficits were never an issue. Timescales were initially fairly short, although they became extended (partly because of the suspension of devolution).

Tools techniques and methods: Included survey of public attitudes, commissioned research, study and visits to other jurisdictions, two major public consultation exercises.

Attitude to the progression of the evaluation: The Northern Ireland Office Minister, Ian Pierson, declared at an early stage that he wanted the number of council reduced drastically from 26 to between five and eight.

Disseminating the report: See pp. 174 ff.

Responding to the report: The outcome of the review and response was a series of publicly available Ministerial statements, rather than a one-off definitive document. Doing so helped the Executive outline its plans without a high-profile definitive document around which critics could coalesce.

In summary, the Review of Public Administration in Northern Ireland took place in contexts that pointed towards the necessity of a 'tight-grip' approach to reviewing public service delivery in Northern Ireland. Specifically, the power-sharing settlements (which emerged from Good Friday Agreement) and the devolution settlement needed to be beyond the scope of the review. This is precisely what happened, and the outcome was marginal refinements, rather than radical reform.

Conclusion

The core argument of this chapter is that evaluating policies to ascertain their success, or otherwise, is an intensely political process. Policy evaluations are moulded, constrained and enabled by the strategic choices of those elites who have to the power over evaluation formats, terms of reference, funding and more. They are neither all-powerful in doing so, nor guaranteed to succeed in their aims. Different strategic approaches can be taken, and much depends on the context of each individual issue. On balance, however, the analysis presented here helps explain why tight-grip policy evaluations are the norm, with the exception of times when there is a strong and powerful coalition of interests waiting to launch an attack on government at the slightest indication of success being 'proved'.

The key to understanding all of the foregoing is the issue of policy success: in particular, the process, programme and political goals policy-makers have when they are establishing evaluations. Once we understand that policy-makers can prioritize these three sets of goals in many different ways, we understand that evaluating programmes is only one aspect of policy evaluation. Often, for example, evaluations are designed to steer evaluations towards political success (for example, keeping governance agendas on track, making 'token' policy seem feasible solutions to wicked problems), supported by sufficient process legitimacy to make the evaluation an authoritative statement. Politics, with a large 'P' and a small 'p' is everywhere in policy evaluations.

Appendix 7.1

Contexts and feasibility of tight-, relaxed- and loose-grip evaluation strategies

		Most feasible (low-risk)	Some feasibility but caution needed (medium-risk)	Least feasible (high-risk)
Degree of politicization	Low	• TIGHT GRIP When the level of politicization is low, the most feasible option for government to pursue its evaluation aims is to keep tight control of the evaluation process. The issue is not sufficiently controversial to generate opposition to such an approach.	• RELAXED GRIP • LOOSE GRIP There is some danger in terms of: **Programmes:** That leeway is given to evaluators and the issue becomes politicized in a way that could not have been foreseen, and the programme goals are compromised; **Politics:** Politicization creates unexpected problems for government's agenda management.	None
	Medium	• TIGHT GRIP When politicization of an issue is moderate, the most feasible option for government to pursue its evaluation aims is to keep a tight rein on the evaluation process. Despite the issue bringing a degree of controversy – and, hence, holding potential for opposition to emerge – maintaining a tight grip will usually be enough to steer the evaluation process and enable government to cope with the type of criticism that is a routine feature of governing.	• RELAXED GRIP There is some danger in terms of: **Programmes:** That leeway is given to evaluators and the issue becomes even more controversial and the programme goals are compromised; **Politics:** An increased level of politicization creates unexpected problems for government's agenda management, and even its own reputation.	• LOOSE GRIP If an issue is already moderately political and little or no steering is given to limit the evaluation process, there is high risk with regard to: **Programmes:** The evaluation is critical of the programme in a way that was not expected; **Politics:** Government has to cope with criticism of its values, aims and agenda.
	High	• TIGHT GRIP When an issue is highly politicized, the most feasible option for government to pursue its evaluation aims is to keep tight control of the evaluation process. Doing so might attract criticism for being too interventionist, but is least likely to create	• RELAXED GRIP If an issue is already highly political and a reasonable amount of leeway is given to evaluators and the evaluation process, there are risks in terms of: **Programmes:** The evaluation is critical of the programme in failing to meet goals and	• LOOSE GRIP The risks to success in adopting a loose-grip evaluation in the face of high politicization, are: **Process:** The evaluation is perceived as generally legitimate and successful, but from government's point of view it rebounds and

	greater political problems than those it seeks to solve.	producing undesirable outcomes; **Politics:** Government has to cope with criticism of its values, aims and agenda, as well as criticism of its competence to govern.	government's point of view it rebounds and become a legitimized critique of government goals and policies; **Programmes:** The scope of the evaluation becomes so broad that it scrutinises either the veracity of the original policy itself or related policy areas. The impact for policy-makers is a disturbance to agendas, beyond what reasonably could have been conceived; **Politics:** The evaluation produces findings that jeopardize government reputation, electoral prospects and/or political direction.
Degree of urgency	**Low**	• TIGHT GRIP When an issue is not urgent, the most feasible option for government to pursue its evaluation aims is to keep tight control of the evaluation process. Doing so avoids creating space for lengthy discussions and generating views with the capacity of challenging those of government.	• RELAXED GRIP • LOOSE GRIP There is some danger in terms of: **Programmes:** Leeway is given to evaluators who end up taking much longer than expected to produce a report. The issue then becomes urgent and programme goals are compromised unless a report can be produced on time; **Politics:** Time delays created unexpected political problems for government. It is criticized for not having foresight.	None
	Medium	• TIGHT GRIP When there are moderate time pressures for an evaluation report to be produced, the most feasible option for government is to keep a tight grip on the evaluation process. Doing so avoids lengthy discussion and ensures the report is delivered on time.	• RELAXED GRIP There is some danger in terms of: **Programmes:** Leeway is given to evaluators and the issue becomes much more urgent than previously anticipated, and programme goals prove difficult to achieve; **Politics:** The emergence of increased and unexpected time constraints leads to criticism of government for not being vigilant about time constraints.	• LOOSE GRIP If time pressures are reasonably strong and there are few or no constraints on the evaluation process, there is the danger of a loose grip in terms of: **Programmes:** The evaluation is critical of the programmes in a way that was not expected **Politics:** Government has to cope with criticism of its values, aims and agenda.

Degree to which electoral and reputational issues at stake	• TIGHT GRIP	• RELAXED GRIP	• LOOSE GRIP
High	When time is at a premium and policy-makers need to act quickly and produce an assessment of policy – for example, in response to a scandal or crisis – the most feasible option for government to pursue its evaluation aims is to keep a tight rein on the evaluation process. Doing so enables a rapid appraisal of what it 'working' and what is not, as well as fending off criticism that government did not act sufficiently quickly.	If an issue is already subject to severe time pressures for an evaluation and government gives a reasonable amount of scope to evaluators and the evaluation process, there are risks with regard to: **Programmes**: The evaluation is in danger of not being delivered on time and information is not available to understand how best to achieve programme goals; **Politics**: Government has to cope with criticism for failing to appreciate the urgency of the matter.	The risks to success in adopting a loose-grip evaluation in the face of severe time pressures, are: **Process**: The evaluation process is too slow and fails to meet deadlines; **Programmes**: Existing programmes with inbuilt defects lack proper appraisal, leading to the perpetuation of 'failing' programmes; **Politics**: Government is criticized for being careless and lacking the capacity to govern vigilantly and effectively.
Low	When the issue has little or no reputational/electoral repercussions, the most feasible option for government seeking to pursue its evaluation aims is to keep tight control of the evaluation process. Although government could be criticized for its strong control tactics, the issue does not have the capacity to damage government's reputation or electoral prospects.	• RELAXED GRIP • LOOSE GRIP There is some danger in terms of: **Programmes**: Freedom is given to evaluators and a report is produced which is critical of the programme in a way that was not foreseen; **Politics**: Leeway is given to evaluators and the issue becomes damaging to reputation or electoral prospects in a way that could not have been envisaged. It also poses difficulties for government's agenda management.	None
Medium	When politicization of an issue is moderate, the most feasible option for government is to keep a tight rein on the evaluation process. The issue does bring a degree of controversy and, hence, potential for opposition to emerge. However, maintaining a tight grip will usually be enough to steer the evaluation process and allow government to cope with criticism as part of the regular business of governing.	• RELAXED GRIP There is some danger in terms of: **Programmes**: A degree of autonomy is given to evaluators, and the programme and its goals are subject to unexpected and difficult criticism; **Politics**: Some freedom to evaluators produces a report that unexpectedly creates problems for government's agenda management and its reputation.	• LOOSE GRIP If an issue has reasonably strong implications for government's reputation or electoral prospects, the risks of allowing substantial freedom to evaluators is: **Programmes**: The evaluation is critical of programme goals and the means of achieving them; **Politics**: Government has to cope with a report that is critical of its values, aims and agenda, as well as the oppositional coalitions that converge around the report.

	• TIGHT GRIP	• RELAXED GRIP	• LOOSE GRIP
High	When an issue has high potential to damage government's reputation/electoral prospects, the most realistic option for government in pursuit of its evaluation aims is to keep a tight grip on the evaluation process. Doing so might attract criticism for being too controlling, but is least likely to avoid opening out far greater political problems that would happen with a report that is a damaging critique of government.	If an issue has high potential to damage government's reputation/electoral prospect and a reasonable amount of freedom is given to evaluators and the evaluation process, there are risks in terms of: **Programmes:** The evaluation is critical of the programme in terms of failing to meet goals or produce good outcomes; **Politics:** Government has to cope with criticism of its values, aims and agenda, as well as criticism of its fitness to hold political office.	The risks to success in adopting a loose-grip evaluation strategy when the issue brings high reputational/electoral stakes for government, are: **Process:** The evaluation is perceived as generally legitimate and successful, but from government's point of view it backfires and become a legitimized critique of government goals and policies; **Programmes:** The scope of the evaluation becomes so broad that it scrutinizes either the merits of the original policy itself or related policy areas. The impact for government is a disturbance to agendas, beyond that envisaged; **Politics:** Evaluators are given substantial autonomy to produce findings that jeopardize government reputation, electoral prospects and/or political direction.
Strength of pressures (including from within government) for a particular evaluation outcome — Low	• TIGHT GRIP • RELAXED GRIP • LOOSE GRIP — When there are little or no pressure for an evaluation outcome of success or failure, any strategy is feasible. None bring risks of any significance involved in particular types of stakes involved in particular types of evaluation outcomes being produced.	None	None
Medium	• TIGHT GRIP — When pressures to produce a particular evaluation outcome are reasonably strong, the most realistic option for government to pursue its evaluation aims is to keep a tight grip on the evaluation process. Doing so will usually be enough to steer the evaluation process in the desired direction,	• RELAXED GRIP — There is some danger in terms of: **Programmes:** Leeway is given to evaluators and the issue becomes subject to greater criticism than foreseen, generating greater opposition to programme goals; **Politics:** The evaluation is critical of government and its policies.	• LOOSE GRIP — If reasonably strong pressures exist for a particular type of evaluation outcome, and an issue is already moderately political and little or no steering is given to constrain the evaluation process, there is danger with regard to: **Programmes:** The evaluation is critical of

194

Strength of likely opposition to an evaluation outcome steered by government	TIGHT GRIP	RELAXED GRIP	LOOSE GRIP
High	• TIGHT GRIP with criticism not being sufficiently strong to derail or seriously delegitimate this strategy. When there are very strong pressures for a particular evaluation, it is very difficult for government to do anything other than keep a tight grip on the evaluation process. Doing so will attract criticism, but government will have very strong support and the move and will help prevent the publication of a report that will cause even greater political damage.	• RELAXED GRIP If there are very high expectations that a particular type of evaluation outcome is produced, relaxing the grip on evaluation is likely to lead to risk in terms of: **Programmes**: The evaluation is critical of the programme goals, outputs and outcomes; **Politics**: Government has to cope with criticism of its values, aims and agenda, as well as criticism from those who had sought a particular type of evaluation outcome.	the programmes in a way that was not expected; **Politics**: Government has to cope with criticism of its values, aims and agenda. • LOOSE GRIP The risks to success in adopting a loose-grip evaluation in the face of very strong pressures for a particular evaluation finding are: **Process**: The evaluation might be legitimate, but a government seeking particular outcomes from the evaluation is very unlikely to get the report it desires; **Programmes**: The scope of the evaluation becomes so broad that it scrutinizes either the veracity of the original policy itself or related policy areas The impact for policy-makers is a disturbance to agendas and coalitions; **Politics**: The evaluation produces findings that are in stark contrast to those who wanted particular outcomes from the evaluation. The outcome is damaging criticism, overt and covert, that the government is being unresponsive to genuine pressure and incapable of judging the seriousness of an issue.
Low	• TIGHT GRIP When the level of opposition is liable to be low, the most feasible option for government to pursue its evaluation aims is to keep a tight rein on the evaluation process. The issue is unlikely to generate any serious opposition to government taking this approach.	• RELAXED GRIP • LOOSE GRIP There is some danger in terms of: **Programmes**: That leeway is given to evaluators and the issue creates criticism to a level that was not envisaged, and the programme goals are compromised; **Politics**: Opposition is generated because a relaxed or loose grip evaluation creates space for opposition to flourish.	None

	Column 1	Column 2	Column 3
Medium	• TIGHT GRIP When the level of opposition is moderate, government is best to pursue its evaluation aims by tightly steering the evaluation process. Doing so will usually be sufficient to ward off criticism of excessive intervention.	• RELAXED When opposition is likely to be moderate, the risk to government of a relaxed grip approach is: **Programmes:** The programme is subject to a level of criticism that is perhaps unnecessary; **Politics:** Freedom has been given to criticize government and its policies to a level that is counterproductive to government and its goals.	• LOOSE GRIP When opposition is likely to be moderate, the risk to government of a relaxed grip approach is: **Programmes:** The programme is subject to severe and unnecessary criticism; **Politics:** Evaluators have been given substantial freedom to criticize government and they are liable to do so, with damage to government's values, agenda and trajectory.
High	• RELAXED When government is faced with the likelihood of very strong opposition against its heavily steering the evaluation process, the most feasible option is to allow evaluators and the evaluation process a measure of freedom. The benefits of doing so are liable to be greater than the risks of giving in to the pressures, or of appearing to 'fix' the evaluation.	• LOOSE GRIP When there is liable to be to be very strong opposition to government heavily constraining the evaluation process, bowing to the pressures for a loose grip evaluation runs the risk in terms of: **Programmes:** Become subject to severe criticism; **Politics:** Government solves one problem and confronts another. The evaluation forms the basis for a major attack on the government's reputation, agenda and direction.	• TIGHT GRIP When there is liable to be to be very strong opposition against government constraining the evaluation process, doing precisely this runs risks in relation to: **Programmes:** Perpetuating problematic programmes because they do not receive serious scrutiny; **Politics:** Government develops or confirms its reputation as dictatorial and out-of-touch.

Chapter 8

Reflections: Cultivating, Sustaining, Learning from and Predicting Success

Introduction

We have come a long way in understanding the nature of policy success accompanying political discourse, and the feasibility of strategies for achieving and evaluating success. We now need to go further and locate the nature of success within broader societal trends and tendencies. Hence, the current chapter picks up on many of the themes in previous chapters and develops them further into 'bigger picture' thinking on success. It contains explicit arguments in the interests of generating debate, although it attempts to be even-handed in putting forward and critiquing a number of different positions. It deals with issues to which academic theory has, at least in some instances, paid virtually no attention, yet the issues themselves crop up in the real world of politics. It deals with competing perspectives on:

- the transferability of conditions for success to other sectors and jurisdictions.
- the capacity of successful programmes to be enduring
- whether we are more liable to learn from successes or failures
- our ability to predict success.

Are the conditions for cultivating success the same in different policy contexts?

Policy-makers want to succeed, whatever the policy sector, jurisdiction or broader context. With an incredible volume of policy and political activity taking place in different jurisdictions throughout the world, it is little wonder that policy-makers might wonder if the successes of others have some validity to help them achieve their own goals. Are such hopes realistic? Can the factors that help cultivate success in one context be applied beneficially elsewhere? There are many different conceptual and applied strands to policy analysis (and, indeed, political science) that would answer in the affirmative. It is useful to identify these and the supporting arguments by discussing success in terms of process, programmes and politics. Counter-arguments are also considered, with a position taken that we are best served by an approach that cuts across aspects of both.

An argument: conditions for success are universal

A considerable amount of academic literature and political life is devoted to the idea that there are certain activities and ways of working that result in successful policy-making. In other words, successful process is considered to be a cross-boundary and cross-policy issue. Academic literature such as that on public deliberation (Gutmann and Thompson 2004; Fischer 2009), policy design (Schneider and Ingram 1997), and incremental bargaining (Lindblom 1965; Braybrooke and Lindblom 1970) assumes that healthy, legitimate policy-making will occur if certain principles and practices are followed (see Chapter 6). For example, Schneider and Ingram (1997: 5) argue that:

> Policy designs that enable citizens to participate, learn, and create new or different institutions, and that break down divisive and negative social constructions of social groups lay the foundations for self-correcting policy dynamics and a more genuine democratic society.

It is not only academics that promote principles and practices for successful policy processes. Policy and political practitioners, ranging from local councillors to governing bodies in international organizations, can actively promote certain forms of policy-making (often tied in to receipt of funding) on the assumption that it cultivates success. Examples include:

- the Improvement Service in Scotland, which supports local authorities by promoting a number of practices such as partnership working and knowledge exchange
- the Australian Commonwealth government's seven principles of good practice in consultation exercises
- the Organisation for Economic Co-operation and Development's (OECD) promotion of 'environmental democracy', including opportunities for public participation in environmentally-relevant decisions.

Conditions for programme success are also proposed by many academics and practitioners. For example, advocates of free markets argue that the market mechanism is the most efficient and effective allocator of resources in society. Hence, regardless of the policy area, the assumption is that markets bring success and, therefore, governments should withdraw from many areas of life and leave decision to individuals, families, private organizations and so on. In essence, if a facet of public policy is the choice of inaction (Dye 2005: 1), then the best thing government can to do be successful, it is argued, is to withdraw. For example, a paper produced in this vein for the Adam Smith Institute by the Vice-Chancellor of the UK's only private university (Buckingham University) argues that UK universities are a pale shadow of the American, Ivy League universities. The solution proposed is that they should be freed from state control and funding in order to generate income through endowments and fees (Kealey 2006).

The promotion of conditions for programme success is not the reserve simply of free market advocates. Policy history is replete with examples of fads, trends and waves that have been promoted on a grand scale as the solution to achieving successful policies. They include Keynesian demand management, control of the money supply, public ownership, privatization of utilities, public–private partnerships, regulation, deregulation and much more. During the debt crisis of the 1980s, both the International Monetary Fund and the World Bank made privatization of utilities a condition of loans. In response to the global financial crisis of 2008 onwards, 'stimulus plans' have been adopted in countries as diverse as the UK, US, Australia, Spain, Germany, Chile, Vietnam and China. Such examples fall under the broad rubric of policy transfer and policy diffusion (Dolowitz and Marsh 2000; Rose 2005). In essence, the principle is that a policy that is successful in one jurisdiction can be successfully exported elsewhere.

Conditions for political success, it often argued, are also generic. For example, US foreign policy since World War II has been based on the assumption that the 'spread of democracy' will work in countries such as Korea, Vietnam, Nicaragua, Iraq, Afghanistan and Somalia. If we also remember that political success includes easing the business of governing, enhancing reputations and winning elections (see Chapters 2 and 3), then generic advice exists to help fulfil these aspirations. For example, Clinton's advisor Dick Morris provides advice such as 'Stand on Principle', 'Divide and Conquer' and 'Mobilize your Nation at a Time of Crisis.' He argues that:

> All politics is the same. It really doesn't matter whether one seeks the presidency of the United States, a seat as a state representative, the chairmanship of a local Rotary club, or the presidency of one's senior class. The strategies and tactics that work for one will work for another.

> *(Morris 2002: xii)*

A trip to any large bookstore is liable to reveal similar thinking in the many leadership books containing generic advice, or even golden rules such as 'think like a winner', 'great leaders persuade', and 'don't be popular, be principled'.

The list could go on, but the key point is an argument of universal applicability, amounting to: 'apply these principles and policy will be successful'.

In summary, therefore, this argument captures much of the dynamic of contemporary policy influence. Conditions for success are routinely 'discovered' and promoted with vigour as *the* solution to solving society's problems.

An argument: conditions for success are different in every context

The argument here is that what works in one context is unlikely to work in another. Context can be a range of factors such as time, space, culture, geographical area, political jurisdiction, political mood and policy sector. Once again, elaboration is useful in terms of the process, programmatic and political aspects of policy.

Successful policy-making process in one context does not mean that the same practice or activity will bring success elsewhere. The Netherlands, for example, has virtually no record of holding referendums (the only exception being the 2005 referendum on the European Constitution). Such absence seems to work in a nation where there is a long-standing tradition of cultural and political diversity, but might be less applicable in Switzerland, where there are roughly three or four referendums per annum in a country where consensus policy-making is paramount (Kriesi 2008). Another example lies in Mark Moore's (1995) call for policy-making to be based on public value, where substantial power is given to public managers. His vision is criticized heavily by Rhodes and Wanna (2007, 2008, 2009), who argue that his prescription is wholly unsuitable for Westminster systems where elected representatives and the people should be the authorisers of policy decisions.

A similar logic applies to programmes. A successful programme in one place or time cannot simply be transplanted elsewhere with the guarantee of success. Even if we leave aside policy transfer pathologies such as incomplete or uninformed transfer (Dolowitz and Marsh 2000), the argument here is that context is crucial to success or failure. China has heavily censored Google Internet searches and online postings, because it suits its purposes of cracking down on activities that it considers damaging to national unification and social order. It seems highly unlikely that these same measures would work, for example, in Spain, Germany, France or the Netherlands, where there are well-entrenched norms and rights to access. More broadly, the EU is an exemplar of the benefits of diversity, with its preponderance of legal directives that involve the setting of broad goals, but leaving substantial autonomy for member states in terms of achieving these goals. The outcome is that across a vast range of issues – from the level of VAT on goods and services, to the maximum length of the working week and the regulation of telecommunications – many countries do things very differently in order to protect 'national interests'.

The argument about political success follows on. A government might be successful in pursuing a governance strategy that 'works' for it, but this same strategy would be unlikely to be work elsewhere, because context is crucial to cultivating success. For example, it is virtually impossible to imagine that the respective governments of one-party and multi-party states would be able to swap strategies in connection with issues such as the elections, the media and civic engagement, and continue on the same 'successful' course.

In summary, this argument encourages scepticism about many of the claims of policy and political evangelists that we can succeed only if we do X or Y. It would tend to suggest that conditions for success need to be considered on a case-by-case basis. To use an analogy, it would criticize the 'one-size-fits-all' approach to policy success as akin to having only one tool in the toolbox.

An argument: success as familial

This argument is something of a mid-way position between the two. It suggests that both positions have something to offer, as long as we do not subscribe wholesale to their views. Some elaboration is needed.

Just because context is a vital ingredient in any recipe for success, so the argument goes, does not mean that every context is utterly unique. Contexts can share similarities in a 'family' way, which can lead to the conditions for success in one context being conducive to conditions for success in another. Political science categorizes polities in many different ways such as majoritarian versus consensus democracies, presidential systems versus parliamentary systems, federal states versus unitary states, republics versus constitutional monarchies, secular versus non-secular states, liberal democratic regimes versus authoritarian regimes, and communist systems versus capitalist systems. The policy dynamics of any two countries within these categories in terms of matters such as political parties, interest groups and civil society might share substantial similarities. Hence, there is some chance, all things being equal, that what works in one context will be of value in another. For example, public deliberation in public policy-making is more liable to be a success for government in a liberal democratic regime as opposed to an authoritarian one. In the latter case, free and open deliberation without retribution would pose a challenge to established authority.

Familial contexts could also relate to the nature of power relations within a policy community. For example, a strategy of policy-making secrecy, with regard to the processes and outcomes of national security decisions, would be unlikely to work if this same level of secrecy was applied to national elections. Charging for public services is more liable to work for entry to swimming pools than for 'collective' goods such as police and defence. The corollary, therefore, is that familial contexts in terms of matters such as political system, political ideology and policy sector can help create conditions conducive to policy success.

The important qualifier is that there are no guarantees of success – only less risk of failure. There are several important reasons for such caution. Just because something worked in one context, does not mean that it will also work in a similar context. The literature on historical analogies in crisis policy-making is a case in point. A new crisis will not necessarily unfold in the same way that an apparently similar one did many years ago (Brändström *et al.* 2004). An outbreak of avian influenza, for example, might be contained by bio-security measures on one occasion but not another. History never repeats itself with precision (Collier and Mazzuca 2006). Even small differences in context can have huge repercussions for the appropriateness of particular policy measures.

A related point is that we should not assume that policy-makers are driven by a rational appraisal of policy options (see Chapter 8), and can make comparisons between familial contexts for the purposes of producing successful policy. Policy-making can be driven by many factors such as path dependency, political self-interest, dominant coalitions of interests and the search for 'garbage can' solutions. Governments can very easily ignore 'success' factors elsewhere, if they feel it is in their interests to do so. Similar 'families' might take very different decisions, even when faced with broadly similar circumstances (for example, see 't Hart and Tindall 2009, on various national responses to the global economic downturn).

The overall argument, therefore, is that conditions for success are translatable to a degree, but the best we do is say that some cases are low-risk while others are high-risk. At times, the difficulty might be in knowing which is which. Perhaps, therefore, we are hitting on a pertinent point. Policy-making instinct for 'what will work' is of value across time and across jurisdictions. Perhaps this is one of the few criteria capable of cultivating policy success.

How sustainable are policy programme successes?

We might assume that successful programmes would continue to be successful, perhaps being subject only to minor refinements. Indeed, we might wonder why this would not happen, on the grounds of 'if it ain't broke don't fix it'. However, policy success, as we know from previous chapters, is not simply a matter of a policy working or being broken. A programme can, for example, work for some interests but not others, or meet one objective but fall short on another. In order to explore the issue of how sustainable programme successes actually are, we need to identify some of the main factors that can help and hinder the perpetuation of successful programmes. The 'all things being equal' caveat applies, although this point will be addressed directly at the end.

Factors helping sustain successful programmes

A number of diverse, but often overlapping, factors might help create conditions that are conducive to the perpetuation of 'successful' programmes.

Dominant power

We know from Chapters 2, 3 and 4 that an important aspect of programme success is the issue of 'success for whom'. Policies that benefit powerful interests or coalitions of interests are more liable to persist than those that do not have this same level of political support. If, for example, a privately-owned regional airport in a small town receives tax subsidies from the local authority and is the biggest employer in the area, then it is in a very strong position for these subsidies to continue. Much of policy analysis focuses directly or indirectly on issues of power, whether it be Marxist models (for example, Miliband 1973) or groups and networks (Pross 1992; Baumgartner and Leech 1998). The common thread is that policies are held in place by powerful interests whose values and preferred policy instruments are enshrined in public policies.

Inheritance/path dependency

Literature on policy inheritance (Rose 1990; Rose and Davies 1994) and path dependency (for example, Wilsford 1994; Pierson 2000; Kuipers 2004; Peters 2005) reveals many differences, but there is a recurring theme in terms of the 'past' being a primary shaper of new policy choices. Pierson (2000) makes a point that can be applied to both: existing policy trajectories generate increasing returns and high costs of exit. For example, a polity that relies on a property tax (based on market value) for householders 'locks in' systems for valuation, administration and collection, as well as coalitions of interests who support and/or benefit from the programme. Pragmatically, it is easier for any new government to continue with this same tax regime, rather than incur the financial, bureaucratic, and political costs of disruption to a new system such as a local income tax or local sales tax. The more general point is that policy continuity is an important feature of public policies and, hence, we might expect this particularly to be the case with programmes that are successful.

Stable value paradigms

Stability of successful programmes is also assisted when there is stability in the dominant societal paradigms that inform policy choices. In Japan, for example, a highly centralized and competitive education system has changed little over decades, rooted in long-standing beliefs that it is the role of the national government to promote equal access to high quality education (Adolino and Blake 2001: 291–4). Also, many countries such as France, Canada, Australia and the UK no longer practice capital punishment, because of a moral belief in rehabilitation rather than 'barbaric' retribution. Jacobs (2009) argues that the values of decision-makers act as a filter through which complexity and causal factors are simplified, ruling in certain choices and ruling out others. The broad tendency is towards a self-reinforcing dynamic, rather than one of ongoing deep learning. When core beliefs and values are the intellectual foundation for policy choices, powerful barriers exist to policy change.

Cross-party agreement

Programmes are more liable to be sustainable when there is cross-party agreement on the programmes goals and policy instruments. For instance, if government and opposition parties agree on the need for a nuclear defence programme, there is a very high likelihood that the programme will continue. Similarly, if the parties agree on the number and size of local authorities, this configuration is liable to remain stable. When governing and opposition parties concur, policy will tend towards continuity, because there is no significant legislative opposition to support any policy alternatives.

Absence of viable alternatives

A further reason for the continuation of a successful policy is that, even when minor problems arise, there are no operationally and politically feasible policy alternatives; hence, the most practical solution is to stick with the existing policy and refine it. For example, sale and consumption of cigarettes is legal in all western nations, despite that fact that there are clear links between tobacco consumption and considerable health pathologies to large sections of the population. The alternative of banning cigarettes would be politically disastrous for any government, as well as producing logistical problems likely to be reminiscent of prohibition in the US, which created an underground market for alcohol. Therefore, governments can continue with the successful aspects of a legal drug (it generates substantial revenue for government and, arguably, contributes to social stability by providing an outlet and pacifier for people's anxieties), and content themselves with refining the basic policy by means of a combination of public health warnings and banning of smoking in public places.

Flexibility

As any structural engineer knows, tall buildings are designed to 'give' in order to cope with high winds. Many policy programmes are similar. Flexibility in terms of policy instruments and/or their implementation can allow them to cope with problems. For example, income tax rates, levies for toll roads, dates for space shuttle launches and immigration quotas can all be altered from time-to-time, rather than being fixed for as long as the programme operates. Flexibility in programme design allows for the refinement of successful policies.

Overall, the foregoing factors are conductive to maintaining 'successful' programme trajectories. They will tend to cultivate either policy stasis or refinements in the same mould, rather than producing new pathways or directions. The Conclusion to the book will develop this point further.

Factors hindering the sustainability of successful programmes

Countervailing forces might also be at play. Many of them mirror the previous factors, although the two sets can co-exist.

Power realignment

Dominant power can be challenged. Whether we subscribe to a pluralist vision of countervailing democratic pressures to prevent one interest from dominating for too long, or a marxist vision of the contradictions of capitalism pulling against private accumulation and exploitation, power balances can change and realignments occur. Therefore, if a feature of programme sustainability is 'success for whom', a feature of policy disruption to that sustainability can be the ascendancy of those who are otherwise losers or marginalized by the 'successful' programme. Baumgartner and Jones (1993), in their influential study of agenda-setting and American politics, point to the long-term fragility of policy monopolies dominating policy sub-systems. They argue, in their case study of nuclear power, that:

> The breakup of the pro-nuclear-policy subsystem in the United States proceeded as follows: opponents exploited divisions within the community of experts; images in the popular media changed; opponents were able to obtain the attention first of regulators then of Congress, the courts, and state regulators; finally, the market responded.
>
> (*Baumgartner and Jones 1993: 79*)

Changes in the balance of power within policy sectors and society more generally might create conditions conducive to undermining established policy trajectories.

Failures

Crises, disasters, fiascos and scandals can punctuate establishing policy pathways and their legitimating frameworks (Bovens and 't Hart 1996; Birkland 2007; Drennan and McConnell 2007). Many policy programme successes (including the durable variety, see Chapter 3) seem to be successful until events disturb the beliefs and assumptions underpinning policies. These events might be exogenous shocks, or failures emanating from policy design. Cobb and Primo (2003), in their study of airline crashes in the US, show that a strong and successful aviation safety record is periodically disrupted by an airline crash, with huge agenda-setting implications and airline regulation coming under intense scrutiny. Dramatic failures, especially those involving human interest and loss of life, can pose serious challenges to the legitimacy of existing programmes. Importantly, however, failures can be the product of a slow build-up. De Vries (2002), in his work on generational change and public policy, argues that dominant trends, and the political elites who support them, prioritize some issues and neglect others. The seeds of failure build up and can become painfully apparent, eventually giving way as societies evolve and new generations of policy-actors are installed.

Emergence of new value paradigms

For whatever reason, societal paradigms and the underlying assumptions about societal goals and priorities can change; swiftly (in the case of punctuations), or slowly over years and decades. Such change can feed through – and, indeed, be part of – factors that undermine the perpetuation of otherwise 'successful' policies. For example, traditional laws limiting marriage to a male–female union have been reformed in counties such as South Africa, Spain, Sweden, the Netherlands, Belgium, Canada and Norway. In many countries, societal values have changed gradually to the point that a 'successful' policy (meeting the goal of allowing only male–female marriages) was considered anachronistic in a modern world that is more sensitive to equal rights and minority interests.

Cross-party disagreement

When the main political parties disagree on the nature of a particular problem and its solution, they are more liable to criticize government policy and offer policy alternatives. Of course, we should not overestimate the ability of parties to reverse the policies of their predecessors (Rose 1984; Hogwood 1992). Nevertheless, party differentiation on an issue is a potential agenda-setter for policy change.

Existence of one or more suitable policy alternatives

The matter of 'suitability' is a value judgement. Pragmatically, for present purposes, I consider 'suitable alternative' to be a policy option that has strong potential to be both technically and politically feasible. For example, there are many ways for government to maintain levels of consumer demand in the face of changing economic circumstances. Measures range from lowering interest rates and reducing sales taxes, to raising tax thresholds, or providing one-off rebates. When feasible alternatives exist, sponsors and supporters of existing and 'successful' policy cannot afford to become complacent.

Rigidity

Some policies have little or no inbuilt capacity for adaptability, and/or even the political will to encourage such malleability. Indeed, part of the attraction for policy-makers can be the desire to produce unwavering 'flagship' policies. The strengths of such programmes can also be their weakness. They might be able to produce success in the short-term, but are vulnerable to failure under longer-term pressure. Rigid programmes are liable to be the product of rigid politics, where leaders stake their reputation a sole solution to a problem, whether it is refusing to support a war, signing an international agreement, or championing a huge infrastructure project. When the first flushes of success begin to disappear, their staunch ideological commitment to the policy leaves little room for manoeuvre.

In sum, the continuation of programmes that are successful from government's point of view cannot be guaranteed. Many factors ranging from coalitions of 'losers' to adversary politics can help set the agenda for change.

What factors help determine whether a policy success will be sustainable or unsustainable?

It is difficult, if not impossible, to provide a definitive answer to this question. There certainly might be an element of luck involved. Dowding (2003: 306) supports Barry's definition of luck as 'getting what you want without trying'. So, for example, Schwartz (2006) explores precisely this issue in relation to Australia's economic resurgence of the 1990s. He concludes that success was more likely to be a matter of intent, rather than a matter of fortunate circumstances that rescued otherwise dysfunctional policies. However, he recognizes that many different interpretations can be applied, including the possibility that success can also be attributable to path dependency, rather than intent or luck. Perhaps the more general lesson here is that the sustainability of a successful policy depends on the balance of forces for and against change. Each case needs to be studied on an individual basis, and even then we cannot escape the role of judgement in ascertaining the causes of success.

Are we more liable to learn from successes or failures?

A starting point: the nature of change and learning

The issue of whether we tend to learn from successes or failures is an important one – particularly because many media, political party and ordinary citizen commentators suggest that learning only comes about when dramatic failures take place. The argument is, for example, that a new train protection system only happens after a tragic rail crash happens, or extra resources for school security only come about when there is a school shooting or a major security incident. The further logic is that, in the absence of such extraordinary failures, public policies tend to persist with many difficult problems and lower-level failures, while never learning from those policies that are 'successful'. A statement that captures this entire argument would be something like: 'We gave more money for X and it worked. Do we really need a disaster to happen before we invest more resources in Y?' This question of whether we are more liable to learn from successes or failures is a tough one to answer. However, I will attempt to do so in very broad terms but need, first, to identify and explore just how complex the issues are.

First, there is the nature of 'learning', as well as its relationship to change. In many respects, what constitutes learning is very similar to the debates on what constitutes success (Chapter 2). Broadly speaking, two schools of thought can be identified. A foundationalist school of thought assumes that learning is an indisputable fact. Much of the literature on organizational learning falls into this category (for example, Argyris 1999; Toft and Reynolds 2005). For instance, learning can be:

- correction of errors – for example, reforming a safety procedure to ensure that it fulfils the role it is meant to perform
- realignment of goals – for example, a new organizational mission to help guide its activities.

Very similar assumptions are pervasive in dominant government discourses about public policy. Political life is replete with government statements such as 'we have learned from our mistakes', 'we have learned to adapt to new challenges' and 'we have learned what really matters'. All contain Hegelian-type assumptions that learning is part of a journey towards higher and higher forms of knowledge. A school governing body, for example, might encourage greater participation from parents in the running of the school, and consider the results to be so worthwhile that participation is encouraged in other activities of schooling. Or, a hospital might need to review its breast cancer screening processes in light of faulty results being released. Extrapolating the arguments here, the assumption is that whether we are learning from successes or failures, the common theme is that learning is a form of improvement for the greater good.

A constructivist or anti-foundationalist approach sees learning as in the eye of the beholder. As Fischer (2003: 11) suggests:

> learning for one person may not be learning for another person with a different political ideology. No amount of data, regardless of how well tested and verified it might be, will convince a person that anything important or useful has been presented if, in his or her view, the findings lead to policy judgements that take him or her in the wrong direction ... For such a person, the findings will not be considered learning per se. Or, alternatively, if they are, they will not be viewed positively.

Therefore, no matter the trajectory of public policy, some people will find it desirable and some will find it undesirable. Much depends on whether people identify with the values behind the policy, their support for the specific instruments used, the degree to which they are liable to be affected, and so on. For example, decriminalizing the use of cannabis might be considered a successful move by many (on the assumptions that it is not a significant danger to health and will ease the demands on police), while others would consider the move to be a failure (because the drug creates a culture conducive to use of harder to drugs, and also conveys a general 'soft' on crime message).

Not only does the debate between foundationalism and constructivism get us off to a difficult start, but also the situation is compounded if we consider the nature of what constitutes policy change. It includes difficult issues such as the nature of policy change itself (Howlett and Cashore 2009) and the time period under study (Kay 2006). For present purposes, there is benefit in simplifying around reasonably consistent approaches to levels of change (see, for example, May 1992: Hall 1993: Sabatier and Jenkins-Smith 1993; Rose and Davies 1994):

- *symbolic change* – political rhetoric of change, but little or no change takes place
- *organizational change* – refinements in rules and procedures of public organizations involved in implementing public policy

- *legislative/policy directive change* – new legislation and/or new policy decisions
- *societal change* – deeper paradigm changes in societal values and beliefs.

Naturally, placing change in certain categories requires judgement, and is especially difficult when change can conceivably straddle more than one category. For example, the creation of the Department of Homeland Security (DHS) after the 9/11 attacks was certainly policy/institutional change, but was it also a paradigm change? One could equally argue 'yes' (never before has there been an integrated vision to protect the US from internal and, particularly, external threats) and 'no' (the creation of the DHS is simply a refinement of the core belief that the US needs to protect itself from internal and, especially, external threats).

Despite such methodological difficulties, combined with the foundationalist versus constructivist tensions, it is possible to take things forward in a similar vein to the way in which the nature of success was tackled in Chapter 2. I argue, therefore, for a 'realist' definition of learning. Broadly, it encompasses both. Policies can change, but the desirability of these changes varies; hence, they might be framed as learning by some interests and not others. Hypothetical examples from the progress, programme and political dimensions will suffice.

In process terms, if government introduces a measure that allows for every school with less than 50 pupils to be exempt from the normal requirement to consult parents regarding school closure, then clearly a policy process change has taken place that could be viewed positively by local authority decision-makers (because it increases their formal capacity to rationalize schools), but negatively by parents (because they have no formal input into the process). Similarly, from the programme angle, if government bails out a financial institution, this policy change might be supported or opposed, depending on whether one believes that it is the role of government to intervene in cases of market failure. Echoes of such differences can also be found in the political aspects of policy. New governance agendas, whether they lean towards Keynesian interventionism or free market promotion, will be recognized as change by all concerned, but the desirability of the move is likely to generate competing and often hostile views. More generally, these hypothetical examples indicate that change and, especially, learning are not purely objective phenomena.

Learning from success

As explored in Chapter 1, very few academic analysts write about policy success, let alone whether we can actually learn from success. Hence, an examination of the issues involved needs to be amalgamated from a number of sources. Learning from success equates broadly with what Baumgartner and Jones (2002) describe as 'positive feedback'. Such ideas are rooted in systems theory and, in particular, the features of systems with inbuilt self-correcting features and tendencies towards equilibrium. In this case we are dealing with political systems. Baumgartner and Jones (2002: 13) define positive feedback as 'a self-reinforcing process that accentuates rather than counterbalances a trend'. They recognize that positive feedback can be incremental, unpredictable and even chaotic. Nevertheless, it amounts to positive returns breeding further positive returns. The implication is that governments can learn from success. Policies 'work', and the benefits that accrue mean that there is a process of continual improving and refining the trends already in existence. For example, Pollitt and Bouckaert (2004), in their examination of public management reforms world-wide, discern intentional trajectories of continual reform-building in areas such as budgeting, accounting and auditing.

There are many reasons why societies might engage in forging pathways that continually build on success. If we take some of the main public policy models as our focal points, we can identify different rationales for learning from success:

- ideas – ideational bandwagon, as problems are seized upon by elites as the opportunity to continue with a reform movement that is already under way
- psychology and agency – calculation of decision-makers that successes need to be continued
- institutions – lock-in whereby institutional feedback mechanisms are self-reinforcing and, therefore, reforms will tend to follow established patterns
- groups – coalitions of interests are dominant and have the capacity to strengthen this dominance through the ongoing production of 'similar' policies
- structural power – structural interests such as class, race and gender have the capacity to reinforce, and even strengthen, this dominance.

Models and concepts of public policy also contain the seeds of countervailing forces. Accordingly, some reasons why positive feedback might not be generated include:

- ideas – dominant thinking derailed by crisis; further reforms in the same mould would suffer from lack of legitimacy
- psychology and agency – calculation by decision-makers that a continuation of similar policies would be too risky
- institutions – lock-in is punctuated; matters cannot go on as they are

- groups – dominant coalition of interests is threatened, if reforms are taken too far
- structural power – dominant positions of structural interests such as class, race, and gender are threatened, unless there is a brake put on reform momentum.

Similar issues and forces are at play regarding learning from failure – although the emphasis is on rebuilding after negative events, rather than perpetuating established policy trajectories.

Learning from failure

As detailed in Chapter 1, literature on failure is much more extensive than literature on success. It covers failures in various forms such as crises, disasters, scandals, policy failures and organizational pathologies (see, for example, Hogwood and Peters 1985; Reason 1990; Tiffen 1999; Rosenthal *et al.* 2001). One consequence of this breadth is that more attention has been paid to what happens after failure, including inquiries, learning, exploitation and blame games (see Lipsky and Olson 1977; Ellis 1994; Weaver 1986; Hood 2002; Kitts 2006; McConnell *et al.* 2008; Boin *et al.* 2009). Learning from failure accords roughly with what Baumgartner and Jones describe as 'negative feedback'. Specifically, they state that:

> A negative feedback system includes a homeostatic process or a self-correcting mechanism. Just as a thermostat adjusts to falling temperatures by putting out more heat, homeostatic devices work to maintain stability. Whatever the direction of the outside force, the homeostatic device operates in the opposite way; the result is to maintain steady outputs in the face of changing external pressures. The key element of any negative feedback system is simply that the system reacts to counterbalance, rather than reinforce, any changes coming in from the environment.
>
> (*Baumgartner and Jones 2002: 8–9*)

One does need to view political life in systems terms of political pluralism to understand the basic idea that failures create countervailing forces. Dominant but ailing political ideologies can give birth to counter-reform movements, just as much as rail crashes can generate calls for new safety systems.

Several reasons can be identified, pointing to why societies might learn from failures. Again, the main public policy models are our starting point, but they have been distilled into simple rationales:

- ideas – legitimacy of dominant ideas is compromised or shattered by failures; new thinking is necessary to restore legitimacy
- psychology and agency – new leaders use failure to help forge a fresh agenda, or existing leaders accept that failures are unacceptable and something needs to change
- institutions – failure is evidence of diminishing returns from existing policies and a new direction is needed
- groups – dominant coalitions of interests are threatened by failure; reform is need to limit the damage
- structural power – dominant structural interests such as race, class and gender are compromised by the failure; policy reform is needed to mini-mize the damage.

Yet, learning from failure is not inevitable; there are countervailing forces that can be couched in similar terms to the above:

- Ideas – failures are considered to be a challenge to core ideological beliefs that need to be protected as much as possible; change needed is marginal or, perhaps, even symbolic
- psychology and agency – avoidance of new jerk reactions and/or playing blames games to avoid responsibility and need for change
- institutions – complex institutional interdependencies make change too difficult to achieve
- groups – powerful coalitions do not concede that failure requires signifi-cant change, and are strong enough to do so
- structures – powerful structural interests are so entrenched across all walks of life that one failure is not enough to cause fundamental change to the means through which their dominance is maintained.

This analysis only takes us so far. We are aware of capacities and constraints on change and learning, but now need to blend them together. Consideration now needs to be given as to whether learning from success is more prevalent than learning from failure.

Learning from success and failure: a balance sheet

In the realm of public policies, tendencies and counter-tendencies, capacities for stasis and change can co-exist. The strength of each will depend on the specific policy contexts. In many respects, therefore, it might seem foolish to speculate about broader tendencies and trends. Nevertheless, one intention of this book on policy success is to stimulate debate about an issue that has been largely neglected in the policy sciences. Hence, in the interests of furthering discussion,

I would suggest, perhaps controversially, that we are more liable to learn from successes than from failures. There are two main reasons for making such a statement.

First, learning from failure is not as pervasive or as deep-rooted as we might think. More specifically, change and learning tend to take place primarily at the symbolic and organizational levels – and, to a lesser degree, at the legislative/core policy level, and, to a much lesser degree, at the paradigm level. Certainly, change does occur in the latter two. For example, the 1996 Port Arthur massacre in Tasmania in 1996 led to new gun control legislation in Australia (Reynolds 1997). In the 1970s, the world economic crisis ushered in a shift to the free market right in most liberal democracies throughout the western world (see, for example, Prasad 2006), while the 2008 global financial crisis has brought a revival of Keynesian-type thinking and public sector ownership as a means of avoiding and/or coming out of recession. I would argue that, particularly in the paradigm case, these are the exceptions that prove the rule. Change and learning from failure tends to be fairly mundane and low-level, despite the political rhetoric of 'lessons to be learned' that typically emerges after crises and disasters. Not everyone would agree. Birkland (1997, 2007), in his studies of the agenda-setting implications of disasters, argues that public expectations after disaster are so high that it is difficult for policy-makers not to engage in reform and learning. Yet, most studies of post-crisis reform (for example, Stanley and Manthorpe 2004; Boin *et al.* 2008) suggest that change tends not to be as profound as we might think. There are far more studies of lower-level symbolic and organizational change after crisis. Examples include:

- the Jerusalem banquet hall collapse in 2001 – which produced an inquiry lasting over two years, but with no changes in building construction standards (Schwartz and McConnell 2009)
- the 1986 Space Shuttle Challenger disaster – which produced a number of procedural and design 'fixes', rather than cultural change within NASA or broader changes in government funding regimes (Boin 2008).

Reasons for impediments to change and learning include blame games as barriers to reform, vested interests resistant to change, format of inquiries and membership steered down particular routes, complex systems of governance generating policy overlap and complexity that is difficult to change (see Drennan and McConnell 2007). The Virginia Tech shootings exemplify. The power of the National Rifle Association in the US has survived the shock and pressure from many school shootings in the US, such as those at Columbine High School (1999) and Virginia Tech (2007). Reform has tended to be at the secondary level (such as better systems of detecting students at risk) and only occasional refinements of existing legislation, without compromising the broader constitutional right to bear arms or the power of the National Rifle Association.

Second, policy continuity is generally more pervasive than policy change, and policy continuity equates broadly with reinforcing, adapting and 'improving' on existing policy trajectories. Of course, there are exceptions such as 'big ticket' party election manifesto issues, and the existence of small, cumulative changes over time. In essence, however, the vast bulk of public policy theories point to change being through small steps. This applies to, among others, bounded rationality, incrementalism, the policy cycle, policy inheritance, new institutionalism, and the advocacy coalition framework. They differ on the reasons for policy change being gradual. Lindblom (1965), for example, argues that incremental bargaining is the most politically viable means of bringing about change. Rose (1990) argues the policy-making choice is at the margins, and is dominated by the inheritance of the past. Nevertheless, they all empha-size the overwhelming importance of continuity. They point towards public policy as principally a process of refining and building on 'what works' (from the point of view of dominant coalitions, political viability, policy-makers' self-interest or whatever our view of the policy process).

Let us now couch this argument about learning tending to be from successes rather than failures in terms of the three aspects of policy that have formed the basis for the analysis in this book: process, programmes and politics.

Process success, as discussed in Chapters 2 and 3, is rooted in government producing a sustainable coalition of interests in order to preserve its broad goals and instruments in 'legitimate' policy, although the caveat is always necessary that framing such outcomes as 'success' depends on whether one identifies with the government's goals. To relate this to the issue of learning principally from success rather than failure, it can be argued that any government tends to produce policies in roughly the same way from day to day, month to month and even year to year. The issue of country-specific policy styles aside (see Richardson 1982), individual policy sectors tend to have their own process values, with reforms being produced after similar type process, whether it be consultation exercises with stakeholders or examination of policy choices. German banking policy, for example, has relied heavily on a consultative and informal policy style (Busch 2008), while policy-making surrounding school spending and social welfare in France conforms to a 'hill climbing model' similar to incrementalism, rather than exhaustive searching for solutions (Le Maux 2009).

Programme success is a more-or-less interrupted achievement of what gov-ernment set out to achieve, and an absence of performance failures of any significance. Again, the qualifier is necessary that not everyone will agree on government goals or how to assess and interpret policy outcomes, and so the contestability of 'success' is inescapable. This point aside, it can be argued that complex programme outcomes tend to be evaluated broadly as successes, setting the agenda for policy refinement and reform that maintains the same balance of policy instruments. As Chapter 7 indicates, a tight grip is the dominant form of policy evaluation, and tight-grip strategies tend to reinforce existing programme pathways. For example, the aftermath of the 1998 Sydney water contamination crisis set in motion reform processes, dominated by the ongoing agenda of a neo-liberal governance framework and its accompanying rationale – a 'successful' trajectory, as far as the conservative coalition government was concerned (Sheil 2000; McConnell 2008).

Political success involves enhancing the electoral prospects of government, sustaining its capacity to govern, as well as sustaining its broad values and direction. Once again, the 'realistic' definition of success in this book recognizes that multiple interpretations will always exist and, hence, all of these characteristics of political success might be met with dismay from some quarters. Regardless, the issue of the dominance of learning from successes applies just as much to politics as it does to programmes and process. Put crudely, governments are more liable to keep forging ahead with their vision and trajectory, unless there is a compelling reason to do otherwise. Of course, change and learning can be a product of failure, but they are not part of day-to-day politics. Governments will generally try their utmost to hold onto the vision and pathways they cherish.

Can we predict policy success?

In some industries, prediction is crucial. Wind tunnels and computer modelling are used to test aerodynamics of new aeroplanes, and drugs are subject to intensive human and animal testing. Success of many products requires a substantial amount of upfront investment. In the natural sciences such as biology and chemistry, hypothesis testing forms the basis of prediction.

One might expect that public policy-makers would seek the same level of rigour when formulating and introducing new policies. Yet, we are dealing here with the social sciences and radically different views on whether the discipline, including public policy, is amenable to modelling. In terms of whether or not it is possible to predict policy success, three different positions can be distilled from a broad range of literature.

An argument: prediction is desirable and feasible

Some social science perspectives, particularly rational choice theory and behaviouralism, hold positivist assumptions that the world can be quantified and understood to the point that prediction is possible because we have grasped the 'present' and the dynamics that drive policy choices (utility maximization, in the case of rational choice theory; observed regularities, in the case of behaviouralism). More generally, prediction is often considered a necessary condition for 'theory'. According to Brady (1993: 194), 'unless we [political science], as a profession, can offer clear theories of how elections, institutions, and policy are connected and deduce predictions from these stories, we shall simply be telling ad hoc stories'.

Free-market icon Milton Friedman also argued that a theory should be judged by 'whether the theory works, which means whether it yields sufficiently accurate predictions' (Friedman 1953: 15). In more applied terms, one strand of policy analysis places forecasting and use of tools such as time-series analysis and linear trend estimation as a crucial activity that increases the chances of policy success and reduces the chances of failure (see Dunn 2004). In the mid-1960s, with an emphasis in the US on long-term planning and the use of mainframe computing, the RAND Corporation developed the Delphi forecasting technique. The logic is that success in the future can be ascertained by using appropriate techniques in the present. One policy area where modelling is particularly prevalent is the macro-economy, in order to inform government on the likely impact of policies such as tax reforms and interest rate adjustments. However, prediction also takes place in fields such as transport (new road usage), health care (demand for services at peak times) and welfare benefits (take-up rate of a new benefit).

Some non-positivist strands within political science are also sympathetic to prediction. From different parts of the political spectrum, we find books and articles devoted to looming failures, for example *Water: The Looming Crisis in India* (Ray 2008) and *Brave New World of Health Care: What Every American Needs to Know about Our Impending Health Care Crisis* (Lamm 2003). One of the most controversial is Samuel P. Huntington's (1997) *The Clash of Civilizations and the Remaking of World Order*, with its thesis that cultural conflicts will dominate global politics, rather than economic or ideological ones. Some also predict success. On a broad political level, Daniel Bell's (1960) *The End of Ideology: On the Exhaustion of Political Ideas in the Fifties* and Frances Fukuyama's (1992) *The End of History and the Last Man* are from the same mould. They amount to arguments that 'political' success in the future is virtually guaranteed, because major ideological conflicts have dissipated and the liberal democratic paradigm has dominated. On a programmatic level, politicians are prone to prediction success, whether it be defeating terrorists, winning wars, improving health care, or reducing homelessness.

An argument: prediction is foolish and impossible

Social science traditions such as new institutionalism and particularly constructivism argue that the political world cannot be reduced simply to immutable facts. It is highly complex and subject to multiple interpretations.

Hence, it is not amenable to modelling in laboratory conditions or projecting into the future based on our experiences. As Pawson (2006: 167) argues:

> one must be modest in reflecting faithfully the limited authority of evidence itself. Good science is not futurology: we should always be humble about predicting the path ahead of what we know about the one already trodden.

There are many more specific reasons, according to such arguments, why prediction is not possible. For example, the implementation literature reveals that one of the many reasons for implementation is the existence of unforeseen shocks to knock a programme off course (Mazmanian and Sabatier 1989; Wanna 2007; Hill and Hupe 2009). The crisis and disaster literature reinforces this argument. The world is never free from unforeseen and disastrous episodes. Indeed, if we think about two of the biggest events to shock the western world in recent times (the 9/11 attacks and the global financial crisis), political science was unable to predict either one. Furthermore, it is not possible to eliminate policy risks in a plural and contingent world (Shapiro and Bedi 2007a, 2007b). Unexpected political resistance and dramatic events might be just around the corner. As Machiavelli (1961: 123) argued:

> no government should ever imagine that it can adopt a safe course of action; rather, it should regard all possible courses of action as risky. This is the way things are: whenever one tries to escape one danger one runs into another.

More generally, this position would suggest that politics is often subject to intangible phenomenon (such as political moods and turning points), and the vagaries of complex interactions of forces range from decision-maker psychology to global market forces means that it is not possible to predict the future.

An argument: we cannot predict but we can have foresight

This perspective takes its cue from by Peter Schwartz (1996) in his book *The Art of the Long View: Planning for the Future in an Uncertain World*. In essence, it suggests that we cannot predict the future, but we can, at least, engage in scenario building and dialogue in order to produce 'better' public policy decisions. As Ringland (2002: 256) argues, in her book on scenario planning in public policy, scenarios are a type of 'sixth sense'.

Many public policy scholars and advocates would not necessarily subscribe specifically to this view, but they would hold some similarities in arguing that if we engage in good practice in decision-making, then we can be much more confident that successful public policy can be produced. The policy design literature typifies (Schneider and Ingram 1997), as does that on public deliberation (Gutmann and Thompson 2004; Gastil 2008). Both would argue that, if we involve a wide range of interests in decision-making, there is a high chance that the outcome will be 'good' policy; that is, legitimate, with commitments to implementation and most potential implementation traps dealt with in advance.

Striking a balance

Overall, we have three broad positions. Which, if any, has the greatest validity? In the interests of stimulating debate on the issue, I would suggest that the most applicable is a variation on the 'long view' argument. We know enough about the present to make educated, and even instinctive, judgements about what will 'work' (and what will not), although we should not get carried away and turn our judgements into predictions. Three rationales can be put forward for adopting such a position.

First, we should accept that our ability to engage in accurate prediction is disproved by the realities of public policy. As we know from this book, all the examples of failure ranging from foot and mouth disease in the UK to Hurricane Katrina in the US, policies do have elements of failure that have gone against the interests and assumptions of policy-makers. Of course, one might argue that the problem here is *not* policy failure but, rather, the inability of policy-makers to predict that a policy was liable to fail and, hence, they should have exercised better judgement in their decision-making. However, I would argue that, even with the best will in the world, prediction in all instances is impossible. The political world will always be the subject to the vagaries of unforeseen events (Shapiro and Bedi 2007b).

Second, we can accept the foregoing argument without taking the logic to its extreme. The political world is not a haphazard mix of policy and dynamic contexts in which 'anything can happen'. Political scientists are very good at identifying patterns of regularity, whether it is path dependency, rational self-interest, or dominant groups/networks/coalitions. Of course, they disagree about the nature of the continuity but, nevertheless, a common denominator is the identification of forces at work, which tend to explain (largely) continuity and (to a lesser extent) change.

Third, if we accept that contingencies are important, but so also are patterns of regularity, we need only reflect on the argument in Chapter 6. One of its main contentions is that some strategies for policy success might be more or less risky in terms of their ability to produce policy success. Of crucial importance is context, in terms of facilitating and/or being a barrier to success. Taking the argument further, it can be suggested that while we cannot predict success, or be aware of every 'shock' that might happen, we can at least be aware that some policies are riskier than others, depending on factors such as degree of issue politicization, extent of political opposition and degree of urgency. Risk assessments are informed judgements, rather than utter guesswork or concrete prediction. As Althaus (2008) demonstrates, in her study of political risk, 'gut instinct' is the principle means by which policy-makers assess risk. We cannot predict the future, but we can at least use our intuition to map out one or more plausible scenarios of whether policy options might succeed or fail.

Conclusion

In this chapter, we have been able to locate the nature of policy success within arguments and debates about societal trajectories and tendencies. The issues should culminate in a greater understanding of the complex phenomenon of policy success. It would be perfectly acceptable to content ourselves now with the journey we have taken and stop with satisfaction. However, the analysis has raised deeper questions about how we understand public policy and the appropriateness of existing models of policy analysis. Hence, the discussion and argument needs to take one final leap. The Conclusion will argue that we need to rethink our understanding of public policy and its dynamics.

Conclusion: Rethinking Public Policy and Shining a Light in Dark Corners

I have taught many officials and public/civil servants over the past twenty years or so, and a regular message in my conversations with them is that the political world often seems to be chaotic and irrational, or dominated by 'quick fixes' and policies that are incapable of dealing effectively with the problem, despite the upbeat talk of their political masters. The more I developed the policy success heuristic, the more convinced I became that it is the key to unravelling many aspects of real politik that public policy theories rarely, or even never, write about. Indeed, in doing so, the success heuristic can also add value to virtually any broader policy analysis perspective.

Such bold statements require more detailed exposition. Hence, in this final chapter I do so, and suggest than we need to rethink our understanding of the nature and trajectory of public policy-making. First, the chapter outlines briefly the main contemporary conceptual models of policy processes and puts forward some reasons why they remain, for many analysts, attractive lenses through which to view the world of public policy, as well as some reasons why they can be found wanting. Second, it briefly recaps the main aspects of a policy success heuristic, before examining in detail the ways in which it shines a light into the dark corners of public policy. This refers to aspects of public policy such as hidden agendas, placebo policies and 'policy on the hoof', which are much talked about but rarely examined in academic terms. Finally, it uses these understandings to turn the spotlight back on established theories and puts forward some reasons why a policy success heuristic should be given serious consideration, as both a supplement to and a direct alternative to established models of the policy process. Sharing some ground with Weiss (1972, 1988) and her study of policy evaluation, it brings an element of realpolitik back into our analysis of public policy. It certainly does not reject theory. Rather, it is based on a theoretical framework that can help explain policy-making in a more grounded way than some of the more abstract models of the policy process than have found favour over the past few decades.

Contemporary models of the policy process: a brief summary

Since the early 1950s, political science has come a long way in producing models that genuinely aid our understanding of policy-making (deLeon 1988; John 1998; Howlett *et al.* 2009). No longer do we have to rely on what is now known as the 'old institutionalism', with its traditional texts pointing to formal rules and constitutions as the guide to opening up the 'black box' of policy-making. The main contemporary models are well-known in academic circles, and so I summarize them here only briefly, but want to go into further detail about why they are attractive propositions – yet, propositions that still cannot capture much of the realities of public policy. There is overlap between some of the models, but there is also sufficient differentiation for us to say that they each have something distinctive to offer analysts of public policy.

Policy cycle

With its origins in Lasswell (1956) and his attempt to produce a policy science of democracy where political science becomes harnessed for the greater good (see Farr *et al.* 2006), the policy cycle is probably the simplest and most immediately accessible model of the policy process. It begins from the assumption that public policies are produced through a sequence of processes. There are many variants, and different texts will produce different assumptions about what constitutes a stage. However, the nearest to a default position is that outlined by Howlett *et al.* (2009). They suggest five stages in the policy cycle:

1. agenda setting – process by which problems come to the attention of government;
2. policy formulation – process of formulating and appraising different options and consulting relevant interests;
3. decision-taking – the adoption of a particular course of action;
4. implementation – the process of putting policies into practice;
5. evaluation – the monitoring of policy outcomes in order to refine and improve policies.

One of the ongoing attractions of the model for many seeking to understand policy processes is that it captures much of the official rhetoric surrounding public policies. Ministers and government officials often make statements such as:

*   'we are aware there is a problem and we are currently exploring options'
*   'we are examining the feasibility of different policy options and we will consult in due course'

- 'no decision has yet be made. There is still a process of scrutiny and discussion to take place'.

Indeed, if any policy analysis model were to represent the public rhetoric of governments, it is likely that it would be the policy cycle. It implies that policy-making is 'above' politics and is conducted in a progressive and considered manner, with the ultimate goal of taking the decision that best accords with the public interest. However, the model has been much criticized for many reasons, including ignoring the role of power in shaping policy process, the coexistence of many stages at the same time, the fact that many decision are often taken in advance of consultation, and the inability of the model to cope with complex systems of multiple decisions rather than simply one decision (see, for example, Jann and Wegrich 2007; Sabatier 2007). Nevertheless, the policy cycle persists as a model, because it is an easy first route into understanding policy processes, as well as the nearest we have to the public face of public policies.

Yet, beyond the conventional critiques of the policy cycle, there are other issues that it does not address. For example, what happens when a government 'does nothing' in order to achieve a particular outcome. An example might be deciding not to intervene in an industrial dispute because it wants the matter to be resolved by an employer and trade unions. Such inaction would certainly constitute public policy by many definitions of same (see, for example, Dye 2005), but it is not so easy to think about it in policy cycle terms, because is not a programme with resources attached to it that can then be put into practice and formally evaluated. Somehow, we need a model that adequately captures realities such as 'inaction', but still has appeal because it captures the rhetoric of governments.

Rational choice

Rational choice has its roots in an economic understanding of the world. It takes many key assumptions of economics (particularly of the libertarian variety) and applies them to politics. Key figures have studied different aspects of political life; for example, Downs (1957) on elections and parties, Buchanan and Tullock (1962) on voters and parties, Niskanen (1971) on bureaucracy. The common theme at the heart of rational choice (sometimes known as 'public choice theory') is that the political world is driven by self-interest (Hindmoor 2006). Self-interest is considered a deductive 'fact', and so the purpose of research is to examine the way in which self-interest is at play in different contexts. Midwinter describes the central assumptions thus:

> The public choice approach has developed an economic model of politics which assumes that voters, politicians and bureaucrats engage

in maximizing behaviour in the pursuit of their own self-interest. Voters seek to maximize their consumption of public goods at minimal costs, politicians to maximize votes, and bureaucrats to maximize budgets.

(Midwinter 1989: 50)

The enduring appeal of rational choice is that it places at stage centre what many people consider to be the driving force for those engaging in politics: self-interest. It closely connects with writings and assumptions that politics is corrupt, or that there is a disconnect with citizens, or that it lacks legitimacy. Yet, for all its power and a plethora of case studies 'proving' its worth, it is surprisingly quiet on many of the intricacies and multiple goals of policy-making. Most policy studies are dominated by discussion of preference ranking in order to achieve a particular outcome but, as this book has shown, policy-makers might have many different process, programme and political goals that they need to juggle. In essence, therefore, rational choice has not 'joined the dots' and an approach is needed that does so.

New institutionalism

New institutionalism is a relatively recent addition to the conceptual toolkit of policy studies. It emerged incrementally from the mid-1980s onwards (see March and Olsen 1984) as a challenge to rational choice and behaviouralist approaches to politics. It has developed many variations. Peters (2005) suggests at least seven, including historical institutionalism, sociological institutionalism, rational choice institutionalism and sociological institutionalism. Despite such diversity, the common thread is the assumption that we can obtain greater analytical leverage if we begin with institutions, rather than actors or groups. Institutions provide forums for structuring and resolving debates. In contrast to the old institutionalism and its focus on formal rules, the new institutionalism examines the role of power and values. One of the most interesting features of the new institutionalist approach, especially the historical version, is its focus on the past as a prime shaper of the future. Public policy decisions are 'path dependent', in the sense that new decisions are shaped and constrained by increasing returns generated by the costs of continuing with existing trajectories and the high costs of alternative trajectories (Pierson 2000).

New institutionalism has substantial appeal to many. Its emphasis on the constraints of the path and the fact that policy decisions do not start from a blank slate appeals to many scholars who find substantial continuity within policy sectors, regardless of election promises or adversary politics. However, many of its applications are in the field of international political economy (for example, Blythe 2002; Thelen 2004), rather than public policy and policy analysis. Therefore, there are few studies taking a new institutional approach that would consider, for example, the role of policy evaluations in helping maintaining continuity, or the role of policies in maintaining governance continuity, precisely because they *do not* fix problems. Once more, a new perspective is needed to help fill a gap in our understanding.

Groups and coalitions

Studying the role of interest groups in policy processes has a long history (see Baumgartner and Leech 1998). The approach was one of the first to question the conventional wisdom of constitutions, because they indicate that power resides outside government and its relationship with citizens *per se*. Debates began seriously in the US in the 1950s cold war climate of the post-war period, the majority with normative implications that group influence was a manifestation of political pluralism (see particularly Truman 1951; Hunter 1953; Dahl 1961). Discussion shifted to the extent that some analysts viewed groups as being more important than legislatures in the policy-making process (Richardson and Jordan 1979), and then to broader assumptions that coalitions of interests are the primary means of understanding the shaping of public policies (Sabatier and Jenkins-Smith 1993; Baumgartner and Jones 2009).

The modern appeal of such models has waned slightly with the rise of new institutionalism, but a strong influence remains. The multitude of groups lobbying for policy influence, many with massive financial backing and, potentially, veto power over government policy, make it an attractive policy analysis position. Yet, for all the persuasive powers of group/coalition perspectives, they tend to study public policy-making from the outside in. In other words, they do not deal in depth with why policy-makers would want to listen to some groups more than others, apart from the fact that they can provide policy-related information to inform decision-making and are strategically placed to help implement policies. Such issues on their own are not to be dismissed, but the groups/coalition approach does not go far enough in identifying the strategic benefits to policy-makers of producing policies that (broadly) enshrine the values and preferred policy instruments of interest coalitions.

Socio-economic models

Put crudely, socio-economic models argue that public policies are driven by 'big business'. There have been many variations down the years, from C. Wright Mills (1956) and his writings on the power elite in US society, to Charles Lindblom (1977) and his views on democratic pluralism with a big business bias, and the marxist works of Miliband (1973) and Poulantzas (1973) on the role of the ruling classes. The role of the socio-economic model is particularly influential in state theory (see, for example, Block 1990; Jessop 2002), but less so in the contemporary world of public policy. The reasons for this relative decline are debatable, and might include anything from Marxism having gone out of favour since the collapse of the Soviet Union, to the reality that many socio-economic analyses of public policy-making tend not to deal with micro-level policy factors. This latter issue is one where a policy success framework can help flesh out the role of socio-economic power in shaping public policy.

The policy success heuristic: a summary

Policy success straddles objective facts and interpretations. Governments might achieve goals, but not everyone would perceive 'successes' because they do not support those goals and/or the values underpinning them. Chapter 2 explores such issues in detail, and produces what I consider to be a realistic and pragmatic definition of success. Hence:

> A policy is successful insofar as it achieves the goals that proponents set out to achieve. However, only those supportive of the original goals are liable to perceive, with satisfaction, a policy success. Opponents are likely to perceive failure, regardless of outcomes, because they did not support the original goals.

Before taking the argument further, we need to contend with the nature of 'policy'. Therefore, if public policy accords broadly with what government chooses to do and not to do, the governments 'do' many things. A useful way of dividing up what government does is: produce policies (process), put them into practice (programmes) and govern, including the contestation of periodic elections (politics). The corollary is that government might 'succeed' in each of these aspects of policy. Hence, policy success can be sub-divided into:

Process success: preservation of government's policy goals and instruments, having done so with constitutional/quasi-constitutional legitimacy, with the support of a sustainable coalition of interests behind it and, in some instances, symbolizing innovation and influence.

Programme success: The deployment of policy instruments that result in meeting objectives, achieving desired outcomes, creating benefit for intended groups/interests and meeting criteria that are valued in the relevant policy domain.

Political success: Enhancing electoral prospects or the reputation of government and leaders, sustaining government's capacity to govern through agenda management, and sustaining the broad values and direction of government.

Commonsense and the real world of public policies make us aware the policies might not achieve such goals; they might fail. Hence, at the broad policy level, success is mirrored by policy failure:

> A policy fails insofar as it does not achieve the goals that proponents set out to achieve. Those supportive of the original goals are liable to perceive, with regret, a policy failure. Opponents are also likely to perceive failures, with satisfaction, because they did not support the original goals.

Such failures, as Chapter 4 argued, can be found in the process, programme and political realms of policy. For example, a government might fail to get its preferred policy option passed through a legislature. Or if it is passed, the programme might fail to do what was intended and could wreak immense damage on the reputation of government.

In reality, however, most policies fall somewhere between the extremes of unblemished success and abysmal failure. They might exhibit complex mixes of successes, failures and shortfalls. Whereas many studies have hitherto made loose reference to 'partial successes', 'mixed successes' and more, this book has adopted a more systematic approach and produced a spectrum, from success to failure, with specific categories along the various points in between. Therefore, at the broad policy level (leaving aside the process, programme and political dimensions for a moment), we may have:

> *Durable success*: Policies that fall short of their aims to small or modest degrees. However, they tend to be quite resilient, relative to the other categories towards the failure end of the spectrum, because of lack of significant space for contestation over performance and decision-making, and fairly low or manageable levels of controversy.

> *Conflicted success*: Policies that display quite substantial departures from original goals and/or because the issue itself is intrinsically controversial. Success is heavily contested between supporters and opponents as a consequence of the political space opened up.

> *Precarious success*: Policies operating on the edge of failure. There are major shortfalls or deviations from original goals (although there might be a few minor successes somewhere within), to the point that there are high-profile and bitter conflicts over the future of the policy.

As detailed in Chapter 3, each of these categories has its own sub-variants in the process, programme and political dimensions of policy. Importantly, placing case study characteristics on points of the success–failure spectrum might differ in each of these three spheres. This point will prove crucial shortly, because it paves the way for enhancing our understanding of many of the contradictions and seeming illogicalities of public policies.

Policy-makers will typically strive for success, but success in one realm might mean sacrificing success in another. Hence, policy-making is a risky business.

For example, as argued in Chapter 6, a policy-maker might succeed in pushing an unpopular bill through the legislative process, but generate the risks of pushing the programme towards failure. The reason is that the bill did not receive a level of scrutiny that would have ironed out implementation problems. This, in turn, can produce failure-inclined political outcomes. Hence, the initial 'quick fix' is at risk of rebounding at a later stage on government's capacity to steer its agenda down particular pathways. At times, policy-makers might be prepared to take such risks on the assumption that they will deal with any difficulties at a later stage.

Policy success: shining a spotlight in the dark corners of public policy

A policy success heuristic illuminates many features of public policy that have been given scant attention in the literature and, indeed, are virtually absent in the main models of public policy. Let us consider a number of such areas.

Good politics but bad policy

The phrase 'good politics but bad policy' is commonplace along journalists and political commentators, but the phenomenon it refers to has rarely been given serious consideration by scholars of policy analysis. The policy success heuristic can accommodate this phenomenon with ease, because it recognizes that policy-makers can have multiple goals, some of which might be met while others are not. Indeed, policy-makers might not actually expect some goals to be met, because some goals have been sacrificed to make way for the attainment of others.

In the language of this book, 'good politics but bad policy' refers to successful politics but unsuccessful programmes. The starting point for comprehending this vital issue rests with an important duality. Policy programmes are not simple bundles of instruments to regulate, allocate, redistribute and so on. They also have a range of symbolic impacts, such as leadership strength, decisiveness, determination, compassion and impartiality, or (if things do not go well) weakness, indecisiveness, floundering, lack of compassion and bias. Symbolism is at the heart of politics (Edelman 1964, 1977; Stone 2002). Therefore, programmes are not just agenda-setters in the sense that they create pathways of instruments to deal with problems, they are also agenda-setters because of the impressions created by the intervention (or non-intervention), its timing and its style. Therefore, the programmatic aspect of policy can have political repercussions in:

- assisting/damaging electoral prospects and reputations

- creating the impression of tackling/not tackling a problem
- indicating government's agenda priorities and intended direction for the future.

One corollary is that policy can serve political functions, yet be weak in programmatic terms. The Anglo-French *Concorde* is one such example. In the 1960s, a joint British and French initiative to design and build a supersonic aircraft cultivated political success by creating a sense of cooperation and national pride at a time when Britain was looking towards Europe while its Commonwealth powers were declining. However, in programme terms, it was a conflicted or even a precarious success, because of massive cost overruns and poor sales (Hall 1982).

In sum, there are many public policy problems where political pay-offs for government are far greater than programmatic pay-offs. Many programmes simply do not live up to the political rhetoric that surrounds them. George W. Bush's 'No Child Left Behind' legislation to improve the learning of students, regardless of race or class, has generated scores of critical studies, including some that suggest that inequality in the classroom has become worse, because the policy exacerbates racial, ethnic and economic inequalities (Hursh 2007). In the words of Edelman (1977: 146) this is an example of 'the political viability of unsuccessful policies', whereby policy action and symbolic reassurance are pivotal in masking underlying inequalities and the harsh realities of policies 'on the ground'. Edelman's argument neatly encapsulates one of the key contradictions of public policy. Political success can thrive, despite poorly performing policies. The policy success heuristic can help explain what might be an otherwise puzzling phenomenon.

Symbolic/placebo policies

A related topic is policies that give the appearance of dealing with a problem, but in reality will do little or nothing. A few scholars have written about the phenomenon (for example, see Stringer and Richardson 1979; Gustafson 1983), but none locate it within a wider policy analysis framework.

Placebo drugs have little or no medicinal qualities, but can nevertheless improve a patient's response to illness, because they perceive it to be a 'real' drug. Similarly, symbolic policies are also 'feel good' policies', but do not contain the ingredients that are necessary to tackle the problem, other than in a superficial or marginal way. They are 'political successes', because they help ease the business of governing by making problems manageable, and giving the impression of government competence and capacities to tackle problems, but the specific programmes themselves are likely to do little to address deep causal factors of the problem at hand.

All policies have a symbolic dimension because, by virtue of having put particular measures in place, they create the impression of government action (or even inaction) to deal with a problem. Therefore, in the strictest sense, all policies are 'symbolic policies'. Yet, the usage of the term here is narrower, because it deals with programmes with particularly high symbolic value, attempting to tackle particularly complex issues that have no clear solutions. These refer to 'wicked issues' such as drug abuse and homelessness, where problems are immensely complex and there is an absence of definitive solutions (Head and Alford 2008). There is a strong placebo or symbolic aspect to many of the ensuing policy responses such as public information campaigns, *ad hoc* programmes or regulatory reforms, but they cannot hope to offer a clear solution to problems rooted in almost overwhelming complexity (in the case of drugs, everything from individual psychologies and peer influences, to urban deprivation and the power of international drug cartels). Many such responses are of symbolic value, because they give the impression of active and positive intervention. Indeed, they often perform better in terms of measures of political success, than they do in measures of programme success. Laufer (2003), in her study of France's equal employment policies, argues that the symbolic value of a comprehensive policy framework to reduce gender inequalities has been strong but, because of a lack of support from relevant actors in both the labour and management communities, in programme terms it has been weak.

A policy success heuristic recognizes that the value for policy-makers of many policies is not what they do in programme terms, but what they *appear* to do. Their success is in the political sphere, rather than the programme sphere.

Quick fixes

We all know the term 'quick fix', with its implication that a short-term and swiftly produced solution stores up problems for the future. The same applies in policy terms. A Google search for 'quick fix' and 'policy' found the terms being applied to policies as diverse as global warming, copyright reform, bank lending, trade policy and tunnel construction. The policy success heuristic can help us think more holistically about these phenomena.

Policy-makers might need to deal with particularly difficult policy problems in times that are typical of the normal rhythms of policy-making, or when the pace of decision-making is increased in crisis and disastrous situations. In the later cases, policy frameworks are shattered by events, and something needs to be done to restore public confidence and deal with acute problems ('t Hart 1993). In both sets of circumstances, a 'quick fix' process success, resulting in policy-makers obtaining approval for legislation or policy decisions, might simply store-up vulnerabilities for programme and political outcomes that lean towards the failure end of the spectrum.

A good example is the rapid creation in the US of the Department of Homeland Security as a response to the 9/11 attacks. In process terms, it was a success (most realistically, a durable success), because the government achieved its aim of introducing legislation to conduct the largest reorganization in the history of US public service. However, in programmatic terms it is widely regarded as tilting heavily towards the failure end of the spectrum (most probably, a conflicted success) being beset by numerous problems because of the disruption, complexity and lack of coherence that it creates (May *et al.* 2009). Process success and programme success do not always go hand in hand. Indeed, the 'fix' of short-term process success can store up vulnerabilities for programme and political failure.

Policy on the hoof

A Google search for this term yielded such results as 'Should Gordon Brown Stop Making Policy on the Hoof?', 'Government Making up Tax Policy on the Hoof' and 'The Wrong Moment to Make Policy in the Hoof'. The term refers to a phenomenon that implies that public policy decisions were taken quickly and without proper thought for the consequences. Another way of saying this is that the policy was produced without a comprehensively 'rational' appraisal of all available policy options and their likely impact. Those with an interest in public policy know that such rationality rarely operates, for reasons ranging from political incrementalism to path dependency. Nevertheless, the term refers not to a 'norm' but, rather, to a type of policy-making tied to a particular policy-making episode that it seems is ill-considered. Indeed, the term 'policy on the hoof' seems nothing but derogatory. Policy made 'on the hoof' appears to have no redeeming qualities. Yet, is this the case? I would argue otherwise. Why would any policy-maker seek to do something with zero purpose? They answer is they would not. Doing something, even under difficult circumstances, is an attempt to achieve success in one form of another. A hypothetical example will illustrate.

Imagine the situation where a government transport minister receives a phone call saying that a leading newspaper is about to run a story revealing that a new government subsidy that helps employees buy bicycles so they can cycle to work and reduce the demand on public transport is backfiring because of corrupt practices. Many people are buying bicycles for family members – not for themselves; suppliers are inflating prices in order to maximize their revenues, and some people are selling their subsidy to others. The minister appears to panic and decides to terminate the policy forthwith. He says that an investigation will be conducted, and proposals for a new and improved scheme will emerge at some time in the future.

This example might well be open to accusations of policy 'on the hoof', because there was not time to think through the repercussions of abandoning the scheme, even for the short term. However, if we think about this example through the lens of the policy success heuristic, it takes on a different perspective. The minister might have been attempting to achieve:

Political success: That is, keeping his or her his reputation intact by being swift and decisive, and trying to ensure that a problem was quickly defused in order not to distract from the government's broader agenda and trajectory.

Programme success: That is, he or she feels that, under the circumstances, the government's dealing with the problem of lack of people cycling to work is best left to the decision of individuals (a voluntary policy instrument), rather than government subsidy (a 'treasure' policy instrument) (see Hood and Margetts 2007 on the tools of government). In terms of definitions of public policy that are similar to those of Dye (2005), who argues that public policy includes decisions not to act, the minister's view is likely to be that policy success is best served by choosing *not* to have a programme at all (at least, for the moment), rather than have a 'bad' one.

When viewed in this way, policies conducted 'on the hoof' have an element of rationality to them, in that they seek to achieve particular goals, even if we think they are misguided or downright stupid in doing so.

Hidden agendas

The accusation that policy-makers have a 'hidden agenda' behind their public commitments to a particular aspect of process, programmes or politics is surprisingly common, despite the fact that policy-makers have made no direct attempt to tackle the topic. A Google search revealed many examples of such accusations, including hidden agendas behind tax cuts, coal nationalization, mathematics education policy, mental health policy, privatization of public pensions, reform of immigration policy and minimum wage provision. At the time of writing in late 2009, a high-profile example is the accusation that the Scottish government and the UK government conspired to secure the release of convicted Lockerbie bomber Abdel Baset al-Megrahi, because doing would help improve trade relations with Libya.

A policy success heuristic provides a framework for helping us understand what might be 'hidden'. Specifically, what might be hidden from view are attempts to attain aspects of success in one or more of the three spheres of policy; that is, processes, programmes and politics. As argued in previous chapters, policy-makers often make trade-offs, prioritizing their goals, seeking success in some aspects of policies but not others. Symbolic policies are one example where 'successful politics' takes priority over 'successful programmes'. Some hypothetical examples are:

Process and politics: A consultation process masking the fact that the decision has already been taken. Therefore, the hidden process agendas are: that the government is seeking to preserve its policy goals and preferred policy instruments; and by consulting, it is obtaining legitimacy in doing so. The hidden political agendas are: that the consultation exercise is helping sustain government's capacity to govern by filtering out dissent from the policy-formation process; and helping sustain the broad direction in which government policy is headed.

Programmes and politics: An income tax decrease just prior to an election can have the hidden political agenda of seeking to enhance government's electoral prospects.

Hidden agendas are attempts by policy-makers to hide the fact that they want to succeed in something, but cannot legitimately say so for fear of breaching constitutional guidelines and/or appearing not to act in the public interest.

The policy success heuristic: adding value to established policy theories

The analysis above points to numerous ways in which a policy success heuristic can help us understand many public policy phenomena that lurk in the dark corners and on the fringes of academic policy analysis. Most of us know they exist, and would accept their status as credible policy phenomena (albeit difficult to research) but, to date, they tend to remain part of the chatter of journalists, academics and policy-actors. Yet, a policy success heuristic is of value beyond such realms. It has the potential to add value to almost all the main policy models. The only exception is the policy cycle. Its simplicity, and rational assumptions about the driving forces and sequences of public policy-making and implementation have been criticized so widely that its utility is limited primarily to being a means of dividing up the policy process into convenient 'stages' as a precursor to deeper analysis, or as an indicator of the idealized rhetoric of policy-makers. I have deliberately avoided aligning the policy success heuristic with any particular theory. Instead, by providing a framework that allows analysts of all intellectual perspectives to think about policy success, I would argue that it has qualities that hold the potential to be incorporated into almost any perspective.

Rational choice theories are predicated on the self-interest of policy-actors. A policy success framework assumes that policy-makers will always strive for some form of success (process, programme and politics), even if this involves prioritizing some successes over others. Striving for success is not the same thing as seeking self-interest, but there is much common ground. Seeking success might involve seeking self-interest (for example, seeking re-election, obtaining approval for a preferred policy that will benefit a minister's career). As Hindmoor (2006) suggests, rational choice theorists are incredibly adaptable in the face of criticism of their assumptions. Some might want to examine preferences for success, as well as the priorities placed on them. A policy success framework helps 'join the dots' for rational choice theorists.

New institutionalism focuses particularly on continuity and path dependency. As argued in Chapter 8, a policy success heuristic leads us to the conclusion that there is substantial continuity, over time, in policy process, programmes and politics. Partly, this is because they 'succeed' in doing the job they were meant to do. Policy-making process could, in theory, be fashioned in many different ways, continually realigning balances of power and rethinking policy problems and solutions. By and large, however, they do not do so. Institutional processes, with formal rules and informal balances of power, broadly 'succeed' for those who have the capacity to shape them; that is, executives and legislatures. There is potential for new institutional theorists to think not just of the change constraints and capacities of institutional frameworks, but also the 'successes' that are brought about by the ongoing adoption of a particular institutional framework. At times, such successes might simply be placebo policies, as part of an ongoing process of managing wicked issues down the policy agenda.

Group and coalition theory places power – individually and, particularly, collectively – at the heart of many explanations of the policy process. Such a perspective is compatible with a policy success framework. For example, it can help explain why some policy sectors manage to exhibit ongoing dominance by a few key groups. Their values become enshrined in process, programme and political norms, which then perpetuate, legitimate and evaluate certain types of policies as 'successes'. In effect, frameworks for creating, achieving and perpetuating policy successes are part of the 'mobilization of bias' (Bachrach and Baratz 1970) that prevents non-dominant interests from any real influence. Of course, such dominance is not entrenched forever and, indeed, can be subject to regular perturbations (Baumgartner and Jones 2009). Additionally, a policy success framework can help explain government-group interactions by making us aware that, when policy-makers strive to 'succeed', interest group power forms part of government's success discourse, whether they are wholeheartedly or reluctantly accepting interest/coalition values and preferred policy instruments. The point here is not to validate the model as such, but to suggest that there is a place for an analysis of policy success in group and coalition perspectives of public policy.

Finally, socio-economic models, from the neo-pluralism of Lindblom to the Marxism (or neo-Marxism) of Miliband, Poulantzas, Offe and others, might find benefit in a policy success framework. Marxist theorists are often highly critical of each other and, hence, it is difficult to generalize. Put crudely, however, we can say that, if policies uphold a system of contradictory class rule (from engaging in expenditures that promote capitalist accumulation and producing policies with frameworks that legitimate liberal democracy as a particular form of capitalism), then policy successes do the same. They succeed for some interests but, in so doing, generate vulnerabilities to failure further down the line. Once again, the point is not to demonstrate the veracity or otherwise of marxist analyses. It is to suggest that a policy success heuristic might help a marxist or neo-marxist analysis to flesh out some of the policy intricacies and contradictions of state policy.

The policy success heuristic as a new model of public policy

Once we grasp the phenomenon of policy success, not only do we have a better understanding of many of the dark corners of public policy – often talked about, but rarely researched – but we also enhance our ability to explain and understand the world. Therefore, we need to rethink the way we understand public policy and give 'policy success' a pivotal role in this process. As argued, with the exception of the policy cycle, there is potential for it to be factored into any of the main public models. However, I would argue that its potential does not stop as an 'add on' to existing analytical frameworks. It is a model in its own right. It helps provide an understanding of public policy, from the forces driving it to the seeming illogicalities and contradictions that bedevil it. It has strong elements of 'political agency' in its focus on the interests and choices of policy-makers, as well as strong emphasis on 'structure', because of the contextual constraints and power frameworks within which they operate.

At worst, the policy success heuristic has more explanatory power than the policy cycle model and, at best, it can provide a more credible explanation than other models as to why particular decisions are taken. For these reasons and more, I would argue that, if we want to understand 'what is going on here?' when we examine a particular policy case, we could do much worse than think about an explanation revolving around policy-makers striving to achieve various combinations of process, programme and political success, making trade-offs between them while juggling feasibilities and risks.

Bibliography

Abraham, T. (2004) *Twenty-First Century Plague: The Story of SARS* (Aberdeen, Hong Kong: Hong Kong University Press).

Adolino, J. R. and Blake, C. H. (2001) *Comparing Public Policies: Issues and Choices in Six Industrialized Countries* (Washington, DC: CQ Press).

Alesina, A., Roubini, N. and Cohen, G. D. (1997) *Political Cycles and the Macroeconomy* (Cambridge, MA: MIT Press).

Alford, J. (2008) 'The Limits to Traditional Public Administration, or Rescuing Public Value from Misrepresentation', *Australian Journal of Public Administration*, 67: 3, 357–66.

Althaus, C. (2008) *Calculating Political Risk* (Sydney: University of New South Wales Press).

Althaus, C., Bridgman, P. and Davis, G. (2007) *The Australian Policy Handbook*, 4th edn (Crows Nest, NSW: Allan & Unwin).

Ambrose, P. (2005) 'Urban Regeneration: Who Defines the Indicators?' in Taylor, D. and S. Balloch (eds) *The Politics of Evaluation: Participation and Policy Implementation* (Bristol: Policy Press), pp. 41–56.

Amnesty International (2008) *State of Denial: Europe's Role in Rendition and Secret Detention*, (London: Amnesty International), http://www.amnestyusa.org/stoptorture/pdf/Europe%20renditions%20whole%20doc%20low%20res.pdf, accessed
22 March 2009.

Andersson, T. and Tengblad, S. (2009) 'When Complexity Meets Culture: New Public Management and the Swedish Police', *Qualitative Research in Accounting & Management*, 6: 1–2, 41–56.

Anheier, H. K. (ed.) (1999) *When Things Go Wrong: Organizational Failures and Breakdowns* (Thousand Oaks, CA: Sage).

Argyris, C. (1999) *On Organizational Learning*, 2nd edn (Oxford: Blackwell).

Arnstein, S. A. (1969) 'A Ladder of Citizen Participation', *Journal of the American Institute of Planners*, 35: 4, 216–24.

Ashworth, J. and Heyndels, B. (2005) 'Government Fragmentation and Budgetary Policy in "Good" and "Bad" Times in Flemish Municipalities', *Economics and Politics*, 17: 2, 245–63.

Bachrach, P. and Baratz, M. (1970) *Power and Poverty: Theory and Practice* (New York: Oxford University Press).

Balloch, S. and Taylor, D. (2005) 'What the Politics of Evaluation Implies' in Taylor, D. and S. Balloch (eds) *The Politics of Evaluation: Participation and Policy Implementation* (Bristol: Policy Press), pp. 249–52.

Barber, M. (2007) *Instruction to Deliver: Tony Blair, Public Services and the Challenge of Achieving Targets* (London: Politico's).

Bardach, E. (2009) *A Practical Guide for Policy Analysis: The Eightfold Path to More Effective Problem Solving*, 3rd edn (Washington, DC: CQ Press).

Barker, A. (1998) 'Canada's Party System in the 1990s', *Journal of Legislative Studies*, 4: 2, 107–27.

Barrett, W. and Collins, D. (2007) *Grand illusion: The United Story of Rudy Giuliani and 9/11* (New York: HarperCollins).

Barroso, J. M. (2007) 'We Are All New Europeans Now', Speech to Lithuanian Parliament, 29 March, http://www.europaworld.org/week302/barrosospeech15407.htm, accessed 17 July 2009:

Barry, J. (2005) *The Great Influenza: The Epic Story of the Deadliest Plague in History* (New York: Penguin).

Baumgartner, F. R. and Jones, B. D. (1993) *Agendas and Instability in American Politics* (Chicago: University of Chicago Press).

Baumgartner, F. R. and Jones, B. D. (2002) 'Positive and Negative Feedback in Politics' in Baumgartner, F. R. and Jones, B. D. (eds) *Policy Dynamics* (Chicago: University of Chicago Press), pp. 3–28.

Baumgartner, F. R. and Jones, B. D. (2009) *Agendas and Instability in American Politics*, 2nd edn (Chicago: University of Chicago Press).

Baumgartner, F. R. and Leech, B. L. (1998) *Basic Interests: The Importance of Groups in Politics and Political Science* (Princeton, NJ: Princeton University Press).

Bell, D. (1960) *The End of Ideology: On the Exhaustion of Political Ideas in the Fifties* (Glencoe, IL: Free Press).

Bevir, M. and Rhodes, R. A. W. (2003) *Interpreting British Governance* (London: Routledge).

Birkland, T. A. (1997) *After Disaster: Agenda Setting, Public Policy, and Focusing Events* (Washington DC: Georgetown University Press).

Birkland, T. A. (2007) *Lessons of Disaster: Policy Change after Catastrophic Events* (Washington, DC: Georgetown University Press).

Birrell, B., Hawthorne, L. and Richardson, S. (2006) *Evaluation of the General Skilled Migration Categories Report* (Canberra: Department for Immigration and Multicultural and Indigenous Affairs) http://www.immi.gov.au/media/publications/research/gsm-report/, accessed 2 November 2008.

Birrell, D. (2008) 'The Final Outcomes of the Review of Public Administration in Northern Ireland. Tensions and Compatibility with Devolution, Parity and Modernization', *Public Administration*, 86: 3, 779–93.

Bishop, P. and Davis, G. (2002) 'Mapping Public Participation in Policy Choices', *Australian Journal of Public Administration*, 61: 1, 14–29.

Block, F. (1990) *Revising State Theory: Essays in Politics and Postindustrialism* (Philadelphia, PA: Temple University Press).

Blythe, M. (2002) *Great Transformations: Economic Ideas and Institutional Change in the Twentieth Century* (Cambridge: Cambridge University Press).

Bogdanor, V. (ed.) (2005) *Joined-up Government* (Oxford: Oxford University Press).

Boin, A. (2008) 'Learning from Crisis: NASA and the Challenger Disaster' in Boin, A., McConnell, A. and 't Hart, P. (eds) *Governing After Crisis: The Politics of Investigation, Accountability and Learning* (Cambridge: Cambridge University Press), pp. 232–54.

Boin, A., 't Hart, P. and McConnell, A. (2009) 'Towards a Theory of Crisis Exploitation: Political and Policy Impacts of Framing Contests and Blame Games', *Journal of European Public Policy*, 16: 1, 81–106.

Boin, A., 't Hart, P., Stern, E. and Sundelius, B. (2005) *The Politics of Crisis Management: Public Leadership under Pressure* (Cambridge: Cambridge University Press).

Boin, A., McConnell, A. and 't Hart, P. (eds) (2008) *Governing after Crisis: The Politics of Investigation, Accountability and Learning* (Cambridge: Cambridge University Press).

Boin, A., McConnell, A., 't Hart, P. and Preston, T. (2010 forthcoming), 'Leadership Style, Crisis Response and Blame Management: The Case of Hurricane Katrina, *Public Administration*.

Booker, C. and North, R. (2007) *Scared to Death: From BSE to Global Warming: Why Scares Are Costing Us the Earth* (London: Continuum).

Bostrom, N. and Ćirković, M. M. (eds) (2008) *Global Catastrophic Risks* (Oxford: Oxford University Press).

Bovens, M. (2010) 'A Comment on Marsh and McConnell: Towards a Framework For Establishing Policy Success', *Public Administration*.

Bovens, M. and 't Hart, P. (1996) *Understanding Policy Fiascoes* (New Brunswick: Transaction).

Bovens, M., 't Hart, P. and Kuipers, S. (2006) 'The Politics of Policy Evaluation' in Moran, M., Rein, M., and Goodin, R. E. (eds) *The Oxford Handbook of Public Policy* (Oxford: Oxford University Press), pp. 319–35.

Bovens, M., 't Hart, P. and Peters, B. G. (1998) 'Explaining Policy Disasters in Europe: Comparisons and Reflections' in Gray, P. and 't Hart, P. (eds) *Public Policy Disasters in Western Europe* (London: Routledge), pp. 195–214.

Bovens, M., 't Hart, P. and Peters, B. G. (ed.) (2001a) *Success and Failure in Public Governance: A Comparative Analysis* (Cheltenham: Edward Elgar).

Bovens, M., 't Hart, P. and Peters, B. G. (2001b) 'Analysing Governance Success and Failure in Six European States' in Bovens, M., 't Hart, P. and Peters, B. G., (eds) *Success and Failure in Public Governance: A Comparative Analysis* (Cheltenham: Edward Elgar), pp. 12–26.

Bovens, M., 't Hart, P., Peters, B. G., Albæk, E., Busch, A., Dudley, G., Moran, M. and Richardson, J. (2001c) 'Patterns of Governance: Sectoral and National Comparisons' in Bovens, M., 't Hart, P. and Peters, B. G. (eds) *Success and Failure in Public Governance: A Comparative Analysis* (Cheltenham: Edward Elgar), pp. 593–640.

Boyne, G. A. (2003) 'What Is Public Sector Improvement?', *Public Administration*, 81: 2, 211–27.

Boyne, G. A. (2004) 'Explaining Public Service Improvement: Does Management Matter?', *Public Policy and Administration*, 19: 4, 100–17.

Brady, D. W. (1993) 'The Causes and Consequences of Divided Government: Toward a New Theory of American Politics?', *American Journal of Political Science*, 87: 1, 183–94.

Brändström, A., Bynander, F. and 't Hart, P. (2004) 'Governing by Looking Back: Historical Analogies and Crisis Management', *Public Administration*, 81: 1, 191–210.

Brändström, A. and Kuipers, S. (2003) 'From "Normal Incidents" to Political Crises: Understanding the Selective Politicization of Policy Failures', *Government and Opposition*, 38: 3, 279–305.

Braybrooke, D. and Lindblom, C. E. (1970) *A Strategy of Decision: Policy Evaluation as Social Process* (New York, NY: Free Press).

Brett, J. (2007) *Exit Right: The Unravelling of John Howard* (Quarterly Essay, Black Inc).

Bringing Them Home: National Inquiry into the Separation of Aboriginal and Torres Strait Islander Children from Their Families (1997) (Sydney: Human Rights and Equal Opportunity Commission).

Brown, G. (2009) Prime Minister's Roadmap to Copenhagen Speech, 26 June, Department of Energy and Climate Change, http://www.decc.gov.uk/en/content/cms/news/pm_speech/pm_speech.aspx, accessed 21 July 2009.

Buchanan, J. M. and Tullock, G. (1962) *The Calculus of Consent* (Michigan, MI: University of Michigan Press).

Burkhalter, H. J. (1994) 'The Question of Genocide: the Clinton Administration and Rwanda', *World Policy Journal*, 11: 4, 44–54.

Burns, D. (1992) *Poll Tax Rebellion* (Stirling: AK Press).

Busch, A. (2008) *Banking Regulation and Globalization* (Oxford: Oxford University Press).

Butler, D., Adonis, A. and Travers, T. (1994) *Failure in British Government: The Politics of the Poll Tax* (Oxford: Oxford University Press).

Cabinet Office (1999) *Professional Policy Making for the Twenty First Century* (London: Cabinet Office).

Cairney, P. (2009) 'The Role of Ideas in Policy Transfer: The Case of UK Smoking Bans since Devolution', *Journal of European Public Policy*, 16: 3, 471–88.

Campbell, K., Dufresne, M. and Maclure, R. (2001) 'Amending Youth Justice Policy in Canada: Discourse, Mediation and Ambiguity', *Howard Journal of Criminal Justice*, 40: 3, 272–84.

Campbell-Smith, D. (2008) *Follow the Money: The Audit Commission, Public Money and the Management of Public Services, 1983–2008* (London: Allen Lane).

Carson, L. and Martin, B. (1999) *Random Selection in Politics* (Westport, CT: Praeger).

Carty, R. K., Blais, A. and Fournier, P. (2008) 'When Citizens Choose to Reform SMP: The British Columbia Citizens' Assembly on Electoral Reform' in Blais, A. (ed.) *To Keep or Change First Past the Post: The Politics of Electoral Reform* (Oxford: Oxford University Press), pp. 140–60.

cbcnews.ca (2008) Newfoundland and Labrador Premier Danny Wilson discussing a judicial inquiry into errors and delays in breast cancer results, 13 May.

ChannelNewsAsia.Com (2008) Singapore's Minister Mentor, Lee Kuan Yew, discussing Singapore's Institutes of Technical Education, 21 February.

Chapman, S., Alpers, P., Agho, K. and Jones, M. (2009) 'Australia's 1996 Gun Law Reforms: Faster Falls in Firearm Deaths, Firearm Suicides, and a Decade without Mass Shootings', *Injury Prevention*, 12: 6, 365–72.

Chari, M. and Heywood, P. M. (2009) 'Analysing the Policy Process in Democratic Spain', *West European Politics*, 32: 1, 26–54.

Charles, M. B., Ryan, R., Castillo, C. P. and Brown, K. (2008) 'Safe and Sound: the Public Value Trade-Off in Worker Safety and Public Infrastructure Procurement', *Public Money & Management*, 28: 3, 159–66.

Christensen, T. and Lægreid, P. (2007) 'Introduction – Theoretical Approach and Research Questions' in Christensen, T. and Lægreid, P. (eds) *Transcending New Public Management: The Transformation of Public Sector Reforms* (Ashgate: Aldershot), pp. 1–16.

Clarke, L. B. (1999) *Mission Improbable: Using Fantasy Documents to Tame Disasters* (Chicago: University of Chicago Press).

Clarke, L. B. (2006) *Worst Cases: Terror and Catastrophe in the Popular Imagination* (Chicago: University of Chicago Press).

CNN International (2005) 'Cheney: Iraq Will Be "Enormous Success Story" ', CNN International, 24 June, http://edition.cnn.com/2005/POLITICS/06/23/cheney.interview/index.html, accessed 21 July 2009.

Cobb, R. W. and Primo, D. M. (2003) *The Plane Truth: Airline Crashes, the Media and Transportation Policy* (Washington, DC: Brookings Institution).

Cobb, R. W. and Ross, M. H. (eds) (1997) *Cultural Strategies of Agenda Denial: Avoidance, Attack and Redefinition* (Kansas: University Press of Kansas).

Cohen, S., Eimicke, W. and Heikkila, T. (2008) *The Effective Public Manager: Achieving Success in a Changing Government*, 4th edn (San Francisco, CA: Jossey-Bass).

Cole, M. and Parston, G. (2006) *Unlocking Public Value: A New Model for Achieving High Performance in Public Service Organizations* (Hoboken, NJ: John Wiley & Sons).

Collier, R. B. and Mazzuca, S. (2006) 'Does History Repeat?' in Goodin, R. E. and C. Tilly (eds) *The Oxford Handbook of Contextual Political Analysis* (Oxford: Oxford University Press), pp. 472–89.

Committee on Foreign Affairs (2007) 'Extraordinary Rendition in U.S. Counterterrorism Policy: The Impact on Transatlantic Relations', Joint Hearing before the Subcommittee on International Organizations, Human Rights, and Oversight and the Subcommittee on Europe of the Committee on Foreign Affairs, House of Representatives, 17 April, Washington, D.C. (City: House of Representatives: Washington, D.C.).

Considine, M., Lewis, J. M. and Alexander, D. (2009) *Networks, Innovation and Public Policy: Politicians, Bureaucrats and the Pathways to Change Inside Government* (Basingstoke: Palgrave Macmillan).

Cooper, C. and Block, R. (2006) *Disaster: Hurricane Katrina and the Failure of Homeland Security* (New York, NY: Times Books).

Cornelius, W. (2001) 'Death at the Border: Efficacy and Unintended Consequences of US Immigration Control Policy Population and Development Review', *Population and Development Review*, 27: 4, 661–85.

Corporate Research Associates Inc. and Kelly Sears Consulting Group (2008) *Evaluation of the Recruitment of Policy Leaders Program – Summary Report*, Public Service Commission, http://www.psc-cfp.gc.ca/abt-aps/inev-evin/2008/rpl-rlp-eval-eng.htm, accessed 22 July 2009.

Cowley, P. (2005) *The Rebels: How Blair Mislaid His Majority* (London: Politico's).

Creighton, J. L. (2005) *The Public Participation Handbook: Making Better Decisions through Citizen Involvement: A Practical Toolkit* (San Francisco, CA: Jossey-Bass).

Crick, B. (1962) *In Defence of Politics* (London: Weidenfeld & Nicolson).

Cullen, M. (2005) Post Budget Speech to Wellington Chamber of Commerce, 20 May http://www.scoop.co.nz/stories/PA0505/S00556.htm, accessed 21 July 2009.

d'Ombrain, N. (1997) 'Public Inquiries in Canada', *Canadian Public Administration*, 40: 1, 86–107.

Dahl, R. A. (1961) *Who Governs? Democracy and Power in an American City* (New Haven, CT: Yale University Press).

Daly, P. H., Watkins, M. and Reavis, C. (2006) *The First 90 Days in Government: Critical Success Strategies for Public Managers at All Levels* (Boston, MA: Harvard Business School Press).

Davidson, E. J. (2005) *Evaluation Methodology Basics: The Nuts and Bolts of Sound Evaluation* (Thousand Oaks, CA: Sage).

Davies, H. T. O., Nutley, S. M. and Smith, P. C. (eds) (2000) *What Works? Evidence-Based Policy and Practice in Public Services* (Bristol: Policy Press).

Davies, J. E. (2009) 'The Limits of Joined-Up Government: Towards a Political Analysis', *Public Administration*, 87: 1, 80–96.

de Mesquita, B. B., Smith, A., Siverson, R. W. and Morrow, J. D. (2003) *The Logic of Political Survival* (Cambridge, MA: MIT Press).

de Vries, M. S. (2002) 'The Changing Functions of Laws and its Implication for Government and Governance', *International Review of Administrative Sciences*, 68: 4, 599–618.

Dekker, S. (2006) *The Field Guide to Understanding Human Error* (Aldershot: Ashgate).

deLeon, P. (1988) *Advice and Consent: The Development of the Policy Sciences* (New York: Russell Sage Foundation).

Delta Commission (2008) *Working Together with Water: A Living Land Builds for Its Future* http://www.deltacommissie.com/doc/deltareport_full.pdf, accessed 16 August 2009.

Dolowitz, D., Greenwold, S. and Marsh, D. (1999) 'Policy Transfer: Something Old, Something New, Something Borrowed, but Why Red, White and Blue?', *Parliamentary Affairs*, 52: 4, 719–30.

Dolowitz, D. P. and Marsh, D. (2000) 'Learning from Abroad: The Role of Policy Transfer in Contemporary Policy-Making', *Governance*, 13: 1, 5–23.

Douglas, M. (1992) *Risk and Blame: Essays in Cultural Theory* (London: Routledge).

Douglas, M. and Wildavsky, A. (1982) *Risk and Culture: An Essay on the Selection of Environmental Dangers* (Berkeley, CA: California University Press).

Dowding, K. (2003) 'Resources, Power and Systematic Luck: A Response to Barry', *Politics, Philosophy & Economics*, 2: 3, 305–22.

Downs, A. (1957) *An Economic Theory of Democracy* (New York: Harper & Row).

Drennan, L. T. and McConnell, A. (2007) *Risk and Crisis Management in the Public Sector* (London: Routledge).

Dror, Y. (1983) *Public Policymaking Re-Examined*, 2nd edn (New Brunswick: Transaction).

Dryzek, J. S. (2006a) 'Policy Analysis as Critique' in Moran, M., Rein, M. and Goodin, R. E. (eds) *The Oxford Handbook of Public Policy* (Oxford: Oxford University Press), pp. 190–203.

Dryzek, J. S. (2006b) *Deliberative Global Politics: Discourse and Democracy in a Divided World* (Cambridge: Polity Press).

Dunleavy, P. (1995) 'Policy Disasters: Explaining the UK's Record', *Public Policy and Administration*, 10: 2, 52–70.

Dunn, W. N. (2004) *Public Policy Analysis: An Introduction*, 3rd edn (New Jersey: Pearson Prentice Hall).

Dye, T. R. (2005) *Understanding Public Policy*, 11th edn (New Jersey: Pearson Prentice Hall).

Easton, D. (1953) *The Political System* (New York, NY: Knopf).

Edelman, M. J. (1964) *The Symbolic Uses of Politics* (Urbana: University of Illinois Press).

Edelman, M. J. (1977) *Political Language: Words That Succeed and Policies That Fail* (New York: Academic Press).

Edelman, M. J. (1988) *Constructing the Political Spectacle* (Chicago: University of Chicago Press).

Edelstein, D. M. (2008) *Occupational Hazards: Success and Failure in Military Occupation* (Ithaca, NY: Cornell University Press).

Eliadis, P., Hill, M. M. and Howlett, M. (eds) (2005) *Designing Government: From Instruments to Governance* (Montreal and Kingston: McGill-Queen's University Press).

Ellis, R. J. (1994) *Presidential Lightning Rods: The Politics of Blame Avoidance* (Lawrence, KS: University of Kansas Press).

Epstein, C. (2008) *The Power of Words in International Relations: Birth of Anti-Whaling Discourse* (Cambridge, MA: MIT Press).

Evans, M. (ed.) (2004) *Policy Transfer in Global Perspective* (Aldershot: Ashgate).

Evans, M. (2009) 'New Directions in the Study of Policy Transfer', *Policy Studies*, 30: 3, 237–41.

Fagerberg, J., Mowery, D. C. and Versbagen, B. (eds) (2009) *Innovation, Path Dependency and Policy: The Norwegian Case* (Oxford: Oxford University Press).

Falkner, G., Teib, O., Hartlapp, M. and Leiber, S. (2005) *Complying with Europe: EU Harmonisation and Soft Law in the Member States* (New York: Cambridge University Press).

Farnsworth, S. J. (2008) *Spinner in Chief: How Presidents Sell Their Policies and Themselves* (Boulder, CO: Paradigm).

Farr, J., Hacker, J. S. and Kazee, N. (2006) 'The Policy Scientist of Democracy: The Discipline of Harold D. Lasswell', *American Political Science Review*, 100: 4, 1–9.

Fischer, F. (1995) *Evaluating Public Policy* (Chicago: Nelson-Hall).

Fischer, F. (2003) *Reframing Public Policy: Discursive Politics and Deliberative Practices* (Oxford: Oxford University Press).

Fischer, F. (2009) *Democracy and Expertise: Reorienting Policy Inquiry* (Oxford: Oxford University Press).

Fischer, F. and Forester, J. (1993) *The Argumentative Turn in Policy Analysis and Planning* (Durham, NC: Duke University Press).

Flaherty, J. (2007) Speech by the Honourable Jim Flaherty, Minister of Finance for Canada, to the Canada China Business Council, 19 January, Department of Finance, Canada, http://www.fin.gc.ca/n07/07–005_1-eng.asp, accessed 21 July 2009.

Flathman, R. J. (1966) *The Public Interest: An Essay Concerning the Normative Discourse of Politics* (New York, NY: John Wiley & Sons).

Flinders, M. and Curry, D. (2008) 'Deliberative Democracy, Elite Politics and Electoral Reform', *Policy Studies*, 29: 4, 371–92.

Flyvbjerg, B., Bruzelius, N. and Rothengatter, W. (2003) *Megaprojects and Risk: An Anatomy of Ambition* (Cambridge: Cambridge University Press).

Fol, S., Dupoy, G. and Coutard, O. (2007) 'Transport Policy and the Car Divide in the UK, the US and France: Beyond the Environmental Debate', *International Journal of Urban and Regional Research*, 31: 4, 802–18.

Fortna, V. P. (2004) *Peace Time: Ceasefire Agreements and the Durability of Peace* (Princeton, NJ: Princeton University Press).

Franklin, B. (2004) *Packaging Politics: Political Communications in Britain's Media Democracy*, 2nd edn (London: Hodder Arnold).

Friedman, M. (1953) *Essays in Positive Economics* (Chicago: University of Chicago Press).

Fukuyama, F. (1992) *The End of History and the Last Man* (New York, NY: Free Press).

Gastil, J. (2008) *Political Communication and Deliberation* (Thousand Oaks, CA: Sage).

Gastil, J. and Levine, P. (2005) 'A Nation That (Sometimes) Likes to Talk: A Brief History of Public Deliberation in the United States' in Gastil, J. and Levine, P. (ed.) *The Deliberative Democracy Handbook: Strategies for Effective Civic Engagement in the Twenty-First Century* (San Francisco: Jossey-Bass), pp. 1–19.

Gauld, R. and Goldfinch, S. (2006) *Dangerous Enthusiasms: E-Government, Computer Failure and Information System Development* (Dunedin, New Zealand: Otago University Press).

Gee, J. P. (2005) *An Introduction to Discourse Analysis*, 2nd edn (Abingdon: Routledge).

Gerstein, M. (2008) *Flirting with Disaster: Why Accidents Are Rarely Accidental* (New York, NY: Union Square Press).

Geuras, D. and Garofalo, C. (2005) *Practical Ethics in Public Administration*, 2nd edn (Vienna, VA: Management Concepts).

Goldfinch, S. (2006) 'Rituals of Reform, Policy Transfer, and the National University Corporation Reforms of Japan', *Governance*, 19: 4, 585–604.

Gray, C. (2003) 'The Millennium Dome: "Falling from Grace" ', *Parliamentary Affairs*, 56: 3, 441–55.

Gray, C. (2008) 'Arts Council England and Public Value: A Critical Review', *International Journal of Cultural Policy*, 14: 2, 209–14.

Gray, P. (1998) 'Public Policy Disasters in Europe: An Introduction' in Gray, P. and 't Hart, P. (eds) *Public Policy Disasters in Western Europe* (London: Routledge), pp. 3–20.

Gray, P. and 't Hart, P. (eds) (1998) *Public Policy Disasters in Western Europe* (London: Routledge).

Green, H., Trache, H. and Blanchard, D. (2001) 'An Experiment in French Urban Policy: Evaluation and Reflection on the Implementation of the Zones Franches Urbaines', *Planning Theory & Practice*, 2: 1, 53–66.

Gregory, F. (2007) 'An Assessment of the Contribution of Intelligence-Led Counter-Terrorism to UK Homeland Security Post 9/11 within the 'Contest' Strategy' in Wilkinson, P. (ed.) *Homeland Security in the UK: Future Preparedness for Terrorist Attack since 9/11* (London: Routledge), pp. 181–202.

Guardian, The (2002) Article in connection with A-level results, 22 September.

Guardian, The (2009) 'Copenhagen Reaction: Delegates Speak', 19 December.

Gupta, D. K. (2001) *Analyzing Public Policy: Concepts, Tools, and Techniques* (Washington, DC: CQ Press).

Gustafson, G. (1983) 'Symbolic and Pseudo Policies as Responses to Diffusion of Power', *Policy Sciences*, 15: 3, 269–87.

Gutmann, A. and Thompson, D. (2004) *Why Deliberative Democracy?* (Princeton, NJ: Princeton University Press).

Hajer, M. and Wagenaar, H. (eds) (2003) *Deliberative Policy Analysis: Understanding Governance in the Network Society* (Cambridge: Cambridge University Press).

Hall, P. A. (1993) 'Policy Paradigms, Social Learning and the State: The Case of Economic Policy Making in Britain", *Comparative Politics*, 25:3: 275–96.

Hall, P. G. (1982) *Great Planning Disasters* (Berkeley, CA: University of California Press).

Hamilton, S. and Micklethwait, A. (2006) *Greed and Corporate Failure: The Lessons from Recent Disasters* (Basingstoke: Palgrave Macmillan).

Hansard (2006) Canadian Conservative MP Dean Del Mastro in defence of his government's handling of hospital waiting times, 39th Parliament, 13 June: col. 1235.

Harlow, C. (2002) 'Accountability, New Public Management, and the Problems of the Child Support Agency', *Journal of Law and Society*, 26: 2, 150–74.

Hartz-Karp, J. (2005) 'A Case Study in Deliberative Democracy: Dialogue with the City', *Journal of Public Deliberation*, 1: 1, Article 6.

Hay, C. (2002) *Political Analysis* (Basingstoke: Palgrave Macmillan).

Head, B. J. and Alford, J. (2008) 'Wicked Problems: Implications for Policy and Management', Paper delivered to the Australasian Political Studies Association Conference, 6–9 July (Brisbane, Australia).

Head, B. W. (2008) 'Three Lenses of Evidence-Based Policy', *Australian Journal of Public Administration*, 67: 1, 1–11.

Hearit, K. M. (2006) *Crisis Management by Apology: Corporate Response to Allegations of Wrongdoing* (Mahwah, NJ: Lawrence Erlbaum).

Hermann, M. G., Preston, T., Korany, B. and Shaw, T. M. (2001) 'Who Leads Matters: The Effects of Powerful Individuals. Leaders, Groups, and Coalitions: Understanding the People and Processes in Foreign Policymaking' in Hermann, M. G. and Hagan, J. (eds) *Leaders, Groups, and Coalitions: Understanding the People and Processes in Foreign Policymaking* (Boston, MA: Blackwell), pp. 81–131.

Hill, M. and Hupe, P. (2009) *Implementing Public Policy*, 2nd edn (London: Sage).

Hindmoor, A. (2006) *Rational Choice* (Basingstoke: Palgrave Macmillan).

Hodgson, L., Farrell, C. M. and Connolly, M. (2007) 'Improving UK Public Services: A Review of the Evidence', *Public Administration*, 85: 2, 355–82.

Hodgson, S. M. and Irving, Z. (eds) (2007) *Policy Reconsidered; Meanings, Politics and Practices* (Bristol: Policy Press).

Hogwood, B. W. and Gunn, L. A. (1984) *Policy Analysis for the Real World* (Oxford: Oxford University Press).

Hogwood, B. W. and Peters, B. G. (1985) *The Pathology of Public Policy* (Oxford: Clarendon Press).

Hogwood, B. W. (1992) *Trends in British Public Policy: Do Governments Make Any Difference?* (Buckingham: Open University Press).

Home Office (2008) *Efficiency & Productivity Strategy for the Police Service: 2008–11* (London: Home Office), http://Police.Homeoffice.Gov.Uk/News-and-Publications/Publication/Human-Resources/Efficiency-Productivity-Strategy?View=Binary, accessed 15 April 2008.

Hood, C. (1976) *The Limits of Administration* (London: John Wiley).

Hood, C. (2002) 'The Risk Game and the Blame Game', *Government and Opposition*, 37: 1, 15–37.

Hood, C. C. and Margetts, H. Z. (2007) *The Tools of Government in the Digital Age* (Basingstoke: Palgrave Macmillan).

Hosken, A. (2006) *Nothing Like a Dame: The Scandals of Shirley Porter* (London: Granta).

Howlett, M. (2009) 'Governance Modes, Policy Regimes and Operational Plans: A Multi-Level Nested Model of Policy Instrument Choice and Policy Design', *Policy Sciences*, 42: 1, 73–89.

Howlett, M. and Cashore, B. (2009) 'The Dependent Variable Problem in the Study of Policy Change: Understanding Policy Change as a Methodological Problem', *Journal of Comparative Policy Analysis*, 11: 1, 33–46.

Howlett, M., Ramesh, M. and Perl, A. (2009) *Studying Public Policy: Policy Cycles & Policy Subsystems*, 3rd edn (Ontario: Oxford University Press).

Hughes, C. E. (2007) 'Evidence-Based Policy or Policy-Based Evidence? The Role of Evidence in the Development and Implementation of the Illicit Drug Diversion Initiative', *Drug and Alcohol Review*, 26: 4, 363–8.

Hughes, O. E. (2003) *Public Management and Administration*, 3rd edn (Basingstoke: Palgrave Macmillan).

Hulme, D. and Moore, K. (2007) 'Why Has Microfinance Been a Policy Success in Bangladesh?' in Bebbington, A. and McCourt, W. (eds) *Development Success: Statecraft in the South* (Basingstoke: Palgrave Macmillan), pp. 105–39.

Hunter, F. (1953) *Community Power Structure: A Study of Decision Makers* (Chapel Hill, NC: University of North Carolina Press).

Huntington, S. P. (1997) *The Clash of Civilizations and the Remaking of World Order* (London: Simon & Schuster).

Hursh, D. (2007) 'Exacerbating Inequality: The Failed Promise of the No Child Left Behind Act', *Race Ethnicity and Education*, 10: 3, 295–308.

Ingram, H. and Mann, D. E. (eds) (1980) *Why Policies Succeed or Fail* (Beverly Hills, CA: Sage).

Ingram, H. and Schneider, A. L. (2006) 'Policy Analysis for Democracy' in Moran, M., Rein, M. and Goodin, R. E. (eds) *The Oxford Handbook of Public Policy* (Oxford: Oxford University Press), pp. 169–89.

Israeli, R. (2004) *The Iraq War: Hidden Agendas and Babylonian Intrigue: The Regional Impact on Shi'ites, Kurds, Sunnis and Arabs* (Eastbourne: Sussex Academic Press).

Issalys, P. (2005) 'Choosing among Forms of Public Action: A Question of Legitimacy' in Eliadis, P., Hill, M. M. and Howlett, M. (eds) *Designing Government: From Instruments to Governance* (Montreal: McGill-Queen's University Press), pp. 154–81.

Jacobs, A. M. (2009) 'How Do Ideas Matter? Mental Models and Attention in German Pension Politics', *Comparative Political Studies*, 42: 2, 252–79.

Jacoby, W. (2005) 'Institutional Transfer? Can Semisovereignty Be Transferred? The Political Economy of Eastern Germany' in Green, S. and Paterson, W. E. (eds) *Governance in Contemporary Germany: The Semisovereign State Revisited* (Cambridge: Cambridge University Press), pp. 21–46.

Jagers, S. C. and Hammar, H. (2009) 'Environmental Taxation for Good and for Bad: The Efficiency and Legitimacy of Sweden's Carbon Tax', *Environmental Politics*, 18: 2, 218–38.

Janis, I. L. (1982) *Groupthink* (Boston: Houghton Mifflin).

Janis, I. L. and Mann, L. (1977) *Decision-Making: A Psychological Analysis of Conflict, Choice and Commitment* (New York: Free Press).

Jann, W. and Wegrich, K. (2007) 'Theories of the Policy Cycle' in Fischer, F., Miller, G. J. and Sidney, M. S. (eds) *Handbook of Public Policy Analysis: Theories, Politics and Methods* (Boca Raton, FL: CRC Press), pp. 43–62.

Jansen, J. (2004) 'Autonomy and Accountability in the Regulation of the Teaching Profession: A South African Case Study', *Research Papers in Education*, 19: 1, 51–66.

Jeeves, A. and Jolly, R. (2009) 'Sexually Transmitted Infection and Public Health in South Africa: Educational Campaigns for Prevention, 1935–1948 and 1999–2008', *Social Theory & Health*, 7: 3, 264–83.

Jessop, B. (2002) *The Future of the Capitalist State* (Cambridge: Polity Press).

John, P. (1998) *Analysing Public Policy* (London: Continuum).

Jones, B. D. (2001) *Politics and the Architecture of Choice: Bounded Rationality and Governance* (Chicago: University of Chicago Press).

Jordana, J. (2001) 'Coping with HIV Transmission in Spain: The Case of Blood Control Failure' in Bovens, M., 't Hart, P. and Peters, B. G. (eds) *Success and Failure in Public Governance: A Comparative Analysis* (Cheltenham: Edward Elgar), pp. 532–50.

Jowell, T. (2009) 'London 2012: We Are Delivering Legacy We Promised', *Telegraph.co.uk*, 21 July, http://www.telegraph.co.uk/sport/othersports/olympics/london2012/5879054/London-2012-We-are-delivering-legacy-we-promised-says-Tessa-Jowell.html, accessed 22 July 2009.

Judge, D. (1981) *Backbench Specialisation in the House of Commons* (London: Heinemann).

Judge, D. (1999) *Representation: Theory and Practice in Britain* (Abingdon: Routledge).

Juster, H. R., Loomis, B. R., Hinman, T. M., Farrelly, M. C., Hyland, A., Bauer, U. E. and Birkhead, G. S. (2007) 'Declines in Hospital Admissions for Acute Myocardial Infarction in New York State after Implementation of a Comprehensive Smoking Ban', *American Journal of Public Health*, 97: 11, 2035–9.

Kaplan, R. S. and Norton, D. P. (1992) 'The Balanced Scorecard – Measures That Drive Performance', *Harvard Business Review*, January/February: 71–9.

Kaplan, R. S. and Norton, D. P. (1997) 'Why Does Business Need a Balanced Scorecard', *Journal of Cost Management*, 11: 3, 5–10.

Kay, A. (2006) *The Dynamics of Public Policy* (Cheltenham: Edward Elgar).

Kealey, T. (2006) *Transforming Higher Education* (London; Adam Smith Institute) http://www.adamsmith.org/images/uploads/bulletin/Education_ Kealey_Briefing.pdf, date accessed 17 July 2009.

Kelly, G., Mulgan, G. and Muers, S. (2002) *Creating Public Value: An Analytical Framework for Public Service Reform* (London: Strategy Unit, UK Cabinet Office).

Kerr, D. H. (1976) 'The Logic of "Policy" and Successful Policies', *Policy Sciences*, 7: 3, 351–63.

Kerrouche, E. (2006) 'The French Assemblée Nationale: The Case of a Weak Legislature?', *Journal of Legislative Studies*, 12: 3–4, 336–55.

Kindleberger, C. P. and Aliber, R. Z. (2005) *Manias, Panics and Crashes: A History of Financial Crises* (New York: John Wiley & Sons).

King, A. (ed.) (1976) *Why Is Britain Becoming Harder to Govern?* (London: BBC).

King, M. (2005) 'Epistemic Communities and the Diffusion of Ideas: Central Bank Reform in the United Kingdom', *West European Politics*, 28: 1, 94–123.

Kitts, K. (2006) *Presidential Commissions & National Security: The Politics of Damage Control* (Boulder, CO: Lynne Rienner).

Knoepfel, P. Larrue, C., Varone, F. and Hill, M. (2007) *Public Policy Analysis* (Bristol: Policy Press).

Knox, C. (2008) 'Policy Making in Northern Ireland: Ignoring the Evidence', *Policy & Politics*, 36: 3, 343–59.

Knox, C. (2009) 'The Politics of Local Government Reform in Northern Ireland', *Local Government Studies*, 35: 4, 435–55.

Knox, C. and Carmichael, P. (2006) 'Bureau Shuffling? The Review of Public Administration in Northern Ireland', *Public Administration*, 84: 4, 941–65.

Kriesi, H. (2008) *The Politics of Switzerland: Continuity and Change in a Consensus Democracy* (Cambridge: Cambridge University Press).

Kuipers, S. L. (2004) *Cast in Concrete? The Institutional Dynamics of Belgian and Dutch Social Policy Reform* (Delft: Eburon).

Kusek, J. Z. and Rist, R. C. (2004) *Ten Steps to a Results-Based Monitoring and Evaluation System: A Handbook for Development Practitioners* (Washington, DC: International Bank for Reconstruction and Development/World Bank).

Ladi, S. (2004) 'Environmental Policy Transfer in Germany and Greece' in Evans, M. (ed.) *Policy Transfer in Global Perspective* (Aldershot: Ashgate), pp. 79–92.

Lamm, R. D. (2003) *The Brave New World of Health Care: What Every American Needs to Know About Our Impending Health Care Crisis* (Golden, CO: Fulcrum Group).

Lasswell, H. D. (1936) *Politics: Who Gets What, When, How* (New York, NY: McGraw Hill).

Lasswell, H. D. (1956) *The Decision Process* (College Park, MD: University of Maryland Press).

Laufer, J. (2003) 'Equal Employment Policy in France: Symbolic Support and a Mixed Record', *Review of Policy Research*, 20: 3, 423–42.

Laver, M. and Schofield, N. (1998) *Multiparty Government: The Politics of Coalition in Europe*, 2nd edn (Ann Arbor, MI: University of Michigan Press).

Law, J. (2004) *After Method: Mess in Social Science Research* (Abingdon: Routledge).

Le Maux, B. (2009) 'How Do Policy-Makers Actually Solve Problems? Evidence from the French Local Public Sector', *Economics and Politics*, 21: 2, 201–31.

Leadbetter, C. (2008) *We-Think* (London: Profile Books).

Lehtomäki, P. (2007) *Speech by Minister Lehtomäki at the United Arab Emirates – Finland Business Forum in Abu Dhabi, 17 January,* http://formin.finland.fi/Public/Print.aspx?contentid=85767&nodeid=15699&culture=en-US&contentlan=2, accessed 21 July 2009.

Leiss, W. and Powell, D. (2004) *Mad Cows and Mother's Milk: The Perils of Poor Risk Communication*, 2nd edn (Montreal: McGill-Queen's University Press).

Levi-Faur, D. and Vigoda-Gadot, E. (eds) (2004) *International Public Policy and Management: Policy Learning Beyond Regional, Cultural, and Political Boundaries* (New York: Marcel Dekker).

Lijphart, A. (1999) *Patterns of Democracy: Government Forms and Performance in Thirty-Six Countries*, 2nd edn (New Haven, CT: Yale University Press).

Lindblom, C. E. (1959) 'The Science Of "Muddling Through" ', *Public Administration Review*, XIX: 2, 79–88.

Lindblom, C. E. (1965) *The Intelligence of Democracy* (New York: Free Press).

Lindblom, C. E. (1977) *Politics and Markets: The World's Political-Economic Systems* (New York: Basic Books).

Ling, T. (2002) 'Delivering Joined-up Government in the UK: Dimensions, Issues and Problems', *Public Administration*, 80: 4, 615–42.

Lipsky, M. and Olson, D. J. (1977) *Commission Politics: The Processing of Racial Crisis in America* (New Brunswick, NJ: Transaction).

Lukes, S. (2005) *Power: A Radical View*, 2nd edn (Basingstoke: Palgrave Macmillan.).

Lundberg, T. C. (2007) 'Electoral System Reviews in New Zealand, Britain and Canada: A Critical Comparison', *Government and Opposition*, 42: 4, 471–90.

Machiavelli, N. (1961) *The Prince* (Harmondsworth: Penguin).

Macpherson, C. B. (1966) *The Real World of Democracy* (Oxford: Clarendon Press).

Maginn, P. J. (2007) 'Deliberative Democracy or Discursively Biased? Perth's Dialogue with the City Initiative', *Space and Polity*, 11: 3, 331–52.

Majone, G. (1989) *Evidence, Argument, and Persuasion in the Policy Process* (New Haven, CT: Yale University Press).

March, J. G. and Olsen, J. P. (1984) 'The New Institutionalism: Organizational Factors in Political Life', *American Political Science Review*, 78: 3, 734–49.

Marr, D. and Wilkinson, M. (2004) *Dark Victory* (Crows Nest, NSW: Allan & Unwin).

Marsh, D. and Furlong, P. (2002) 'A Skin Not a Sweater: Ontology and Epistemology in Political Science' in March, D. and Stoker, G. (eds) *Theory and Methods in Political Science*, 2nd edn (Basingstoke: Palgrave Macmillan), pp. 17–41.

Marsh, D. and McConnell, A. (2010a) 'Towards a Framework for Establishing Policy Success', *Public Administration*.

Marsh, D. and McConnell, A. (2010b) 'Towards a Framework for Establishing Policy Success: A Reply to Bovens', *Public Administration*.

Marsh, D. and Stoker, G. (eds) (2002) *Theories and Methods in Political Science* (Basingstoke: Palgrave Macmillan).

Martin, B. (2007) *Justice Ignited: The Dynamics of Backfire* (Plymouth: Rowman & Littlefield).

Marton, R. and Phillips, S. K. (2005) 'Modernising Policy for Public Value: Learning Lessons from the Management of Bushfires', *Australian Journal of Public Administration*, 64: 1, 75–82.

May, J. V. and Wildavsky, A. B. (eds) (1978) *The Policy Cycle* (Beverly Hills, CA: Sage).

May, P. J. (1992) 'Policy Learning and Failure', *Journal of Public Policy*, 12: 4, 331–54.

May, P. J. (2005) 'Policy Maps and Political Feasibility' in Geva-May, I. (ed.) *Thinking Like a Policy Analyst: Policy Analysis as a Clinical Profession* (New York: Palgrave Macmillan), pp. 127–51.

May, P. J., Sapotichne, J. and Workman, S. (2009) 'Widespread Policy Disruption: Terrorism, Public Risks, and Homeland Security', *Policy Studies Journal*, 37: 2, 171–94.

Mazmanian, D. A. and Sabatier, P.A. (1989) *Implementation and Public Policy* (Lanham, MD: University Press of America).

McConnell, A. (1995) *State Policy Formation and the Origins of the Poll Tax* (Aldershot: Dartmouth).

McConnell, A. (1999) *The Politics and Policy of Local Taxation in Britain* (Wirral: Tudor).

McConnell, A. (2003) 'Overview: Crisis Management, Influences, Responses and Evaluation', *Parliamentary Affairs*, 56: 3, 393–409.

McConnell, A. (2008) 'Ripples Not Waves: A Policy Configuration Approach to Reform in the Wake of the 1998 Sydney Water Crisis', *Governance*, 21: 4, 551–80.

McConnell, A. (2009) 'Framing Dilemmas in the Quest for Successful Crisis Management' in 't Hart, P. and K. Tindall (eds), *Framing the Global Economic Downturn: Crisis Rhetoric and the Politics of Recessions* (Canberra: ANU e-press), pp. 315–21.

McConnell, A., Gauja, A. and Botterill, L. C. (2008) 'Policy Fiascos, Blame Management and AWB Limited: The Howard Government's Escape from the Iraq Wheat Scandal', *Australian Journal of Political Science*, 43: 4, 599–616.

McEntire, D. A. (2007) *Disaster Response and Recovery* (Hoboken, NJ: John Wiley & Sons).

McGuigan, J. (2003) 'The Social Construction of a Cultural Disaster: New Labour's Millennium Experience', *Cultural Studies*, 17: 5, 669–90.

McKee, T. and Novotny, T. E, (2003) 'Political Interference in American Science: Why Europe Should Be Concerned About the Actions of the Bush Administration', *European Journal of Public Health*, 13: 4, 289–90.

Midwinter, A. (1989) 'Economic Theory, the Poll Tax and Local Spending', *Politics*, 9: 2, 9–15.

Miliband, R. (1973) *The State in Capitalist Society: The Analysis of the Western System of Power* (London: Quartet).

Miller, G. J. and Robbins, D. (2007) 'Cost-Benefit Analysis' in Fischer, F., Miller, G. J. and Sidney, M. S. (eds) *Handbook of Public Policy Analysis: Theory, Politics, and Methods* (Boca Raton, FL: CRC Press), pp. 465–80.

Milliken, J. (ed.) (2003) *State Failure, Collapse and Reconstruction* (Oxford: Institute of Social Studies).

Mintrom, M. (2003) *People Skills for Policy Analysts* (Washington, DC: Georgetown University Press).

Mitrany, D. (1966) *A Working Peace System* (Chicago: Quadrangle Books).

Mitroff, I. I. and Pauchant, T. C. (1990) *We're So Big and Powerful Nothing Bad Can Happen to Us* (New York: Carol).

Moore, M. H. (1995) *Creating Public Value: Strategic Management in Government* (Cambridge, MA: Harvard University Press).

Morgan, M. G. and Peha, J. M. (2003) *Science and Technology Advice for Congress* (Washington, DC: RFF Press).

Morris, D. (1999) *The New Machiavelli* (Los Angeles, CA: Renaissance Books).

Morris, D. (2002) *Power Plays: Win or Lose – How History's Great Political Leaders Play the Game* (New York: Regan Books).

Mouzos, J. (1999) *Firearm-Related Violence: The Impact of the Nationwide Agreement on Firearms* (Canberra: Australian Institute of Criminology, Series on Trends and Issues in Crime and Criminal Justice).

Moynihan, D. P. (2005) 'Why and How Do State Governments Adopt and Implement "Managing for Results" Reforms?', *Journal of Public Administration Research and Theory*, 15: 2, 219–43.

Mueller, D. C. (2003) *Public Choice III* (Cambridge: Cambridge University Press).

Mulcahy, M., Evans, D. S., Hammond, S. K., Repace, J. L. and Byrne, M. (2005) 'Secondhand Smoke Exposure and Risk Following the Irish Smoking Ban: An Assessment of Salivary Cotinine Concentrations in Hotel Workers and Air Nicotine Levels in Bars', *Tobacco Control*, 14: 384–88.

Nagel, S. (1980) 'Series Editor's Introduction' in Ingram, H. M. and Mann, D. E. (eds) *Why Policies Succeed or Fail* (Beverly Hills, CA: Sage), pp. 7–10.

National Commission on Terrorist Attacks Upon the United States (2004) *Group Politics and Public Policy Final Report of the National Commission on Terrorist Attacks Upon the United States* (New York: W.W. Norton).

New York Times (2000) Jeb Bush, Governor of Florida, commenting in relation to his 'One Florida' educational policy, 15 September.

Nicoll, K. and Edwards, R. (2004) 'Lifelong Learning and the Sultans of Spin: Policy as Persuasion?', *Journal of Education Policy*, 19: 1, 43–55.

Niskanen, W. A. (1971) *Bureaucracy and Representative Government* (Beverly Hills, CA: Sage).

Noh, A. and Tumin, M. (2008) 'Remaking Public Participation: The Case of Singapore', *Asian Social Science*, 4: 7, 19–32.

Norberry, J., Woolner, D. and Magarey, K. (1996) *After Port Arthur – Issues of Gun Control in Australia* (Canberra: Parliament of Australia Parliamentary Library).

Northcott, D. and Llewellyn, S. (2005) 'Benchmarking in UK Health: A Gap between Policy and Practice?', *Benchmarking: An International Journal*, 12: 1, 419–35.

O'Flynn, J. (2007) 'From New Public Management to Public Value: Paradigmatic Change and Managerial Implications', *Australian Journal of Public Administration*, 66: 3, 353–66.

O'Neill, M. K. and Primus, W. E. (2005) 'Recent Data Trends Show Welfare Reform to Be a Mixed Success: Significant Policy Changes Should Accompany Reauthorization', *Review of Policy Research*, 22: 3, 301–24.

OECD (2007) *Fiscal Equalization in OECD Countries*, Working Paper No. 4 (Paris: OECD).

Offe, C. (1984) *The Contradictions of the Welfare State* (London: Hutchinson).

Office for National Statistics (2008) *Social Trends 38* http://www.statistics.gov.uk/downloads/theme_social/Social_Trends38/Social_Trends_38.pdf, accessed 16 April 2008.

Oliver, M. J. and Aldcroft, D. H. (eds) (2007) *Economic Disasters of the Twentieth Century* (Cheltenham: Edward Elgar).

Osborne, D. and Gaebler, T. (1992) *Reinventing Government: How the Entrepreneurial Spirit is Transforming the Public Sector* (Reading, MA: Addison-Wesley).

Oxford English Dictionary (2001) *Oxford English Dictionary* (Oxford: Oxford University Press).

Page, E. C. (2005) 'Joined-up Government and the Civil Service' in Bogdanor, V. (ed.) *Joined-up Government* (Oxford: Oxford University Press), pp. 139–55.

Parsons, W. (2002) 'From Muddling through to Muddling Up: Evidence Based Policy Making and the Modernization of British Government', *Public Policy and Administration*, 17: 3, 43–60.

Patapan, H., Wanna, J. and Weller, P. (eds) (2003) *Westminster Legacies: Democracy and Responsible Government in Asia and the Pacific* (Sydney: University of South Wales Press).

Patashnik, E. M. (2008) *Reforms at Risk: What Happens after Major Policy Changes Are Enacted?* (Princeton: Princeton University Press).

Pawson, R. (2006) *Evidence-Based Policy: A Realist Perspective* (London: Sage).

Pawson, R. and Tilley, N. (1997) *Realistic Evaluation* (London: Sage).

Peachment, A. (ed.) (2006) *The Years of Scandal: Commissions of Inquiry in Western Australia 1991–2004* (Crawley: University of Western Australia Press).

Perrow, C. (2007) *Surviving the Next Catastrophe: Reducing Our Vulnerabilities to Natural, Industrial and Terrorist Disasters* (Princeton: Princeton University Press).

Perry, R. W. and Quarantelli, E. L. (eds) (2005) *What Is a Disaster? New Answers to Old Questions* (Philadelphia: Xlibris).

Peters, B. G. (1986) *American Public Policy: Promise and Performance*, 2nd edn (Basingstoke: Macmillan).

Peters, B. G. (2005) *Institutional Theory in Political Science: The 'New Institutionalism'*, 2nd edn (London: Continuum).

Peters, B. G. and Hornbeek, J. A. (2005) 'The Problem of Policy Problems' in Eliadis, P., Hill, M. M. and Howlett, M. (eds) *Designing Government: From Instruments to Governance* (Montreal and Kingston: McGill-Queen's University Press), pp. 77–105.

Pierson, C. (2003) 'Learning from Labor? Welfare Policy Transfer between Australia and Britain', *Commonwealth and Comparative Politics*, 41: 1, 77–100.

Pierson, P. (2000) 'Increasing Returns, Path Dependence, and the Study of Politics', *American Political Science Review*, 94: 2, 251–67.

Pierson, P. (2004) *Politics in Time: History, Institutions, and Social Analysis* (Princeton: Princeton University Press).

Pincione, G. and Tesón, F. (2006) *Rational Choice and Democratic Deliberation: A Theory of Discourse Failure* (Cambridge: Cambridge University Press).

Pine, J. C. (2007) *Technology in Emergency Management* (Hoboken, NJ: John Wiley & Sons).

Pollack, H. (2007) 'Learning to Walk Slow: America's Partial Policy Success in the Arena of Intellectual Disability', *Journal of Policy History*, 19: 1, 95–112.

Pollitt, C. (2003) 'Joined-up Government: A Survey', *Political Studies Review*, 1: 1, 34–49.

Pollitt, C. (2008) *Time, Policy, Management: Governing with the Past* (Oxford: Oxford University Press).

Pollitt, C. and Bouckaert, G. (2004) *Public Management Reform: A Comparative Analysis*, 2nd edn (Oxford: Oxford University Press).

Poole, S. (2007) *Unspeak: Words Are Weapons* (London: Abacus).

Posner, R. A. (2004) *Catastrophe: Risk and Response* (Oxford: Oxford University Press).

Post, J., M. (2004) *Leaders and Their Followers in a Dangerous World: The Psychology of Political Behavior* (Ithaca, NY: Cornell University Press).

Poulantzas, N. (1973) *Political Power and Social Classes* (London: NLB and Sheed & Ward).

Prasad, M. (2006) *The Politics of Free Markets: The Rise of Neoliberal Economic Policies in Britain, France, Germany, and the United States* (Chicago, IL: University of Chicago Press).

Prasser, S. (2006a) 'Aligning "Good Policy" with "Good Politics" ' in Colebatch, H. K. (ed.) *Beyond the Policy Cycle: The Policy Process in Australia.* (Crows Nest, NSW: Allen & Unwin), pp. 266–92.

Prasser, S. (2006b) *Royal Commissions and Public Inquiries in Australia* (Chatswood, New South Wales: LexisNexis Butterworths).

Pressman, J. L. and Wildavsky, A. B. (1984) *Implementation: How Great Expectations in Washington Are Dashed in Oakland: Or, Why It's Amazing That Federal Programs Work at All, This Being a Saga of the Economic Development Administration as Told by Two Sympathetic Observers Who Seek to Build Morals on a Foundation of Ruined Hopes*, 3rd edn (Berkeley, CA: University of California Press).

Prime Minister of Australia (2008) Address to Heads of Agencies and Members of Senior Executive Service, Great Hall, Parliament House, Canberra, 3 April, (http://www.pm.gov.au/media/speech/2008/speech_0226.cfm, accessed 18 March 2009.

Pross, A. P. (1992) *Group Politics and Public Policy*, 2nd edn (Toronto: Oxford University Press).

Quigley, K. F. (2008) *Responding to Crises in the Modern Infrastructure: Policy Lessons from Y2k* (Basingstoke: Palgrave Macmillan).

Radin, B. A. (2000) *Beyond Machiavelli: Policy Analysis Comes of Age* (Washington, DC: Georgetown University Press).

Ramesh, M. (2004) *Social Policy in East and Southeast Asia: Education, Health, Housing, and Income Maintenance* (London: Routledge).

Ray, B. (2008) *Water: The Looming Crisis in India* (Lanham, MD: Lexington).

Reason, J. (1990) *Human Error* (New York: Cambridge University Press).

Reynolds, C. (1997) 'Issue Management and the Australian Gun Debate', *Public Relations Review*, 23: 4, 343–60.

Rhodes, R. A. W. and Wanna, J. (2007) 'The Limits to Public Value, or Rescuing Responsible Government from the Platonic Guardians', *Australian Journal of Public Administration*, 66: 4, 406–21.

Rhodes, R. A. W. and Wanna, J. (2008) 'Stairways to Heaven: A Reply to Alford', *Australia Journal of Public Administration*, 67: 3, 367–70.

Rhodes, R. A. W. and Wanna, J. (2009) 'Bringing the Politics Back In: Public Value in Westminster Parliamentary Government', *Public Administration*, 87: 2, 161–83.

Richardson, J. (ed.) (1982) *Policy Styles in Western Europe* (London: George Allen & Unwin).

Richardson, J. J. and Jordan, A. J. (1979) *Governing under Pressure: The Policy Process in a Post-Parliamentary Democracy* (Oxford: Martin Robertson).

Ricks, D.A. (2006) *Blunders in International Business*, 4th edn (Oxford: Blackwell).

Riker, W. H. (1962) *The Theory of Political Coalitions* (Newhaven, CT: Yale University Press).

Ringland, G. (2002) *Scenarios in Public Policy* (Chichester: John Wiley & Sons).

Robinson, G. (2001) 'Power, Knowledge and "What Works" in Probation', *Howard Journal of Criminal Justice*, 40: 3, 235–54.

Robinson, N. (2003) 'Fuel Protests: Governing the Ungovernable?', *Parliamentary Affairs*, 56: 3, 423–40.

Rochefort, D. A. and Cobb, R. W. (eds) (1994) *The Politics of Problem Definition: Shaping the Policy Agenda* (Kansas: University Press of Kansas).

Rodousakis, N. and dos Santos, A. M. (2008) 'The Development of Inclusive E-Government in Austria and Portugal: A Comparison of Two Success Stories', *Innovation – The European Journal of Social Science Research*, 21: 4, 283–316.

Rodriguez, H., Quarantelli, E. L. and Dynes, R. R. (eds) (2006) *Handbook of Disaster Research* (New York: Springer).

Roe, E. (1994) *Narrative Policy Analysis: Theory and Practice* (Durham, NC: Duke University Press).

Rose, R. (1984) *Do Parties Make a Difference?*, 2nd edn (Basingstoke: Macmillan).

Rose, R. (1990) 'Inheritance before Choice in Public Policy', *Journal of Theoretical Politics*, 2: 3, 263–91.

Rose, R. (1993) *Lesson-Drawing in Public Policy: A Guide to Learning across Time and Space* (Chatham: Chatham House Publishers).

Rose, R. (2005) *Learning from Comparative Public Policy: A Practical Guide* (London: Routledge).

Rose, R. and Davies, P. L. (1994) *Inheritance in Public Policy: Change without Choice in Britain* (New Haven, CT: Yale University Press).

Rosenthal, U., Boin, R. A. and Comfort, L. K. (eds) (2001) *Managing Crises: Threats, Dilemmas and Opportunities* (Springfield, IL: Charles C. Thomas).

Rosenthal, U., Charles, M. T. and 't Hart, P. (eds) (1989) *Coping with Crises: The Management of Disasters, Riots and Terrorism* (Springfield, IL: Charles C. Thomas).

Rotberg, R. I. (ed.) (2003) *When States Fail: Causes and Consequences* (Princeton, NJ: Princeton University Press).

Sabatier, P. A. (2007) 'The Need for Better Theories' in Sabatier, P. A. (ed.) *Theories of the Policy Process* (Boulder, CO: Westview Press), pp. 3–17.

Sabatier, P. A. and Jenkins-Smith, H. C. (eds) (1993) *Policy Change and Learning: An Advocacy Coalition Approach* (Boulder, CO: Westview Press).

Sager, F. and Risi, C. (2009) 'The Limited Scope of Policy Appraisal in the Context of Referendum Democracy – the Case of Regulatory Impact Assessment in Switzerland' , Paper prepared for Workshop 30, 'The Politics of Policy Appraisal', ECPR Joint Sessions, Lisbon, April 14–19,

Saharso, S. (2007) 'Headscarves: A Comparison of Public Thought and Public Policy in Germany and the Netherlands', *Critical Review of International Social and Political Philosophy*, 10: 4, 513–30.

Sandbrook, D. (2006) *White Heat: A History of Britain in the Swinging Sixties* (London: Abacus).

Sanderson, I. (2002) 'Evaluation, Policy Learning and Evidence-Based Policy Making', *Public Administration*, 80: 1, 1–22.

Scharpf, F. W. (1997) *Games Real Actors Play: Actor-Centered Institutionalism in Policy Research* (Boulder, CO: Westview Press).

Schattschneider, E. E. (1960) *The Semisovereign People: A Realist's View of Democracy in America* (Hinsdale, IL: Dryden Press).

Schneider, A. L. and Ingram, H. (1997) *Policy Design for Democracy* (Kansas: University Press of Kansas).

Schön, D. A. and Rein, M. (1994) *Frame Reflection: Toward the Resolution of Intractable Policy Controversies* (New York: Basic Books).

Schultz, D. (2007) 'Stupid Public Policies and Other Political Myths', Paper prepared for the American Political Science Association Annual Convention, Chicago, 29 August 28–3 September, http://www.allacademic.com//meta/p_mla_apa_research_citation/2/0/9/1/7/pages209173/p209173–1.php, accessed 21 September 2009.

Schwartz, H. (2006) 'Explaining Australian Economic Success: Good Policy or Good Luck?', *Governance*, 19: 2, 173–205.

Schwartz, P. (1996) *The Art of the Long View: Planning for the Future in an Uncertain World* (New York, NY: Doubleday).

Schwartz, P. (2003) *Inevitable Surprises: Thinking Ahead in a Time of Turbulence* (New York: Gotham).

Schwartz, R. and McConnell, A. (2009) 'Do Crises Help Remedy Regulatory Failures? A Comparative Study of the Walkerton Water and Jerusalem Banquet Hall Disasters', *Canadian Public Administration*, 52: 2, 92–112.

Scott, J. (2001) *Power: Key Concepts* (Bristol: Polity Press).

Schaffer, F. C. (ed.) (2007) *Elections for Sale: The Causes and Consequences of Vote Buying* (Boulder, CO: Lynne Reinner).

Shapiro, I. (1999) 'Enough of Deliberation: Politics Is About Interest and Power' in Macedo, S. (ed.) *Deliberative Politics* (Oxford: Oxford University Press), pp. 28–38.

Shapiro, I. (2003) *The State of Democratic Theory* (Princeton, NJ: Princeton University Press).

Shapiro, I. and Bedi, S. (eds) (2007a) *Political Contingency: Studying the Unexpected, the Accidental and the Unforeseen* (New York: NY: New York University Press).

Shapiro, I. and Bedi, S. (2007b) 'Introduction: Contingency's Challenge to Political Science' in Shapiro, I. and Bedi, S. (eds) *Political Contingency: Studying the Unexpected, the Accidental and the Unforeseen* (New York: NY: New York University Press), pp. 1–18.

Sharman, J. C. (2008) 'Power and Discourse in Policy Diffusion: Anti-Money Laundering in Developing States', *International Studies Quarterly*, 52: 3, 635–56.

Shaw, C. (2004) *The Campaign Manager: Running and Winning Local Elections* (Boulder, CO: Westview Press).

Sheil, C. (2000) *Water's Fall: Running the Risk with Economic Rationalism* (New South Wales: Pluto Press).

Simon, H. A. (1957) *Administrative Behavior*, 2nd edn (London: Macmillan).

Sintomer, Y. and de Maillard, J. (2007) 'The Limits to Local Participation and Deliberation in the French 'Politique De La Ville", *European Journal of Political Research*, 46: 4, 503–29.

6, P., Leat, D., Seltzer, K. and Stoker, G. (2002) *Towards Holistic Governance: The New Reform Agenda* (Basingstoke: Palgrave Macmillan).

Slovic, P. (ed.) (2000) *The Perception of Risk* (London: Earthscan).

Slovic, P., Fischoff, B. and Lichenstein, S. (2000) 'Response Mode, Framing and Information Processing Effects in Risk Assessment' in Slovic, P. (ed.) *The Perception of Risk* (London: Earthscan), pp. 154–67.

Smith, A. and Kern, F. (2009) 'The Transitions Storyline in Dutch Environmental Policy', *Environmental Politics*, 18: 1, 78–98.

Snider, L. (2004) 'Resisting Neo-Liberalism: The Poisoned Water Disaster in Walkerton Ontario', *Socio & Legal Studies*, 13: 2, 265–89.

Sofia Echo (2007) The release and return to Bulgaria of the six Bulgarian medics imprisoned for eight years in Libya on HIV-infection charges, 25 July.

Spiegel Online International (2008) Item on a report regarding Germany's welfare state, 26 June.

Squires, P. and Measor, L. (2005) 'Below Decks on the Youth Justice Flagship: The Politics of Evaluation' in Taylor, D. and Balloch, S. (eds) *The Politics of Evaluation: Participation and Policy Implementation* (Bristol: Policy Press), pp. 21–40.

Staelraeve, S. and 't Hart, P. (2008) 'Dutroux and Dioxin: Crisis Investigations, Elite Accountability and Institutional Reform in Belgium' in Boin, A., McConnell, A. and 't Hart, P. (eds) *Governing after Crisis: The Politics of Investigation, Accountability and Learning* (Cambridge: Cambridge University Press), pp. 148–79.

Stamsø, M. A. (2008) 'Grants for First-Time Homeowners in Norway – Distributional Effects under Different Market and Political Conditions', *European Journal of Housing Policy*, 8: 4, 379–97.

Stanley, N. and Manthorpe, J. (2004) *The Age of the Inquiry: Learning and Blaming in Health and Social Care* (London: Routledge).

State of Wisconsin Legislative Audit Bureau (1997) *An Evaluation of the Learnfare Program: Final Report* (Wisconsin: State of Wisconsin Legislative Audit Bureau).

Steenhuisen, B. and van Eeten, M. (2008) 'Invisible Trade-Offs of Public Values: Inside Dutch Railways', *Public Money & Management*, 28: 3, 147–52.

Stoker, G. (2006a) *Why Politics Matters: Making Democracy Work* (Basingstoke: Palgrave Macmillan).

Stoker, G. (2006b) 'Public Value Management: A New Narrative for Networked Governance', *American Review of Public Administration*, 36: 1, 41–57.

Stokes, S. C. (2003) 'Pathologies of Deliberation' in Elster, J. (ed.) *Deliberative Democracy* (Cambridge: Cambridge University Press), pp. 123–39.

Stokey, E. and Zeckhauser, R. (1978) *A Primer for Policy Analysis* (New York, NY: W.W. Norton & Co.).

Stone, D. (2002) *Policy Paradox: The Art of Political Decision Making*, 2nd edn (New York: W.W. Norton).

Stringer, J. K. and Richardson, J. J. (1979) 'Managing the Political Agenda: Problem Definition and Policy Making in Britain', *Parliamentary Affairs*, 33: 1, 23–39.

Studlar, D. T. (2004) 'Tobacco-Control Policy Instruments in a Shrinking World: How Much Policy Learning' in Levi-Faur, D. and Vigoda-Gadot, E. (eds) *International Public Policy and Management: Policy Learning Beyond Regional, Cultural, and Political Boundaries* (New York, NY: Marcel Dekker), pp. 189–219.

Stutz, J. R. (2008) 'What Gets Done and Why: Implementing the Recommendations of Public Inquiries', *Canadian Public Administration*, 51: 3, 501–21.

Sulitzeanu-Kenan, R. (2010) 'Reflections in the Shadow of Blame: When Do Politicians Appoint Commissions of Inquiry?', *British Journal of Political Science*.

Susskind, L. (2006) 'Arguing, Bargaining and Getting Agreement' in Moran, M., Rein, M. and Goodin, R. E. (eds) *The Oxford Handbook of Public Policy* (Oxford: Oxford University Press), pp. 269–95.

Susskind, L. and Cruickshank, J. (1987) *Breaking the Impasse: Consensual Approaches to Resolving Public Disputes* (New York, NY: Basic Books).

Swedish Police (2009) *Tasks and Objectives of the Police*, http://www.polisen.se/en/English/The-Swedish-Police/Tasks-and-Objectives-for-the-Police-/, accessed 18 September 2009).

Sydney Morning Herald (2007) Item on the Workplace Relations Centre at the University of Sydney, 3 October.

't Hart, P. (1993) 'Symbols, Rituals and Power: The Lost Dimensions of Crisis Management', *Journal of Contingencies and Crisis Management*, 1: 1, 36–50.

't Hart, P. (1994) *Groupthink in Government: A Study of Small Groups and Policy Failure* (Boston: Johns Hopkins University Press).

't Hart, P. (2008) 'The Limits of Crisis Exploitation', *Arena Journal*, 29/30: 157–74.

't Hart, P., Rosenthal, U. and Kouzmin, A. (1993) 'Crisis Decision Making: The Centralization Thesis Revisited', *Administration & Society*, 25: 1, 12–45.

't Hart, P., Stern, E. K. and Sundelius, B. (eds) (1997) *Beyond Groupthink: Political Group Dynamics and Foreign Policymaking* (Ann Arbor: University of Michigan Press).

't Hart, P. and Tindall, K. (2009) *Framing the Global Economic Downturn: Crisis Rhetoric and the Politics of Recessions* (Canberra: ANU e-press).

Takeuchi, Y. (1997) 'The Self-Activating Entrance Examination System – Its Hidden Agenda and Its Correspondence with the Japanese "Salary Man" ', *Higher Education*, 34: 2, 183–98.

Tanguay, A. B. (1999) 'Canada's Party System in the 1990s' in Bickerton, J. and Gagnon, A. G. (eds) *Canadian Politics*, 3rd edn (Ontario: Broadview Press), pp. 325–53.

Taylor, I. (2003) 'Policy on the Hoof: The Handling of the Foot and Mouth Disease Outbreak in the UK 2001', *Policy & Politics*, 31: 4, 535–46.

Taylor, D. and Balloch, S. (eds) (2005a) *The Politics of Evaluation: Participation and Policy Implementation* (Bristol: Policy Press)

Taylor, D. and Balloch, S. (2005b) 'The Politics of Evaluation: An Overview' in Taylor, D. and Balloch, S. (eds) *The Politics of Evaluation: Participation and Policy Implementation* (Bristol: Policy Press), pp. 1–17.

Thelen, K. (2004) *How Institutions Evolve: The Political Economy of Skills in Germany, Britain, the Unites States and Japan* (New York, NY: Cambridge University Press).

Thompson, J. B. (2000) *Political Scandal: Power and Visibility in the Modern Age* (Cambridge: Polity Press).

Tiffen, R. (1999) *Scandals, Media, Politics and Corruption in Contemporary Australia* (Sydney: University of New South Wales Press).

Times, The (2009) Item on Guantanamo Bay detention camp, 1 January.

Toft, B. and Reynolds, S. (2005) *Learning from Disasters: A Management Approach*, 3rd edn (Leicester: Perpetuity Press).

Trichet, J.-C. (2004) 'Current Issues on the European Central Bank and the Euro': Speech by Jean-Claude Trichet, President of the ECB, Delivered at the Club International La Redoute Bonn, 27 September 2004, http://www.ecb.int/press/key/date/2004/html/sp040927.en.html, accessed 17 July 2009.

Truman, D. B. (1951) *Governmental Process: Political Interests and Public Opinion* (New York: Alfred A. Knopf).

Tsebelis, G. (2002) *Veto Players: How Political Institutions Work.* (Princeton, NJ: Princeton University Press).

Ugland, T. and Veggeland, F. (2004) 'Towards an Integrated Approach? Food Inspection Reforms in Canada and the European Union', *Policy and Society*, 23: 4, 104–24.

van Gestel, N., Koppenjan, J., Schrijver, I., van de Ven, A. and Veeneman, W. (2008) 'Managing Public Values in Public–Private Networks: A Comparative Study of Innovative Public Infrastructure Projects', *Public Money & Management*, 28: 3, 139–45.

van Outrive, L. (1998) 'The Disastrous Justice System in Belgium: A Crisis of Democracy?' in Gray, P. and 't Hart, P. (eds) *Public Policy Disasters in Western Europe* (London: Routledge), pp. 23–38.

Wagner, W. and Steinzor, R. (eds) (2006) *Rescuing Science from Politics: Regulation and the Distortion of Scientific Research* (New York, NY: Cambridge University Press).

Wallner, J. (2008) 'Legitimacy and Public Policy: Seeing Beyond Effectiveness, Efficiency, and Performance', *Policy Studies Journal*, 36: 3, 421–33.

Wanna, J. (ed.) (2007) *Improving Implementation* (Canberra: ANU E-Press).

Ward, I. (2008) 'An Experiment in Political Communication: The British Columbia Citizens' Assembly on Electoral Reform', *Australian Journal of Political Science*, 43: 2, 301–15.

Washington Post (2003) South Korean Deputy Foreign Minister Lee Soo Hyuck commenting with regard to engaging in nuclear talks with North Korea, the United States, China, Russia and Japan and South Korea 8 September.

Washington Post (2004) George W. Bush commenting on the sudden and unexpected collapse of Saddam Hussein's regime, 20 August.

Weare, C. and Wolensky, E. (2000) 'Winners, Losers, and Efficiency: Achieving Multiple Goals in Japan's Financial System Reforms', *Journal of Comparative Policy Analysis*, 2: 1, 9–37.

Weaver, R. K. (1986) 'The Politics of Blame Avoidance', *Journal of Public Policy*, 6: 4, 371–98.

Weimer, D. L. and Vining, A. R. (2005) *Policy Analysis: Concepts and Practice*, 4th edn (Upper Saddle River, NJ: Pearson).

Weiss, C. H. (1972) *Evaluation Research: Methods of Assessing Program Effectiveness* (Englewood Cliffs, NJ: Prentice-Hall).

Weiss, C. H. (1988) *Evaluation: Methods for Studying Programs and Policies*, 2nd edn (Englewood Cliffs, NJ: Prentice-Hall).

Wildavsky, A. (1987) *Speaking Truth to Power: The Art and Craft of Policy Analysis*, 2nd edn (New Brunswick: Transaction).

Williams, P. D. (2005) 'Peter Beattie's Strategies of Crisis Management: *Mea Culpa* and the Policy "Backflip" ', *Australian Journal of Public Administration*, 64: 4, 41–52.

Wilsford, D. (1994) 'Path-Dependency, or Why History Makes It Difficult, but Not Impossible to Reform Health Care Services in a Big Way', *Journal of Public Policy*, 14: 251–83.

Winship, C. (2006) 'Policy Analysis as Puzzle Solving' in Moran, M., Rein, M. and Goodin, R. E. (eds) *The Oxford Handbook of Public Policy* (Oxford: Oxford University Press), pp. 109–23.

Withington, J. (2005) *A Disastrous History of Britain: Chronicles of War, Riot, Plague and Flood* (Gloucestershire: Sutton).

Wright Mills, C. (1956) *The Power Elite* (New York, NY: Oxford University Press).

Wyplosz, C. (1997) 'An International Role for the Euro?', Report prepared for the European Capital Market Institute, http://hei.unige.ch/~wyplosz/ecmi.pdf, accessed 2 August 2009.

Yanow, D. (2000) *Conducting Interpretive Policy Analysis* (Thousand Oaks, CA: Sage).

Zetter, L. (2007) *The Political Campaigning Handbook: Real Life Lessons from the Front Line* (Petersfield, Hampshire: Harriman House).

Index